"GAMERS," MULTICULTURALISTS AND THE GREAT COMING APART

THE UNITED STATES SINCE 1965

ALFRED CLAASSEN

"Gamers," Multiculturalists, and the Great Coming Apart: The United States since 1965
Copyright ©2021 Alfred Claassen. All Rights Reserved

Published by:
Trine Day LLC
PO Box 577
Walterville, OR 97489
1-800-556-2012
www.TrineDay.com
trineday@icloud.com

Library of Congress Control Number: 2020915204

Claassen, Alfred.
"Gamers," Multiculturalists, and the Great Coming Apart – 1st ed.
p. cm.
Epub (ISBN-13) 978-1-63424-338-4
Kindle (ISBN-13) 978-1-63424-339-1
Print (ISBN-13) 978-1-63424-337-7
1. United States -- Social conditions -- 1960-1980. 2. United States -- Social conditions -- 1980- 3.Social classes. 4.Social mobility. 5. Baby boom generation -- United States. 6. Political culture -- United States.. I. Title

FIRST EDITION
10 9 8 7 6 5 4 3 2 1

Printed in the USA
Distribution to the Trade by:
Independent Publishers Group (IPG)
814 North Franklin Street
Chicago, Illinois 60610
312.337.0747
www.ipgbook.com

CONTENTS

INTRODUCTION

I offer in *"Gamers," Multiculturalists, and the Great Coming Apart* a fresh, interdisciplinary history of the United States since 1965, one that describes and analyzes the changing American society, character, and major events of the time. The central questions it seeks to answer are how and why did the United States change during the 51 years of the global era from 1965 to 2016, how and why has it done so in the new era since 2016, and how and why have the major events of both periods occurred. The narrative begins in 1965 because the wheels of change began turning on the many dimensions of the human during the mid-1960s and particularly that year.[1] Every social institution, aspect of character, and major event was profoundly affected. Like a massive, slow-motion earthquake it played out through rolling, pitching, grinding, jolting, and shaking phases. The time of great upheaval lasted for a decade and triggered innumerable aftershocks at home and abroad.

The epochal transformation beginning in 1965 installed a new paradigm, a new set of basic assumptions framing society and character.[2] That paradigm was global liberalism, and it featured the opening up and spreading of economic, political, social, and cultural markets, moving from relatively prescribed patterns toward free choice in most areas of society and life.[3] It also featured a factious new group identification and attachment hallowing difference and inclusion, pointedly departing from the previous era's relative national unity and harmony.

The openness of the era extended beyond national borders to yield globalization. As the United States and other liberal societies allowed people, products, ideas, and images to flow more freely around the world than ever before, those societies acquired extraordinary sociocultural variation. Indeed early in the era there arrived the point in world history of maximum encounter with sociocultural difference. Non-Western societies for the first time began joining the United States and the West in exposure to the economic and sociocultural markets and in sustained development. Well over half the countries of the world became predominantly liberal by the end of the 20th century.

The thesis of this book is that as the United States led the world geopolitically, economically, and in most other ways during the global era, it underwent a many-sided coming apart. Most fundamentally, it came apart into contentious groups on the basis of identity and into contentious classes on the basis of character. The global-liberal paradigm framed race, ethnicity, lifestyle, and gender in radical and divisive terms that brought destructive consequences. Out of that multiculturalism arose a troubling new upper class of "gamers" who have been highly adapted to the various markets but alienated and withdrawn from leadership into economic and career maneuvering that brought further destructive consequences. The basic disintegration represented by identity politics and self-centered gaming led to the country's also coming apart politically, socially, and morally, leaving it divided, weakened, poorly governed, and internationally vulnerable by the end of the era.

The reign of the global-liberal paradigm ended in the United States after 51 years in 2016 as Donald Trump's presidential campaign and the middle- and working-class movement of American Restoration behind it successfully critiqued and proposed to remedy the fundamental problems wrought by that paradigm and era. Trump and the Restoration were fiercely attacked without letup by an elite organized Resistance, and the country again entered paradigm crisis in which the ground is moving beneath us, all aspects of society and life are open to question, and epochal transformation is under way. The outcome of the comprehensive and profound conflict between the Restoration and Resistance will determine the shape, direction, and condition of the United States during the coming decades. Before turning to the immense and elusive task of interpreting, analyzing, and appraising our present circumstances and alternatives, it is of paramount importance that we first step back and carefully prepare ourselves by taking our bearings on the now completed and better understood global paradigm and era just left behind. For when we democratic citizens interpret what the United States has become, analyze what its circumstances are, and work toward conclusions regarding how it is to conduct itself, we are matching wits with our own elites and those of our international adversaries, neither of whom have our nation's best interests in mind.

A great deal of excellent recent scholarly and journalistic work has clarified key elements of the American experience of the last 55 years. My aim in this book is to bring that work together in a panoramic, 360-degree view of the United States since 1965, broadening and deepening the emerging understanding, and rounding it off with a fresh interpretation of the extremely high-stakes paradigm conflict of the new era. Each of the first seven chapters describes and analyzes a major facet of the global-era United States and the events accompanying it. Chapter 8 then analyzes the tumultuous paradigm conflict between Restoration and Resistance since 2016 and its implications for the future of our country. Incredibly, the American history of the last 55 years has in many ways revolved around the simple narratives propping up two fateful accusations against the United States as we have known it. I lay out essential but never-provided historical context in the epilogue which seriously calls into question those narratives and the accusations teetering upon them.

To place the American experience since 1965 in sharp relief I frequently compare and contrast it with that of the preceding era in this society and with that of other societies, particularly Europe, India, Japan, China, Russia, and the Islamic world during the global era. Although this work draws from across the human sciences and covers a great deal, it focuses on society rather than culture, treating religion, the arts, or popular culture, for example, not in and of themselves but only as they bear upon social institutions, character, and major events. Nor does this book address the natural world except incidentally. Environmental and public-health issues are patently of importance today but outside its scope. What I offer in these pages, in the belief that it is what has been most needed, is comprehensive description and analysis of the U.S. experience of the last 55 years under a unifying narrative. This work is grounded in notions I have presented in an earlier book.[4]

How one should read this book: Readers who approach it settled in the notion that they will be reading it all the way through should by all means do so. There is a logic to the way the chapters unfold. But those who are uncertain whether they want to should first read chapter 4, "The Rise of the Gamers," and then chapter 8, "Trump's American Restoration Meets Asymmetric Top-Gamer Resistance." Chapter 4 is both lively and necessary background. Most of these uncertains will then want to read more.

PART I
THE CONDITION OF GLOBALIZATION

CHAPTER 1

THE PAX AMERICANA:
THE WORLD UNDER U.S. LEADERSHIP

When the United States and the allies emerged victorious from World War II in 1945, they established the Pax Americana,[5] the world order under this country's leadership. Its net national product was then nearly half that of the entire world, its military forces numbered more than 10 million men, and they were widely deployed across the globe. It had suffered relatively light casualties (barely over 1 percent those of the USSR), its homeland was untouched, and it alone among the major participants in the war was free of exhaustion. Above all, the United States possessed a monopoly in atomic weapons. Its international leadership extended over all non-communist countries after the war.

With its wealth, technological base, and organizational capacity steadily increasing, the United States developed and maintained a vast military apparatus. The military might, economic resources, and resolve of the United States have underwritten the remarkable international security regime, but its friends and allies have also provided crucial support. The major economic, political, social, and cultural changes and great events since 1945 have owed more fundamentally to the nature of American international leadership than to any other factor. The extraordinary peace and prosperity the world has known since then owe everything to the Pax Americana.

There is a precedent to the Pax Americana: The ninety-nine years of the Pax Britannica, until its collapse at the onset of World War I in 1914, were more peaceful by far than any similar period that Europe had known since the height of Rome.[6] After the collapse of the British security regime, the years between 1914 and 1945 witnessed terrible and wrenching conflict – a single *31-year crisis* that included the two world wars, most countries' economic doldrums of the 1920s,[7] and the Great Depression of the 1930s. During this 31-year crisis, the developed world substantially reverted to the vicious military aggression and mercantilist economic practice that had been endemic throughout the authoritarian, hierarchically dominated era from antiquity through Napoleon.

Prolonged trench warfare between the greatest powers on earth rocked the world in the Great War as millions of young lives and the finest hopes of a civilization were destroyed. No sooner had World War I concluded than the ill-conceived and vindictive Treaty of Versailles spawned continuing destruction. An ominous succession of events followed as Mussolini seized power in Italy in 1922, Germany slumped into sharp recession in 1928, and the Great Depression began in 1929, leading to Adolf Hitler's accession to power and establishment of the Third Reich in 1933. Japan invaded Manchuria in 1931, and General Franco began his military insurrection in 1936, consolidating power through the bloody Spanish civil war that ensued. Later that year Nazi Germany, Japan, and Italy formed the Axis. Germany seized Austria and the Sudetenland in 1938 and then, with Russia, invaded Poland in 1939, initiating war. The 31-year-crisis culminated in World War II from 1939 to 1945, in which military operations were conducted globally, and 60 million people were killed – among them 27 million Soviet soldiers and civilians, 6 million Jews in the Holocaust, and hundreds of thousands from the atom bombs over Hiroshima and Nagasaki – a war that was several times more destructive than "the War to end all Wars" with which the crisis began.

The Pax Americana has operated within the loose consensus of the world community, the enormous liberal complex made up of the West, India, Japan, South Korea, and dozens of other countries by the end of the global era. China, North Korea, Russia, and the bulk of the Islamic world have lain outside of and actively oppose it. Much of the strength of the Pax Americana has arisen from the fact that, by and large exercised with restraint and conferring great security and economic benefits upon the world, U.S. leadership has for the most part enjoyed acceptance. Its security regime has been benign because the United States has been moderate, democratic, and constrained in its international relations by middle-class values. International responsibility is not something the United States had wanted but a duty it inherited and gladly performed that no other nation could provide.[8] A minimalist security regime relatively respectful of rights and free of the ambition to dictate stands in stark contrast to the heavy-handed impositions of the Nazi, Soviet, and Chinese regimes.

The Pax Americana has been tested in several large military campaigns and numerous small police actions on different continents. Those occasional tests and what they have demonstrated about the power and resolve of the United States and its allies have been of decisive importance for the security regime although, day in and day out, it has operated most effectively via the enormous economic and moral power brought to bear on its behalf by the other leading countries of the world. Although the United States has substantially led by persuasion, this leadership has been possible only because it has had great military and economic might that it was ready to employ, and because its aims have generally been advantageous to most others.

THE EARLY PAX AMERICANA, 1945-1965

U.S. international leadership was vigorously contested by the Soviet Union from the beginning and by communist China from 1949, even as this country enjoyed something approaching hegemony in the rest of the world. During the first two post-war decades of more acute international threat, domestic support for American global leadership was comprehensive and strong, if less than carte blanche.

The post-World War II division of Europe provided a framework within which at the outset there was hope for harmony among the wartime allies. Germany was divided into four zones, one for each of the key allies, with the USSR mostly in the east and the United States, Britain, and France mostly in the west and south. Berlin, an island within the Soviet zone, was also divided into sectors. On the basis of its own huge army and heavy lifting during the war, the Soviet empire extended over Eastern Europe and a large part of Germany at the end of World War II, with the acquiescence of the United States and Britain. The Western allies were receptive to a tolerant, constructive postwar partnership with the Soviets. Stalin, who had expended so very many lives during the war, had other ideas.

Finding fertile ground in many parts of the world, the Soviet Union was on the march. Well before the war was over, Stalin's agents were fomenting disorder and revolution, seeking to spread the communist system and draw in client states. Soviet-oriented communist parties were expanding rapidly across Europe, including in France and Italy. Given the devastation Europeans had endured, the transformations they had undergone, the intellectual and aesthetic undertows they were experiencing, and the political turbulence they were encountering, communism appealed to many.

By 1946 Turkey was facing escalating Soviet demands and Greece, imminent communist overthrow. Resolved not to allow the Soviets control of the Dardanelles, President Harry Truman deployed the Sixth Fleet to the eastern Mediterranean for permanent stationing. He extended substantial economic and military assistance to Greece,[9] where the threat did not subside until 1949.[10] Additionally the Soviets were attempting encroachment in Iran, from which the United States pressured them into stepping back.[11] It was becoming apparent as well that the Yalta Agreement[12] was not going to be implemented as promised. For example, the Soviet Union seemed intent upon not holding the agreed upon democratic elections in Poland and seemed to be preparing to remain in Austria, instead of honoring its commitment to withdraw from that country. Halfway around the world, the civil war in China also resumed in earnest at the end of the war.

As he watched events unfold in light of the record of international aggression by hierarchical societies from imperial Germany to the Axis powers, Winston Churchill became increasingly alarmed. Stalin's resumé – bank robber for the Bolsheviks before World War I, brutal forced industrializer during the late 1920s and early 1930s, and paranoid mass murderer during the late 1930s – heightened Churchill's fears. On March 5, 1946 in Fulton, Missouri he delivered the famous "Iron Curtain" speech, laying out the global threat posed by totalitarian communism and calling for a Cold War to contain its expansion. As President Truman and the U.S. Congress heeded Churchill's warnings, along with those of George Kennan and other prescient observers, of the unfolding communist threat, the United States began resisting Soviet aggression.

The Cold War was a 45-year standoff and series of confrontations – over territory, allies, military advantage, and trading partners – that occurred between the world's leading military powers from 1946 until the disintegration of the USSR in 1991. The Soviet Union and communist China sought to take over or intimidate other countries, but stopped short of all-out war with the Western powers. Throughout the Cold War, the United States and its allies defended the security of the non-communist world and for the most part thwarted overt and covert efforts by communist countries to invade or otherwise overthrow non-communist governments.

The United States let the Yalta violations in Poland slide, but when Stalin began interfering with allied transport of supplies to West Berlin in May of 1948, Truman responded brilliantly; not with tanks but with the Berlin airlift, which resupplied the beleaguered city while galvanizing world opinion against Soviet aggression. The dramatic airlift continued until the blockade ceased in May of 1949. That year, while the focus was on Europe, China fell to the communists. Later the same year, several years sooner than anticipated, the Soviets also exploded their first atom bomb.

Under the circumstances, the United States reversed its almost complete unilateral disarmament in the aftermath of World War II and began rearming to defend the free world. American diplomacy also began building its network of alliances around the communist powers, most importantly NATO but also ANZUS, SEATO, and CENTO, isolating the Soviets and then the communist Chinese. An alarmed and determined, if saddened, American public broadly supported Truman's policies from the beginning. By 1949 popular support for resisting communist aggression was intense.

U.S. resolve was tested in 1950 when North Korea invaded the unprepared South. The United States intervened with UN support, slowed the invasion as it pushed far into the South and then began forcing the North Koreans back toward the 38th parallel.[13] Determined to replace the aggressive communist regime in the North, the allies under General MacArthur moved beyond the parallel, despite loud warnings by the Chinese. A few weeks later, with UN forces far into the North, China invaded in massive numbers, and the United States and its allies were again abruptly pushed down the peninsula. The UN forces regrouped under General Ridgeway's gifted command and again began rolling the Chinese and North Koreans back to a defensible line approximating the 38th parallel a year after the Korean War began. After two years of frustrating negotiations while the fighting continued, public support for the inconclusive struggle declined. A ceasefire was finally achieved in mid-1953 after President Dwight Eisenhower let it be known that if the fighting did not cease, the United States would mount a much larger offensive against North Korea and take the war to China itself,[14] but the war was never formally ended.

The most dangerous Cold War flare-ups after the Korean War were the Berlin crisis and Cuban missile crisis. The Berlin crisis of 1961 was initiated when in violation of treaty commitments the Soviets erected the Berlin wall to halt the flow of refugees into West Berlin from the east. During the Cuban missile crisis of 1962, the United States and Soviet Union stood at the brink of thermonuclear war for several long days over the secret stationing of Soviet nuclear missiles in Cuba, until the Soviets relented and agreed to remove them. In return, the United States assented, reasonably, to withdrawing its nuclear missiles from Turkey, but this part of the exchange would not be publicly known until long afterward.[15] Wisely or not, President John Kennedy was determined to humiliate First Secretary

Nikita Khrushchev and did so, albeit at great risk, in order to punish the latter's chronic bellicosity.

The Korean War in stalemate, the Chinese invaded Tibet in 1954, venturing that the United States was unwilling to confront it in an Asian land war over its conquest of a remote, defenseless neighbor. Having conquered Tibet, the regime aggressively reinterpreted that country's history of relations with India, claiming for China a good deal of Indian territory along the Tibetan border. The Chinese struck again (dangerously) during the Cuban Missile Crisis in 1962, invading India along fronts in Kashmir and the northeast. In the short border war, China took a strip of land to which it had no claim but sought for the completion of transportation links.[16] This acute portion of the Cold War dominated the early Pax Americana of the first two postwar decades.

The liberal and communist worlds competed fiercely for support among less developed countries during the postwar decades, in the process badly distorting the post-colonial transitions of many countries, including Egypt, Angola, Cuba, and Malaysia. The protracted contest imparted a Marxist, conflictual hue to many third-world countries that had experienced comparative harmony during their earlier stages of independence. At the same time, it helped perpetuate their hierarchical traditions by increasing the scale and power of coercive apparatuses and discouraging enterprise. The Cold War, especially while intense, was not conducive to liberalization in the third world. Nevertheless, the Cuban missile crisis came close enough to Armageddon that it understandably gave serious pause to the Americans and their allies as well as to the Soviets. Both sides backed off somewhat afterward.

The Mature Pax Americana, 1965-1991

Entering the global era, the Pax Americana was less forcefully contested from 1965 to 1991 than it had been during its early, acute phase, even as U.S. dominance was somewhat reduced. The Vietnam War was a turning point. Despite its vast power, the United States was unable or unwilling to defeat a third-world opponent in an extended guerrilla war. From 1968 on, the war was effectively lost. It was lost primarily because, for the stakes involved, President Lyndon Johnson was unwilling to risk China's possible entry into the conflict had the U.S. military taken the war early and decisively to North Vietnam. The choice to fight the war in a constricted manner prolonged and doomed it, given the more stringent emerging realities of public opinion in the new era that were shaped in large part by the ensuing frustration. The war was also lost because it had aspects of both an invasion from the communist North and a domestic insurgency in the South, leading to public uncertainty about whether the war was a justifiable defense of the free world or an unjustifiable resistance to a colonial uprising. As the war went on, the moral ambiguity of the U.S. position in Vietnam was felt with growing keenness, eroding domestic and international support for its continuation. It was also the first fully televised war, shocking images of whose violence were constantly being broadcast all over the world. Toward the war's end, the American public was no longer even willing to support continuation of South Vietnam's partially successful though messy combat effort built up under President Richard Nixon and General Creighton Abrams' policy of Vietnamization, and financial assistance was halted.

Modest weakening of the Pax Americana was evident in the U.S. domestic turmoil of the late 1960s and in President Nixon's 1971 decision to take the country off the qualified gold standard, as well as in opposition to the Vietnam War. Unable to afford in such quantities both guns and butter, as the saying went, despite its enormous economy, the United States was undergoing inflation. Simultaneously in the throes of Watergate, it was unable to avert the Yom Kippur War of 1973 or to do more than stand by as Arab petroleum producers first organized an oil boycott to protest the West's tolerance of Israel's policies and then activated OPEC, the international oil cartel, in early 1974. The United States government was able to lead internationally during the global era, especially when doing so sensibly, but it could no longer be as confident that either its own public or those of other liberal countries would follow.

Solid domestic support for defending vital U.S. and allied national security interests around the world held through the mature Pax Americana and beyond, but after the war in Vietnam the public was wary of ethically ambiguous involvements and impatient with ill-conceived, open-ended, or mismanaged ones. There was widespread concern at home and abroad about such limited but questionable U.S. engagements as those in Grenada, Panama, Afghanistan, and Iraq. U.S. power remained predominant globally, but the range of circumstances under which it could be employed was restricted. Democratic peoples around the world had little trouble distinguishing between horror at the threat of Soviet occupation and annoyance and resentment over seemingly arbitrary American intervention, but as the Soviet threat diminished, many were becoming more concerned with U.S. action abroad as well.

Through it all, the Pax Americana reaped a bountiful harvest of beneficial global developments. Among the most important of them, the Cold War with China was suspended in large steps during the 1970s as a result of the normalization of relations achieved by Nixon and Mao Zedong in 1972, the death of Mao and failed coup by the "Gang of Four" in 1976, and the establishment of the Deng Xiaoping regime in 1978. Deng remained the regime's paramount figure until 1992. The most dramatic fruition of the Pax Americana came when after several years of liberalization under Mikhail Gorbachev, the Soviet empire reverted to its Russian core as the Eastern European satellite countries were ceded their freedom between 1989 and 1991. The Baltic States were also soon granted independence, and much of Eastern Europe quickly stepped into the global-liberal mainstream. The other non-Russian republics were given independence as well.

Tyrannical from the outset, Soviet rule had been marked by a series of major uprisings by subject peoples, including in East Berlin in 1953, Hungary in 1956, and Czechoslovakia in 1967, each violently suppressed by Soviet and proxy troops. Propped up by an enormous security apparatus and abject fear of the heavy boot, Soviet rule was illegitimate at its core. Its immorality was widely perceived even in Russia, in part as a consequence of the opening made there to Western culture in the decades following the death of Stalin. The last straw was the debacle of the Soviet war in Afghanistan (1979-89). The Soviets were halted and the tide turned by mujahedeen guerrillas wielding CIA-supplied, shoulder-fired anti-aircraft missiles to devastatingly counter the invaders' air advantage. Its military defeat further discredited the Soviet regime and empire and intensified popular revulsion against them.[17] Overextended in Afghanistan and elsewhere, an economically stressed politburo had quietly decided under Andropov in December of 1981 that thereafter the USSR would not again intervene in Eastern Europe should the subject countries assert their independence.[18]

The leadership of Gorbachev (1985-91) combined with the Soviet military rout and crisis of acceptance to liberalize and bring down the regime and empire. Gorbachev's policies of glasnost and perestroika, respectively openness and restructuring, essentially made public the end of the threat of Soviet intervention that had long hung over the subject countries. Before reform had progressed far at home, it led to the unraveling of the Soviet empire. The spirit of glasnost was nowhere more welcome than in the captive Eastern European countries where free discussion and assembly focused above all on ending Soviet occupation. With a mixture of humanity, courage, and dithering, Gorbachev more or less peacefully acceded power one by one, as the former subject peoples demanded independence.

Several subject nations within Russia proper, including Chechnya, did as well, but, other than the Baltic States, none of these were given independence. The successful unraveling also owed much to Gorbachev's successor Boris Yeltsin's courageous defeat of the attempted hardliner coup in 1991 and the parliamentary uprising in 1993.

Essential to the collapse of the Soviet Union was also the charismatic leadership of President Ronald Reagan, whose decency and rhetoric of freedom were combined with toughness and steadfastness. Reagan's resounding phrases worked their way into the minds of Eastern European subjects, Soviet peoples, and, not least, Gorbachev himself. Amid lofty appeals to justice and high-minded denunciations of Soviet tyranny, the American president undertook a comprehensive military buildup in response to the Soviet invasion of Afghanistan. The Soviets could not withstand the expense of trying to keep up with Reagan's military investment. Nor could they come close to matching such U.S. military technology as anti-missile defense and submarine-detection systems. Held at bay for decades by nuclear deterrence and concerted global resistance, the USSR finally crumbled from within, bringing an end to the Cold War. The United States and its close allies, possessing the world's most thoroughly market-driven economies, were also the most innovative and wealthiest countries and hence, all else equal, those best equipped to win long struggles for survival. Global-liberal societies' economic, military, and moral robustness proved decisive, as it had for their national-liberal predecessors. (The dominant paradigm and society that preceded global liberalism in the United States, those of approximately 1885 to 1965, were relatively focused on the nation state and thus national – rather than global-liberal systems).[19] Throughout the Soviet period, the USSR was a segmentary, tribal, plural state much like Austro-Hungary had been. Even as the Soviet Union engaged in brutal suppression, it prided itself in being made up of autonomous national cultures. When strongly identifying ethnic groups are also highly regionalized, as Armenians, Azerbaijanis, Uzbeks, and others were within the Soviet Union, a country is not merely weakened but in danger of disintegration when in crisis. For the longing of ethnic groups to participate with their fellows is difficult to stop, short of the use of overwhelming force. Such an unnatural political union as the USSR is hard to keep together. Had the Soviets used their absolute power to systematically

Russianize the country, more fully mixing its subject peoples and unifying their language and culture, as the French had during the 17th century, the regime might have collapsed but not the sovereign state with it.

The Eased Pax Americana, 1991-2012

Toward the end of, and following, the Soviet collapse, a decade-long interregnum of multi-lateralism arrived, to which Iraq's invasion of Kuwait presented an early challenge.

Under President George H. W. Bush, the United States undertook the First Iraq War in 1991 with strong involvement of the UN and the participation of many countries. The United States and its allies implemented General Colin Powell's doctrine of overwhelming force and soon reversed the Iraqi conquest, which without U.S. initiative would have been allowed to stand, but they made no attempt to replace the regime. For a time, the slogan became "the new world order," the restrained, civilized, collegial, largely uncontested, post-Cold War projection of a peaceful, liberal world under the leadership of the United States.

Meanwhile, Yugoslavia began to unravel as Slobodan Milošević's brooding Serbian nationalism turned murderous against successive Balkan national communities as they declared independence. When Slovenia and Croatia broke away, Milošević responded violently but was unable to halt the centrifugal movement. Bosnia was more problematic because more ethnically split, primarily between Serbians and Muslims, and its Serbian militias began committing genocide against their Muslim neighbors with Milošević's approval and support.

The world outcry against the atrocities was loud and nearly unanimous, but European countries, in their timidity born of collective guilt over fascism together with half a century of security dependence on the United States, were unable to bring themselves to halt it. Year after year the genocide went on amid barrages of denunciation and innumerable resolutions, but the Europeans would not act. Bush lent moral support and encouraged them to do their share and take responsibility for the problem in their own backyard, but he kept the United States out of the Balkans. President Bill Clinton at first continued Bush's policy of aloofness but after continued genocide and European handwringing the United States entered Bosnia in 1994 with European backing and partial UN support to halt the genocide. As another Serbian genocide was under way in Kosovo two years later, and the Europeans were again paralyzed, Clinton at last intervened with a bombing campaign to stop Serbia's war crimes. U.S. engagement under Clinton with the UN in Bosnia and Kosovo was more hesitant and delayed than it had been under the elder Bush in the Persian Gulf, but it too was consultative, needed, and generally appreciated.

An important consequence of the collapse of the USSR was that India, which had long been cozy with the Soviets, out of lingering colonial resentment toward Great Britain and Jawaharlal Nehru's genteel sympathy for hierarchy, began concerted liberalization and realignment and became an increasingly important member of the world community. The imminent threat to India, whose interests and inclinations lay entirely in peaceful relations with its neighbors and the world, was from Pakistan, bitter internecine struggle having resulted in partition at the very moment of India and Pakistan's independence in 1947. Pakistan claimed all of predominantly Muslim Kashmir and has directed aggression against India throughout the more than seven decades since their independence, waging four wars and an ongoing campaign of terrorism over the contested province. Ceaseless fanning of nationalist sentiment over Kashmir has been the Pakistani security forces' convenient justification for their grotesquely outsized position in the country's politics and economy. They stoked hatred toward India to gain domestic political support and deflect criticism from their immense diversion of resources and chronic mismanagement of the economy. As sensible and restrained opinion in Pakistan began acknowledging around 2010, the best of their country's institutions and traditions needed to be protected from the spreading extremism and volatility in their midst, much of it fostered by the security forces.

As Deng-regime China developed rapidly over the later decades of the global era, it increasingly posed the most serious threat to India as well as to the Pax Americana. China allowed considerable play to economic markets under the new regime – much more than did Maoist China or the USSR – but its markets remained predominantly under the direction of the state and conducted for purposes of the regime and its cronies. Its profile had much in common with that of imperial Germany of the hierarchical societies of the national era. As Germany was the rising hierarchical power of the late 19th and early 20th centuries, China was the rising hierarchical power of the late 20th and early 21st. It shared Bismarck's aim of exploiting the economic markets and strategy of co-opting internal dissent by improving conditions for the population while remaining authoritarian. China also came to share every bit of imperial Germany's hubris, yet China was totalitarian where the imperial Germany was not. China's population at the end of the period was just over four times that of the United States and 50 percent greater than that of the West as a whole.

The Chinese regime's single most hostile act toward the world community was the covert passing of nuclear weapons technology and components to Pakistan from the 1980s on. The regime wagered that it was in its interests to help equip Islamic countries with nuclear weapons in their growing contest with the United States and the West. Its intent was that this proliferation would be costly to the United States and its allies, tie them up, and provide the Chinese regime more room within which to maneuver.[20] Its intent was also to force the United States to reconfigure defense capabilities away from meeting Chinese conventional war threats and toward addressing Islamic insurgencies. Its further intent was to nudge Pakistan and India toward a nuclear stand-off in the expectation that a beleaguered India would be a less substantial counterweight to China. The Chinese rulers calculated that the gargantuan costs and risks of their ghastly, negative-sum action would be borne disproportionately by other countries, leaving China comparatively stronger. Pakistani and, potentially, Iranian nuclear weapons (the latter partly proliferated from Pakistan) posed major threats to everyone in the world, the Chinese people included, but the regime banked that given their well-known resolve, numbers, tight controls, and geographical insularity, these weapons would be less likely to be directed toward them than toward others. China deliberately created the nuclear proliferation that occupied a good deal of the rest of the world's international attention and resources. This strategic move was vintage Deng Xiaoping in its abstruse brilliance. The proliferation was also sufficiently secret and advanced in time from the threat that it fell within Deng's slogan, "Hide our claws."

That such proliferation would leave *China* stronger vis-à-vis the world, at least for a time, is likely correct, but note the reference behind the decision. This action greatly harmed China's true and lasting national interests. Who is to say that a nuclear war between Pakistan and India would not devastate China as well? Trolling in nuclear chaos could make sense only to a threatened elite within the Chinese Communist Party possessing doubtful popular acceptance, whose legacy of machinations haunts China and the world. The decision to proliferate in such a manner speaks more reliably about who the Chinese rulers are than decades of official statements.[21]

Where Deng-regime China was, until recently, for the most part pragmatic, North Korea was an erratic rogue state. From the Korean War on, the regime has stewed in its poisonous juices, glowered across the demilitarized zone, and intermittently taken hostile action against the South, all the while building up its military and cruelly exploiting its people. North Korea undertook extremely costly nuclear weapons development even as its perennial agricultural crisis resulted in widespread starvation. Learning more about this program in 1993 than it wanted to know, the Clinton administration pressured and bribed the North Korean regime into signing a formal accord with the United States and allowing inspections, whereupon the regime went underground with its program. When the deception was discovered by the George W. Bush administration in 2002 and was soon after admitted, North Korea summarily expelled the inspectors. Already committed in Iraq and Afghanistan, Bush did nothing. Seeking to intimidate at every turn, the Kim Jong-un regime's nature has long been abundantly apparent.[22]

Despite Russia's promising change of regime and withdrawal from much of its empire, hopes for a new world order were largely dashed over the next decade. Russia continued to possess a formidable military, including a nuclear arsenal second only to that of the United States, and its turbulent experiment with pseudo-democratic reform under Boris Yeltsin soon proved unserious. The Russian regime once again became fully authoritarian after Vladimir Putin was elected president in 2000, and the country again began presenting problems to the world community increasingly comparable to those the USSR had presented. Russia once more began menacing its neighbors.

Putin's aggression began on a relatively small scale and was carried out surreptitiously for the most part as it occupied two provinces of Georgia and one of Moldova. Putin attempted to assassinate Ukraine's Reform President Viktor Yuschenko with dioxin poisoning in 2004. He may also have murdered Polish President Lech Kaczynski and much of his administration in 2010 by causing their plane to crash while attempting to land in Russia. Putin's covert interference with and corruption of the new regimes of the former Soviet republics and dependencies undermined autonomy and set back development in them.

Muslims were partly in denial of and partly awed and confounded by the West's stupendous military and technological achievements during the 18th, 19th, and early 20th century, as were third-world peoples almost everywhere. Muslims were also revolted and embarrassed by those accomplishments. By the middle decades of the national era, they began looking to Westernizers like Mustafa Ataturk and Gamal Nasser. The most prominent Islamic figures of the early decades of the global era instead sought inspiration and strength in their own tradition. Many young Muslims were receptive to new Islamist forms (i.e., those of totalitarian political Islam) that were developing in Cairo, Damascus, and other centers during the 1950s and early 1960s, particularly around the Muslim Brotherhood. Decades in the making, the Islamist movement began coming into its own during the late 1960s and 1970s in the Middle East.

The Islamic Resurgence, the strengthening of Muslim tradition and aggressive resistance to difference, particularly women's rights, increasingly pronounced since the late 1960s, has presented a many-sided Muslim counter-paradigm diametrically opposed to global liberalism (although there has been important variation in it from country to country). The Islamic Resurgence has been predominantly Islamist, presenting a hardening of Muslim societies' perennial authoritarianism into militancy and totalitarianism. Accordingly, much of the Islamic world has remained strikingly insular and highly intolerant of other traditions, and it has posed threats to non-Muslim societies in many parts of the world.

Distantly analogous to the rise of fundamentalist Christianity in the United States and many third-world countries, the Islamic Resurgence has been associated with the institutionalization and spread of moral and religious discipline in an effort to restore sociocultural coherence to personal and communal life. But the Islamic movement entails a strongly collectivist, outward political thrust almost entirely absent in Christianity. Moreover, where Christian fundamentalism has lain outside of and resisted many aspects of the dominant global-liberal paradigm, the Islamic Resurgence has been paradigmatic in the Muslim world since the mid-1960s.

Bound up with the Islamic Resurgence, a double crescent of conflict containing most of the world's trouble spots has described the boundaries between Islam and its neighbors in Asia, Europe, and Africa, extending from Mindanao through portions of Indonesia, Thailand, India, Pakistan, Xinjiang, Central Asia, the Caucasus, the Middle East, Sudan, Nigeria, Mali, and beyond. Under the Islamic Resurgence, most fundamentalist Muslims in particular have shown neither respect nor tolerance for their neighbors, "infidels" toward whom they feel morally superior and bear accumulated resentments. Large numbers of putatively moderate Muslims everywhere have supported their highly intolerant coreligionists in spirit and with resources. Along many of their frontiers, notably in equatorial Africa, Muslims have been gaining ground through migration, fertility, aggression, terror, and pressured conversion. Many Muslim regimes, in their ambivalent simultaneous admiration for and fear of fundamentalism have encouraged or tolerated Islamist militias, leaving confused sovereignty and porous borders. They have used such non-state actors ambiguously to simultaneously allow and cover internal and external aggression from safe havens. Like Lashkar-e-Taiba and Hezbollah, al Qaeda and ISIS have been Islamist militias, only much more ambitious and far-reaching than the others.

In Israel, the Islamic Resurgence has met with what has appeared to be its nemesis, the adjacent small, prosperous, liberal, Western country that has received the brunt of its wrath but is not going to be intimidated by anyone into yielding its security, although the Jewish state would be a partner to a just and lasting peace which guaranteed its national security.

Given the frame of mind accompanying the Islamic Resurgence, Israel's great strength and success have enraged Muslim populations, as has U.S. support of it. Islam being a highly political religion, the *umma*, the community of all Muslims, is of supreme importance to it.[23] The Islamic Resurgence has manifested strong nationalism from the beginning, only oriented toward the umma rather than the nation-state.[24] Muslims have taken Israel's very existence as an unacceptable travesty. An Islamic Resurgence would have occurred in any event, but the Arab-Israeli conflict has further inflamed what might otherwise have been less radical and xenophobic.

The surface challenge to the world community has been to help assure Israel's security while offering the Palestinians land and statehood. Such a problem would appear to be ready-made for solution via side-payments, reparations, border adjustments, good fences, some UN troops, an end to detached settlements, and a Palestinian capitol in East Jerusalem – but it is not. Prime Minister Ehud Barak offered such an agreement to the Palestinians in 2000, and Yasser Arafat rejected it. Prime Minister Ehud Olmert offered slightly more in 2008, and Mahmoud Abbas rejected it. The fundamental problem is that neither the Palestinians nor the vast majority of other Muslims have been ready to accept a non-Muslim state in their midst. Reconciliation of the Arab-Israeli conflict has foundered on the spirit of the times in the Muslim world.

The Islamic Resurgence has been radical and nationalist partly because of the strength of communal ties to Islam as a whole but also partly because of the cynical efforts of Muslim rulers, particularly oil producers like the Saudis, to deflect anger away from their own authoritarian regimes. For a time, the Islamic Resurgence seemed to pose the great threat toward these regimes. But many Muslim ruling classes of the global era like many before them, Muslim and non-Muslim, consciously employed nationalism to redirect popular anger outward in order to stymie its natural, inward, expression. Stoking nationalism to distract Egyptians from domestic economic and political issues was the modus operandi of the Mubarak regime for decades. Israel has been the Muslim autocracies' all-purpose enemy, although as the United States was drawn into the region, it too increasingly became a target. Nor, mixing fervor and cynicism, have most of the corrupt rulers been impervious to the charismatic radicals' nationalist appeal, so long as their regimes' interests have been secure. While throttling dissent at home, the tyrants long privately chortled at the Islamist gains and U.S. difficulties abroad.

Into this tinderbox appeared Osama bin Laden, the product of extremist Saudi Arabian Wahabi Islam, engineering school, corporate business, and the Afghan resistance to Soviet occupation during the 1980s. His al Qaeda terrorist campaign and especially his spectacular strike on the World Trade Center of September 11, 2001 successfully shifted some Muslim rage from Israel toward the United States and the West, intensifying the Islamist insurgency against the Pax Americana. Bin Laden's influence was considerable in Pakistan before he was killed in May of 2011 in his regime-provided sanctuary.

After 9/11 the United States under President George W. Bush invaded Afghanistan in early 2002 with the support of the allies to depose the Taliban regime that had harbored the terrorists. Bush replaced it with a formally democratic but duplicitous, corrupt, and ineffectual regime under Hamid Karzai that he half-heartedly sought to strengthen with a program of institution building. While the Taliban-dominated insurgency simmered at a relatively low level during its early years with its top command protected in Pakistan, the U.S. president redirected his attention to Iraq where Saddam Hussein was busy being his provocative self though providing a necessary counterweight to Iran and doing so without threatening vital American international security interests.

Still possessing considerable public support soon after 9/11, George W. Bush invaded Iraq in 2003 and quickly destroyed Hussein's regime, only to face stubborn guerrilla resistance. A follow-up effort led by General David Petraeus during the surge of 2007 and 2008 was at last able to install a partially democratic successor regime that showed some early vitality. Expensive, poorly conceived, conducted and justified, and bearing multiple unfortunate side effects, the Iraq War dragged on for eight years. President Barack Obama scaled down troop strength in Iraq, and significant U.S. combat operations ceased there in late 2011. As the United

States departed, the Shi'ite-dominated Maliki government became ominously more autocratic and sectarian vis-à-vis the country's Sunni and Kurdish minorities, while moving closer to Iran.

Following years of secondary attention by the United States, the war in Afghanistan intensified again between 2008 and 2011. Western forces countered Taliban successes for a time, but the Obama White House always opposed the war and wound down U.S. involvement.

The Arab Spring that began in December of 2010 presented what might have been a hopeful new direction for the Islamic Resurgence. Beginning with Tunisia's democratic uprising and going on to those of Egypt, Libya, Yemen, Syria, and other countries, the movement initially brought degrees of self-determination to a few once entirely hierarchical Arab countries in the face of cruel resistance from tyrannical ruling classes, but the activists were turned back everywhere except in Tunisia. The courageous and inspired, mostly young people who supported democratization struggled with intelligence and pride to shunt aside those herding, fleecing, and stifling them. They made beginnings toward throwing off their shackles and instituting much-needed economic, political, social, and cultural reforms, but their cause awaited another day.

The true nemesis of the Islamic Resurgence was neither Israel nor the West; it was the extent to which Muslim publics were susceptible to diversion by radical nationalism. This in turn has been substantially conditioned by the hierarchical origins and history of Islam. Hopes for Arab Spring-like liberalization or for Middle Eastern peace are likely to remain unfulfilled until Muslims find within themselves the resources with which to critique their tradition and extend humanity to their neighbors.

The Pax Americana was fairly effective overall in deterring outright invasion around the world from 1945 through 2012. Public support was relatively strong in advanced liberal countries for halting overt aggression between states, at least insofar as the stakes were high and remedies practicable. In response to clear-cut security threats, global-liberal voting publics, when led by the United States, were usually willing and able to isolate economically and politically, or if necessary turn back by force, any country that would challenge global harmony in such an egregious manner, although they occasionally looked the other way when preoccupied by more pressing concerns. The security regime was less effective in countering insurgencies, which tend to be drawn out and ambiguous, but those too have been reversed when sufficiently threatening to the liberal world order. Although shaken by 9/11, the Pax Americana seemed to face less menacing threats than the Soviet Union had posed, and it remained relatively low key through the George W. Bush and first Obama administrations.

The Precarious Pax Americana and Global Disorder from 2013

Another dangerous phase of the Pax Americana arrived when President Obama partially suspended U.S. international leadership and operation of the Pax Americana, beginning with a reversal of the expected ways of treating international friends and foes. For example, after Poland had gone out on a political limb at the request of the United States in 2008 and accepted NATO anti-ballistic missiles to protect Europe from the threat of Iranian nuclear missiles, he unceremoniously dropped the plans during his first year in office. He snubbed any number of allied leaders the same year. Two years later, at the urging of Britain and France, he unwisely participated in NATO air strikes that enabled Arab-Spring rebels to overthrow Muammar Gaddafi in Libya and that country to slip into chaos. Obama showed disquieting animus toward Israel from the onset. While repeatedly disappointing U.S. allies, he reached out to adversaries of the security regime, as in his "resetting" of relations with Russia and Iran.

Both sides of the administrations peculiar treatment of friends and foes came together in Syria where the 2012 "red line" regarding consequences the Iranian-backed regime would face if it were to employ chemical weapons against its people, became an embarrassment the following year when Bashar al-Assad was allowed to use those weapons without repercussions in suppressing freedom fighters the United States had been supporting. Obama conveyed the impression to opponents of the security regime that he was not oriented toward forcefully restraining their aggression.[25]

U.S. international policy was sufficiently out of character during the first Obama administration that it took the major authoritarian powers four years of experience with it before they would allow themselves to believe that a partial caesura had occurred in the Pax Americana. They began exploiting the opportunity during the second Obama administration, moving into the vacuum created by its ambivalence and inaction to forcibly extend control over land, sea, and airspace belonging to their neighbors or the world, albeit cautiously with the exception of ISIS. Once its adversaries understood that the Pax Americana was partially suspended, they began encroaching upon the liberal world order, first by seeking to establish and progressively enlarge regional spheres of influence.

Accordingly, China restructured its ruling class with a more forward presence of the Red Army under Xi Jinping on November 15, 2012 immediately following the U.S. presidential election. Its bid was under way to exclude U.S. and allied military power from the western Pacific. Insofar as this campaign was successful, it would absorb Taiwan and Finlandize or turn other traditional U.S. allies in the area, including South Korea and Japan. The more of its program China achieved, the greater its momentum would be and the more dangerous and costly the eventual containment of or conflict with it.

While rapidly building up its military amid great secrecy, the Chinese regime began increasingly bullying India and other neighbors over arbitrary territorial claims. In early 2013 it sharply intensified its efforts to extend control over the Spratly Islands and most of the South and East China Seas, to which several other countries had valid claims in international law, but it did not. China created artificial islands in the Spratlys 660 miles from the mainland and 210 miles from the Philippines, building military airfields on several of them. At stake were airspace, surface transportation, fishing, and seabed resource rights that included large undersea petroleum reserves.

The regime also began pushing with increased force and bluster to annex Taiwan, on Beijing's terms. It did so against the agreement between the United States and China signed by Richard Nixon and Mao Zedong in 1972, under which relations between the two countries were normalized. That agreement grounds the understanding in effect between the world community and China regarding Taiwan: There is one China, Taiwan is part of China, and it will one day be reincorporated into China, but only by peaceful means and with the agreement of Taiwan. The agreement provided for transfer of the permanent U.N. Security Council seat from the Republic of China (Taiwan) to the People's Republic, in return for China's acceptance of normalization. China was sowing hatred of the West and Japan and whipping up nationalism for popular support while beginning to expand territorially.

Following Obama's reset with it, Putin's Russia invaded and occupied Crimea in early 2014. Soon after, amid a massive disinformation campaign, it invaded additional territory in eastern and southern Ukraine while paying and/or coercing Russian-speaking locals to join, providing some cover for what it was doing. Russia consolidated control of the occupied portions of Ukraine during 2015. Its conquests in Ukraine were the first open invasion of a sovereign European nation since World

War II. Russia also began harassing numerous European countries with flagrant violations of their airspace and coastal waters. This time around, major authoritarian societies were employing creative, confusing, irregular, asymmetric means of conducting international aggression and propaganda war.

Iran responded to the reset with it by continued extension of influence in the Middle East, sponsorship of terrorism, and development of nuclear weapons and missiles. That country consolidated its control in Lebanon and Syria, increased its control in Iraq and supported the Houthi takeover of Yemen. The United States and Europe reached a controversial nuclear weapons accord with Iran in 2015 that postponed but did not bar it's becoming a nuclear power.

ISIS or the Islamic State in Syria and the Levant grew out of al Qaeda in Iraq, the home base of which was Anbar province, during the Second Iraq War. Headed by Abu Bakr al Baghdadi from 2010 until 2019, ISIS sent its radical forces to fight in Syria when the Arab-Spring uprising began there in 2011. Known for its barbarous beheadings and smashing of artifacts from earlier civilizations, ISIS was committed to a strategy of holding land and forming an Islamist state, which led to an early break with al Qaeda. After conquering large swaths of territory in Syria and Iraq, ISIS proclaimed itself the Caliphate in 2014 and began accepting affiliates in numerous countries across the Islamic world from West Africa to the Philippines.

The onslaught of ISIS was already under way during Obama's first term, but most of its territorial gains came during the second. After long resisting military involvement against ISIS, the American president eventually began hesitant, perfunctory use of air power in Syria and extended military aid to the Iraqi government to fight the radical movement. Coordinating with Iran, Russia then moved ground troops and planes into Syria in September of 2015 to support the Assad regime while expanding its naval base in Tartus. Its targets were overwhelmingly the United States' Sunni allies among the Syrian rebels. The administration began working with some effectiveness in 2016 with Kurdish militias friendly to the West, who began taking territory from ISIS in Iraq and Syria.

On multiple fronts, the Obama administration balked at assuming leadership and largely left the allies to fend for themselves. Although the administration moved some forces to Eastern Europe, it for the most part ceded support of Ukraine to the European allies, who participated in economic sanctions, organized financial support for the country, and sent a few troops to neighboring countries but, like the United States, were unwilling to help arm it to better resist the invasion. Japan and other Asian allies largely had to deal with Chinese aggression by themselves although the United States did send ships through and planes over the South China Sea in sporadic defiance of and protest against China's unilateral advances and proclamations. The administration opposed the Iran-supported Houthi takeover of Yemen but passed on much of the task of dealing with it to the Arab League with Saudi Arabia, Egypt, and Jordan taking the lead.

Obama disengaged from the Pax Americana in part because unlike his predecessors he substantially took the security of the United States and its allies for granted.[26] He also disengaged from it because, even more unlike his predecessors, he did not consider these countries beacons. He identified not with them but with putatively disadvantaged outsiders, a broad social disaffection he shared with many of his contemporaries. Obama's concerns were withdrawing troops from Iraq and Afghanistan, endorsing unconditional Palestinian statehood, releasing prisoners from Guantanamo, normalizing relations with Cuba, fighting ebola in Africa, giving amnesty to illegal immigrants, and allowing large numbers of unscreened Syrian refugees into the country.

The approach of international disorder during Obama's second administration initiated a new phase of the Pax Americana in which the security regime was under sustained challenge and for the first time precarious. The precarious Pax Americana since 2013 has been analogous to the late Pax Britannica from 1871-1914, the period following the Franco-Prussian war and unification of Germany. Once an authoritarian, nationalistic, rapidly industrializing, and broadly developing Germany was unified under a martial Prussia that was filled with hubris from three successful wars, culminating in the quick, lopsided defeat of France – Britain had to wage an increasingly uphill struggle to maintain the international security regime, one that eventually failed. However, the precarious Pax Americana under Obama was different from the late Pax Britannica in that this time around, unlike the last, the potential power was overwhelmingly present in the liberal societies with which to support the security regime.

Much of the grand drama of the modern world continued to be the opposition between liberal and authoritarian societies during the global era. Its major hierarchical regimes were all fundamentally predatory – they aggressed daily against their own people, and only military deterrence kept them from aggressing against other countries. The Pax Americana was built upon the terrible lessons learned during and after the 31-year crisis regarding what happens when liberal societies appease authoritarian societies' demands or stand aside when they conquer. Most Americans understand that the United States is the indispensable nation without whose leadership the peaceful, tolerant, prosperous world we have known since 1945 disintegrates, and they have an understandable dread regarding how bad the consequences might be were that to occur. They also sense that the United States needs its friends and allies just as they need it.

The ultimate flywheel of the Pax Americana had long been that the advanced liberal societies making up the core of the world community possessed tremendous resources, basic unity, capable citizens, dedicated leaders, widespread responsibility, and great potential power when the need arose. Contemporary hierarchical regimes, by contrast, were brittle, one and all. If their aggression were deterred for long enough, they would eventually accumulate unsustainable levels of corruption and discontent and crumble internally. Deterring authoritarian societies from international aggression required sustained alertness and resolve on the part of the United States and its allies, a prolonged arm-wrestle.

As we shall see, the further weakening of the Pax Americana that occurred between 2013 and 2016 had to do with the increased economic might of China but more to do with sociocultural changes in the West. China now had substantial resources, but the massive economic resources of the United States remained in place, and those of Europe, although diminished, also remained enormous. Nevertheless, important sources of U.S. and allied strength were eroding through the global era while some of those of authoritarian societies were building. Among the new sources of American weakness were precipitous declines in unity, leadership, engagement, and responsibility. Tendencies to narrowness, historical obliviousness, and naïve idealism have long been vulnerabilities of liberal societies needing to be overcome, but wisdom and leadership were becoming scarce by the end of the global era, leaving these societies exposed. As government became less dependable, it could be less readily entrusted with tasks, including that of maintaining international security. China and Russia underwent turbulent paradigm conflict respectively during the late 1960s and 1970s and the late 1980s and 1990s, and by the mid-2010s it was the West's turn again. The problem was that the upper classes of liberal societies were withdrawing their sense of responsibility and needed leadership, as if playing chicken with reality. While the Chinese were investing immense sums, the Russians were maintaining their formidable nuclear presence, and both were upgrading their military technology, liberal societies were dropping their defense spending and readiness to dangerous levels. John Gaddis aptly speaks of "a disconnection in our thinking between the security to which we have become accustomed and the means by which we obtained it."[27] Leon Trotsky said it best: "You may not be interested in war, but war is interested in you!"[28]

As we shall also see, the nature of international security regimes determines a great deal about the societies under them. The geopolitics of the global era at the same time gains the fuller context it requires when we examine the profound ways in which society and character changed during its 51 years. The Pax Americana was foundational to the society and time, and so was the global capitalism that arose out of it, to which we now turn.

CHAPTER 2

GLOBAL CAPITALISM

As the United States and the United Kingdom were nearing the end of World War II, the global economy was high on their list of priorities. Having watched the world fall into depression amid mercantilist, competitive currency devaluations and tariff increases, they had learned well the bitter lessons of harsh international monetary and trade practices. They resolved to do better and began putting in place the architecture of a global capitalism that would not become fully ascendant until decades later. In 1944 the United States hosted the Bretton Woods conference at which, with major British input, the bedrock principles and institutions of postwar global free trade were established. The international monetary system issuing from it was based upon a limited gold standard that provided at once for capital controls and for adjustments between currency values. The International Monetary Fund (IMF) was created to monitor national policies and currency values and extend loans to assist countries whose currencies were in jeopardy.[29] The monetary aspects of Bretton Woods endured until 1971 when reconciling countries' divergent monetary and fiscal policies within a quasi-fixed-rate system became unduly cumbersome. A system of floating rates has been in place ever since for the currencies of most countries, although a few have pegged the value of their currencies to that of another nation as, for example, Hong Kong has done with its currency to the U.S. dollar.

After the war the United States and United Kingdom established relatively low tariffs, and in 1947, together with many other countries, set up the current international free trade regime under the General Agreement on Trade and Tariffs (GATT). GATT and its successor, the World Trade Organization (WTO), provided a loose framework within which member nations were encouraged to progressively liberalize trade policies. The infamous Smoot-Hawley Tariff that took effect in 1930 had been 46 percent, which was not unusual for the time. By the early 1980s, average U.S., EU, and Japanese tariffs were reduced to 4.9 percent, 6.0 percent, and 5.4 percent respectively, and by 2009 to 4.3 percent, 3.6 percent, and 3.1 percent.[30] In addition to those brokered through the WTO, a number of important regional multilateral trade agreements were reached among global capitalist countries to facilitate international exchange. They included NAFTA (the North American Free Trade Agreement), joining the United States, Canada, and Mexico in even less restrictive trade in 1994. Yet the most important condition of global capitalism was the simple presence of the Pax Americana's light international order, leaving room for peaceful international trade that created its own momentum.

THE TRIUMPH OF GLOBAL CAPITALISM

Global capitalism was the economic facet of global liberalism. The entire world rather than the nation-state became the economic arena between 1965 and 2016 as the markets spilled across national boundaries in a massive way. Although much of the infrastructure of the world markets had been established earlier, global capitalism did not become dominant until the mid-1960s, for only then did protected, heavily regulated national-capitalist economies largely yield to bracingly open global ones. Some of the characteristic features of global capitalism did not emerge until the 1970s and early 1980s.

Market economies were no longer easily able to sustain barriers to restrict competition and protect national economic interests. Monopolies and cartels in such forms as industrial organizations, trade associations, fair trade agreements, and labor unions had been encouraged during the national era. Many national-era restraints of trade were either swept away or significantly weakened under the vigorous economic competition of the global era, although new ones also arose, including OPEC.

After centuries of inaction in response to the stupendous development of the modern West, the third world became predominantly capitalist during the global era. Most third-world countries substantially cut back hierarchies,[31] privatized former state enterprises, and opened their economic markets. Supply and demand drew and squeezed well over a billion former peasants off the land and into cities and towns for paying jobs. Among non-Western societies, only Japan had liberalized and achieved sustained economic growth prior to the global era, under special circumstances during the 1950s. Virtually all other third-world countries remained traditionally hierarchical until the global period. Japan's postwar recovery complete, it surged to world leadership in many industries during the 1960s and 1970s. Then, early in the global era, the "four tigers" – Hong Kong, Singapore, Taiwan, and South Korea – underwent extensive economic liberalization and achieved sustained growth. From 1965, Singapore under Lee Kwan Yew and his son Lee Hsien Loong pursued free-market policies coupled with mild, benign authoritarian rule, carried out with genius by the elder Lee.

Capitalism broke out of its earlier Western confines and became widely accepted, as a global agora of scores of new and prospering market societies came into being amid economic freedom and unparalleled international trade. Most of Latin America became capitalist during the late 1970s and 1980s, Chile spectacularly so. That country had enjoyed a precociously democratic history earlier in the 20th century but had been dependent upon the export of a few basic commodities, subject to strong price swings. Like numerous other less developed societies of the time, it was also burdened with a costly, inefficient bureaucracy and dysfunctional welfare state. Following the capable and well-intentioned but misguidedly statist leadership of Eduardo Frei, Chile underwent the wrenching turmoil of Salvador Allende's communist expropriations followed by General Augusto Pinochet's brutal repression. Despite the appalling severity with which the latter dealt with the radical opposition, Pinochet undertook thoroughgoing economic reforms based upon Milton Friedman's pro-free-market ideas as implemented by a talented group of University of Chicago-trained economists. Pinochet stabilized the money supply, pruned and restructured social programs, and deregulated the economy. His brilliant, startlingly successful privatization of Chile's social security system was influential worldwide. From the 1970s, Chile enjoyed the strong, sustained, and diversified economic growth that had previously eluded it, becoming an early third-world exemplar of the advantages of working with the markets, not against them.

Mexico first took the opposite turn from Chile's in the global era as President Lopez Portillo hurriedly undertook massive nationalization of the banking system toward the end of his term in 1982. His country liberalized belatedly from the early 1990s under Salinas de Gotari and several successors. Peña Nieto, although from the long-retrograde PRI, attempted to strike against entrenched special interests beginning in 2012, but his country was only able to grow at a disappointing 2 percent rate.[32] Brazil, a star during the 1990s and first decade of this century, settled back to a 1 to 2 percent growth rate and then sank into deep recession in 2015 from which it did not emerge until 2017.[33]

India's Nehru set a mid-century economic course of top-down planning, high subsidies, intrusive controls, and socialist leaning. He bequeathed a legacy of mixed traditional hierarchical and British-elite disdain for economic markets, sapping India's economy for decades, but he did create the elite institutes of technology that were important to its later ascent. Prime Minister P. V. Rao and Economics Minister Manmohan Singh of the Congress Party at last began deregulating the cumbersome economy and opening it to the markets in 1991. The sustained economic development which began that year leveraged the skills, energy, and capital of large, well-educated émigré communities to establish centers of entrepreneurialism in Bangalore and Mumbai. Their software and business services industries soon became global presences. Fluent knowledge of English by much of the country's middle class helped facilitate India's economic development.

Nevertheless, numerous harmful conditions impeded India's economy. Amid pervasive corruption, its bureaucracy, the bulk of whose compensation came in bribes, was dysfunctional. Bureaucrats represented a tiny, largely exploitative portion of the population.

An air of satrapy hung about the Indian civil service and judiciary, both of which were granted extensive legal immunity, leaving officialdom unaccountable.[34] The government was supposed to provide free electricity and water but performed these services poorly when at all, yet private utilities were barred from charging for services. Defense procurement and agricultural regulation were corrupt.[35] India protected its small retail sector by discouraging international chains (until late 2015), slowing growth but augmenting social stability. India's informal economy remained vastly larger than its formal one, in part because being in it enabled employers to escape draconian labor laws. India was burdened as well by an extremely complex tax system.[36]

Several Asian countries, including Hong Kong, Singapore, Taiwan, and South Korea, reached or exceeded first-world economic levels during the 1970s, 1980s, and 1990s, quickly matching the earlier economic miracles of Germany and Japan. South Korea's economy grew at an 8.3 percent rate from 1965 to 1980.[37] By 2010 Singapore had become one of the most prosperous countries in the world per capita. India began sustained GDP growth that ranged between approximately 4 and 10 percent from when it liberalized in 1991 through 2016.[38] India, Brazil, Indonesia, Turkey, and South Korea became economic powerhouses, as did China in the second world (that is, among comparatively developed but predominantly hierarchical countries). Non-Western societies had waited out the early- and national-capitalist periods (1500-1885 and 1885-1965 respectively), but most accepted capitalism during the late 20th century. In doing so they skipped directly from traditional hierarchy into global capitalism.

The Tech Revolution. A third industrial revolution every bit as epochal as its predecessors[39] began unfolding in the United States during the late 1950s. Breakthroughs in electronics delivered the semiconductor, and computers began their ramifying series of new information technologies, bringing steep declines in production costs and marked increases in productivity. Automation displaced industrial workers as farm machinery had displaced agricultural workers during the late 19th century. Industrial employment in most advanced economies stood at about 25 percent of the labor force in 1820, peaked just after World War II at nearly 50 percent (32 percent in the United States), and was again back to around 25 percent by 1980.[40] By 2010 it had declined to about 10 percent of employment in the United States and most first-world economies (but 22, 20, and 17 percent respectively in the robust manufacturing sectors of the German, Italian, and Japanese economies),[41] made redundant by automation, relocation to the third world, and growing demand for services. As part of the tech revolution, robotics began coming into its own in the 21st century, further displacing industrial employment. Yet machines were becoming smarter, safer, more adaptable, more programmable, and less expensive, enabling first-world manufacturing to become more efficient than utilizing cheap labor in the third world and China. Industrial employment may have been down, but industrial production still made up 29 percent of U.S. GDP in 1984 and 20 percent in 2015.[42]

Job replacement through technological development also took place in the service sector even as employment in the sector expanded overall. Drastic reductions in the labor needed to type, file, sort, manipulate, and transfer information occurred during the global era, radically transforming office jobs, just as those in spinning and weaving had been two centuries earlier. New technologies displaced large numbers of secretarial positions.[43] Entire categories of service workers disappeared while other new ones appeared – floor traders were out, software engineers in, for example.

Amid profound technological development and business innovation, an impressive entrepreneurialism arose in the United States under global capitalism, an extremely competitive culture of risk-taking whose epicenter was California's Silicon Valley – like Wall Street in New York, a loose geographical designation but above all a culture and state of mind. Exuding a sense of limitless opportunity, those under its thrall bore the supreme confidence that if someone has a great idea and runs with it, they can achieve astounding things.

Denizens of the Silicon Valley felt that all it takes to succeed is ability, boldness, energy, and perseverance. With or without credentials, two talented young people in jeans and T-shirts who presented a great idea to gatekeeping venture capitalists, angel investors, executives, corporate lawyers, or consultants could raise millions of dollars there. Even though the earlier extreme openness diminished to a degree in this century as engineers succeeded the area's founding figures with their more diverse backgrounds, nowhere else has such opportunity ever been possible. As a consequence, many of the boldest and most creative from all over the world migrated to the United States, to the country's great benefit. Abundant venture capital, outstanding universities, and a highly skilled labor force uniquely combined in the Silicon Valley with extreme entrepreneurialism, creativity, and receptivity to change. Where most cultures in human history have been conservative, this one was radical, spawning generation upon generation of technological change.

The tech phase from the 1960s through the end of the century was primarily about building out the core information technologies of computers, the Internet, cell phones, and networking. Even as that continued, the new phase in the early 21st century became tech, out to conquer the world economy. Legions of extraordinarily capable entrepreneurs and engineers in this phase of the tech revolution were freshly rethinking every corner of the economy, reducing the notion of technology to its essence, which is getting more from less. In their cerebral vision, technology was far more than electronics: It was everything from how banking is conducted to how transportation is organized; how medical knowledge is brought to bear on symptoms to how education is conducted; how customers pay for merchandise to how prospective mates are sorted, and from how materials are made to how cities are laid out. The Silicon Valley's top entrepreneurs and engineers were extraordinarily talented human beings supremely confident that they were taking over the world, and they were doing precisely that. Entire industries large and small began to fall like overripe fruit, including many richly deserving displacement. The Silicon Valley ethos was, "We're the smartest; we're going to win; and if you don't understand how, we don't have the time to tell you."

Technology was rapidly moving toward dominance in the American and the world economies. Apple devoured entire global industries, including much of the world's music industry. In the iPhone, it had the gold-standard smart phone worldwide. It had its eye on conquering television. Google was devouring Madison Avenue in a similar way. Cisco built out large portions of the global communications infrastructure. Facebook reached some 2 billion active users worldwide. Adages like "Software eats labor" and "Tech eats finance" exemplified the limitless confidence and competitiveness of the early 21st century Silicon Valley.

In its crosshairs among vast numbers of other targets were the automobile and energy industries. The established auto industry was on the verge of major disruption at the hands of tech competitors to whom automobiles became computer platforms that ought to do everything for their owners, in addition to providing a superior driving experience. Teslas, for example, got new software updates automatically, had few moving parts, could be recharged at home, and needed minimal repair. The company had no dealer network; its cars were bought online. Dealerships were the old, national-era model. Tesla seemed to have more to fear from other tech companies than it did from GM or Toyota. Google and other companies were far along toward self-driving automobiles, freeing people to use their transportation time productively while dramatically enhancing both safety and the efficiency of urban land use.

Auto and truck drivers seemed to be as obsolete and quaint as elevator operators, not long after which, pilots and air traffic controllers would be too. Mechanical and civil engineers had already largely been replaced by software, and accountants were ripe for the same.

The lack of abundant, inexpensive, clean energy remained a bottleneck throughout the global era, although it was diminishing toward the end. Each previous industrial revolution had its new energy technology – the first, coal-burning steam power and the second, gasoline- burning internal combustion engines. The 1960s and 1970s developed nuclear power, but fission had daunting side-effects that increasingly rendered it politically unacceptable as an energy source. Research and development were going into the quest for alternative energy that was at last bearing fruit in solar, wind, and other efficient alternative energy sources.

The Revolution in Finance. The United States also developed impressive new financial institutions and instruments that greatly facilitated the raising of capital for corporate ventures during the global era. Amid the large interest-rate fluctuations of the late 1970s, a new generation of financial theorists came onto the scene, with whose help finance became highly creative and much more efficient at matching investors with opportunities.

Michael Milken's innovations in high-yield bonds during the 1980s allowed smaller and riskier businesses access to the bond markets. During the 1990s the advent of options markets and rise of exchange-traded funds (ETFs), derivatives mimicking whole exchanges or portions of them such as industries, made possible unprecedented sophistication in hedging. Financial instruments could be devised to manage any conceivable risk that businesses and investors face ,as complex debt deals could be tailored to finely match the needs of companies and financial institutions. Select deregulation and competition between financial exchanges drastically reduced the costs of buying and selling instruments of all kinds, again sharply cutting the costs of doing business. A vast array of new derivatives made investment much less expensive and more efficient, resulting in an altogether more financially driven business environment.

Amid the new financial acuity and prominence, ownership and management increasingly became separated. The advent of rapid-turnover institutional ownership during the 1970s and 1980s, followed by programmed trading, put serious strain upon the traditional role of boards of directors, bringing about a transformation in corporate governance. Plural, diverse, indirect, ephemeral investors had decreasing interest in participating in corporate governance. Shareholder control of corporate affairs was metamorphosing from internal politics or "voice," to the threat of selling or "exit."[44]

By late in the global era, tech was beginning to conquer finance as it had other industries, under the rubric of *fintech* or financial technology, taking apart and reorganizing finance with software. Rethinking the very notion of banking, it considered banks to be lumbering and obsolete: They borrow people's money, impose fees, support branches, pose credit risk, and require backup by the Federal Depository Insurance Corporation (FDIC).

Retail banking is easily performed by software: Paypal and similar services pay bills, and eLoan extends credit. Bitcoin and other crypto-currencies also had powerful implications for banks as they did for other less advanced payment systems. When bills may be securely paid for fractions of 1 percent, and currency exchange becomes a free, frictionless ledger entry, what need was there for banks with their exorbitant fees and systemic risks? Crypto-currencies may or may not prove viable or significant in the long run, but they introduced important notions that were likely to own the future. Similarly revolutionary thinking was beginning to move into the insurance industry.

The Revolution in Management. Large business achieved major productivity gains during the global era and continued to increase market share in the economy. Notable efficiency gains arose from corporations discovering that they do best when they stick to their core missions. For a time, particularly during the 1960s, such high-flying conglomerates as LTV, ITT, and Litton thought it advantageous to diversify and accumulate subsidiaries in many different industries; but it became clear during the 1970s that the need to diversify in such a manner applies only to investors, not to companies. As corporations learned to stay with what they knew best, the economy became more specialized, and each task was performed more efficiently. Unlike the haphazard mergers of the 1960s, those of the 1980s were all about synergies, finding elements of missions that had positive externalities for each other. Yet it took some care to define a core business properly.

Business enterprises learned how to divide and allocate portions of their core missions utilizing much more varied structures than ever before to centralize some tasks and decentralize others as needed, enabling them to respond more effectively to the diverse exigencies that arose.[45] Exotic organizational advances were among the innovations facilitated by the widespread use of management consulting. Relying upon consultants and contracting out disparate services enabled companies to stay trim and agile while meeting extremely well the many one-time-only problems with which they might otherwise have difficulty coping.

Large corporations moved away from the turgid bureaucracy widespread throughout the national period. Lean new entities with flatter organizational structures arose in which layers of management were shed and responsibility widely delegated. The most competitive companies became organized into fast-moving, loosely coordinated enterprises capable of grouping and regrouping as needed. Self-managing teams increasingly utilized changing structures and tactics to run them, attaining degrees of flexibility unprecedented in large firms. Such adaptability took advantage of and demanded highly developed managerial skills and personal autonomy. With so much delegation of authority, a creative, independent spirit reached more deeply into corporate structures than ever before. This decentralization of authority entailed responsive management by alert human beings, not only allowing but requiring abundant input and discretion from below. That the hundred largest Fortune 500 corporations had eight times the inflation-adjusted revenue by the 2010s they did during the 1960s[46] was made possible by decentralization. So productive was decentralization that it diffused widely across the world and well beyond business.

Such management gains were matched by others in marketing as weak retailers of all sizes gave way in market after market to strong ones that were frequently larger. First malls, then discounters and outlets, and then gigantic box stores thrived. Many of the largest, such as Walmart and Europe's Carrefour superstores, became virtual small towns in themselves. In the process, personal service was often sharply cut back and great numbers of clerical and sales positions eliminated. From the late 1990s, Internet shopping accelerated many of these trends and put severe pressure on other forms of retailing. Amazon and other leading e-tailers' facilities dwarfed the scale of traditional retail establishments. They became extremely automated and slashed real estate and labor costs, leaving much of traditional retail dead in the water. Unquestionably there was also human loss in all of this.

The Competitive New Labor Markets. The compensation for the high-level executives, professionals, and technicians upon whom companies most relied went up steeply in the United States from the 1980s, as did the expectations placed upon them. The extraordinary potential rewards were matched by equally exceptional motivation, leading to ambition unimaginable to mid-20th century "organization men."[47] Accordingly, top employees worked more intensely and for longer hours. The great economic incentives and extreme effort were supercharged in start-up companies, whose normal pay was reduced and compensation in large part provided through awards of equity shares and stock options; as well as at investment banks where astronomical salaries lay ahead for those who made the grade. Such promise drove a single-minded new devotion to work that displaced everything else before it. The global markets also brought economic fear that spurred labor. The average annual hours worked in the United States were declining until 1975 but flat overall afterward despite increased incomes. By contrast, France's work hours declined by 20 percent from 1975, Norway's by 18 percent, and Spain's by 16 percent from 1977 until the end of the era.[48]

The experience of being a private-sector employee was extremely different during the global era from what it had been in the mid-20th century. The national-era lifetime communal and moral commitments to each other of company and employee vanished.[49] Not only did many employees participate in the entrepreneurialism of their companies, but many were essentially transformed into entrepreneurs of their own labor; investing in, managing, and marketing their careers, surprisingly often with astuteness and pluck. As they accumulated advantageous education and experience, their value in the labor market appreciated. In the hyper-competitive climate, corporations regularly treated their employees as commodities, and employees sometimes not only treated their corporations as commodities but treated themselves as such. At any time, they could be given ten minutes' notice to clean out their desks and leave the building, and at any time they could give their companies short notice that they would have to find someone else. Many companies churned employees, and some employees churned employers. So turbulent did employment become that serial career change became widely accepted and expected. Job insecurity abounded, as did stoic acceptance of the same.

As the steady but modest employment which most blue-collar workers knew during the national era yielded to the turbulent labor markets of the global era, workers faced waters more bracing than any they had known since the 19th century. Factory employment receded, and once-protected craft jobs became insecure. The working class had been distinct and prominent during the national era, but it became sharply less so through the global era. From a peak of just under 50 percent of the labor force in 1947, union membership in the United States had declined to 11 percent by 2016.[50] The primary remaining area of growing union membership during the global era was among public employees.

Instead of parades of workers with their lunch boxes, it often became lone craftsmen with their enterprise, knowledge, marketing, and equipment aggressively driving their pick-up and panel trucks from job to job for relatively high pay. Their skills and responsibilities went up as did their profits, salaries, and wages. Even janitorial work, yard work, housecleaning, and catering frequently became quite entrepreneurial. Some of the most enterprising hired their fellow workers and managed, marketed, and supported teams of service-providers, reinvesting their proceeds to build successful businesses. Workers became much more exposed to the economic markets during the global period than they had been at mid-century, and many became bourgeois and developed middle-class leanings, including political ones, often becoming resentful of high taxes and subsidies of the underclass, for example. Yet many other workers did not fare well.

Nor were the professions spared as the markets pushed aside long-standing norms and practice in law, medicine, and the academy. Wrested from their once relatively independent, genteel, and secure lives, professionals, like laborers, became free to bob about in the markets. Subject to many of the same market forces as any other business, attorneys competed openly for clients in ways that would have gotten them disbarred for unprofessional conduct a few decades earlier. Yet attorneys were able to maintain many arbitrary and inefficient barriers against encroachment on their turf by nonprofessionals performing routine legal services.

Many physicians were transformed into employees of relentlessly cost-cutting health maintenance organizations (HMOs) and other health service groups. Some even unionized out of desperation, but to little avail. A deathly combination of HMOs, insurance companies, regulations, liability laws, and decreasing Medicare payments constricted most physicians' practices that remained nominally independent. Physicians were also under market assault from those in competing healthcare occupations charging less for their services. In higher education, triumphant administrators attuned to PR, marketing, and raising capital, increasingly shuffled professors around, occupied them with busywork, and held them accountable for attracting quotas of tuition and fee-paying students. Out of convenience for administrators and to cut costs, large numbers of professorships were converted to adjunct positions without benefits or privileges. The "freeway flyer" instructors taking these positions were at the mercy of the markets, driving between campuses and teaching numerous courses of doubtful quality on split shifts for low pay.

Big Government and the Economic Crisis of the 1970s. Paradoxically, at the very onset of global capitalism, the United States underwent another large wave of expanding government with the Great Society programs of the late 1960s and early 1970s. This countercurrent against the capitalist tide brought explosive growth of the welfare state and sharply increased dependency. Between 1960 and 1982, the share of U.S. GNP allocated to welfare expenditures soared from 10.3 percent to 19.3 percent.[51] Eligibility requirements were loosened, and the welfare rolls more than doubled. According to Patterson, the number of Americans "on public assistance grew from 7.1 million in 1960, to 14.4 million in 1974." All of this growth came from expansion of those on AFDC (Aid to Families with Dependent Children), which increased from 3.1 million in 1960 ... to 10.8 million by 1974."[52] Social Security payments were increased several times during the 1970s and indexed against inflation under President Ford. Between 1970 and 1978 alone, disability programs broadened their coverage, eased eligibility requirements, and new awards rose 134 percent.[53] Through the late 1960s and early 1970s, a vast array of welfare services opened lives of relative leisure to those willing to rely upon the dole.

Many new social programs also made their appearance. Food stamps came into being in 1964, and as Neil Gilbert says, "between 1967 and 1978 the average number of monthly participants leaped from approximately 1.5 million to 16 million."[54] Medicare and Medicaid were established in 1965 under Social Security. Large-scale federal involvement in low-income housing arrived in the late 1960s. The newly instituted Department of Housing and Urban Development (HUD), among numerous other activities, cleared slums, built public housing, and offered rent subsidies for those of low income. A series of employment programs from Job Corps to the Comprehensive Employment and Training Act (CETA) was experimented with. A large, ramshackle War on Poverty was mounted under the Office of Economic Opportunity (OEO). Vaguely reminiscent of the New Deal's National Recovery Administration (NRA), OEO encouraged the poor to organize and engage in community action.

A spate of new federal regulatory agencies came in under the Nixon administration. The Environmental Protection Agency (EPA) and Occupational Safety and Health Agency (OSHA) were established in 1970, followed by the Consumer Products Safety Commission in 1973. Many existing regulatory agencies were also expanded, while the Food and Drug Administration (FDA) and other established agencies became much more activist. All had serious initial difficulties balancing their missions with the need of business to conduct itself profitably. With experience, the new agencies and endeavors ironed out some of their largest policy wrinkles.

The slow growth and high inflation of the 1970s, the global era's first economic crisis, followed on the heels of this major new expansion of government. As large sums of money poured into both Great Society programs and the Vietnam War, inflation rose from 2 percent in 1965 to a peak of 13 percent in 1978. Painful recessions afflicted the country in 1970-71, 1974-75, and 1980-81. Economic growth averaged only 2 percent during the 1970s, well below the historic U.S. average of 3.5 percent. As the welfare rolls expanded, social pathologies multiplied.[55] Increasing resistance to irresponsible underclass[56] conduct joined disappointment about the country's economic performance to produce growing opposition to welfare.

The Conservative Reaction and the Heyday of Global Capitalism. As the cultural cachet of the late 1960s and early 1970s waned, a conservative reaction began trimming the excesses from and reorienting big government. The reaction was anticipated in 1976 with the presidential election of Jimmy Carter, a Southern Democrat who promised to cut back government spending, introduce efficiency, and deregulate the economy. Carter's most notable domestic achievement was the extensive deregulation introduced under economist Alfred Kahn, his deregulation czar. The latter's first big project was decontrol of the airline industry via the virtual disbandment of the Civil Aeronautics Board (CAB), opening an era of price and route competition, vigorous expansion, and radical reorganization for the airlines. By the late 1970s deregulation of natural gas pipeline, telecommunications, and banking industries also occurred, as did some initial decontrol of utilities.

The conservative reaction took hold first in the United Kingdom where a solid Tory majority was elected in 1979 under Margaret Thatcher, an able, principled, fiercely determined, and market-oriented prime minister who undertook sharp cutbacks of government involvement throughout the British economy. Conservatism surged in the United States during the 1980s under President Reagan, who, after the inflation and economic doldrums of the 1970s, pursued much of the reaction's program against the excesses of the welfare and regulatory states. Banking and securities regulations were considerably loosened, and trucking was deregulated. Anti-trust enforcement was also relaxed, on the theory that in the absence of domestic competition, expanding international trade and competition offered sufficient protection against monopolism. The notion that regulatory policies ought to be cost effective gained wide currency. A few applications of the new free-market ideas were at once brilliant and radical, as in U.S. experiments with artificial markets in pollution rights.

Reagan's domestic reform proposals were for the most part stymied legislatively by Democratic majorities in both houses of Congress. Nevertheless, his reassuring manner, steadfast commitment, and great charisma enabled him to reach an extraordinary audience with his conservative message. When Reagan arrived on the political scene, conservatism was in marginal repute; when he left office, it was the reigning ideology. Reagan's real power was moral and rhetorical. The force of his character was sustained by a contemplativeness that kept him earnestly in touch with the Protestant moral virtues he had acquired decades earlier in small-town Illinois. As he prepared the way for the end of the Cold War, he also prepared the way for free-market economic policies. Only with Thatcher and Reagan was global capitalism fully under way.

Despite the clamor building against it, welfare was relatively unscathed by the conservative reaction until the 1990s. Some of the most dramatic cutbacks of the era occurred when President Clinton acquiesced to welfare reforms under which able-bodied recipients were required to find work or lose their assistance. Unlike during the 1930s, the inefficiency and heavy-handedness of government were blamed, while the free markets were largely cast in the role of hero. The welfare and regulatory states were pruned and partly transformed toward compatibility with the markets.

More Big Government. Entitlement spending accelerated in the 21st century as medical, disability, and retirement entitlements multiplied and expanded. The Cadillac care and third-party payment written into Medicare early on combined with demographic imbalance and growing monopolism to create increasing financial drain. The extension of disability eligibility to millions of additional claimants lay behind much of the problem. Under the new mandates, the healthcare industry in the United States soared to 17 percent of US GDP by 2014.[57]

Even as the conservative reaction brought about selective deregulation, the U.S. economy continued to undergo increased regulation overall. Dense new regulation grew up around businesses of all sizes, including costly environmental and safety measures. The Sarbanes-Oxley Act of 2002 burdened corporations with reporting requirements and increased their vulnerability to civil and criminal law. Employment law was another area of growing legal intrusion. Employees could be terminated at will during the 1950s unless unionized or in the government sector. Many of them still could be, but some private employees acquired partial property rights in their jobs, protecting them from termination except for documentable cause and/or entitling them to severance pay when discharged. Employees gained much-expanded civil rights with respect to their privacy, speech, and conduct on the job. They won the right to freedom from discrimination or harassment at work and the right to family leaves. As liability claims became more costly, jobs were cut. Nevertheless, the U.S. labor market remained more open than those of almost all European countries.

Civil law was another area of growing economic intervention. The scope for litigation expanded greatly during the global era thanks to an activist bench and creeping special-interest legislation for trial lawyers. Class-action lawsuit requirements loosened dramatically. Fraudulent or dubious personal injury claims sometimes resulted in preposterous awards, transforming the economy. Punitive judgments echoed the confiscatory "liturgies" of ancient Rome, and in many cases property again became insecure. In an atmosphere of rampant predation, unscrupulous law firms began fleecing law-abiding companies with frivolous securities fraud suits. Legal defensiveness distorted a great deal of American business; that of medicine, absurdly. Liberal courts and trial attorneys became the analogs of officials administering the welfare and regulatory states, only in lottery fashion.

On the other hand, regulation was remiss in the insufficiency of its anti-trust oversight. Monopolism again became a major problem as industries underwent horizontal integration through anti-competitive practices. A handful of oligopolistic companies gained control of the automobile rental industry and restricted price competition. Reconsolidation of the oil companies contributed to increased oil prices via manipulation of spot-market trading and refinery output through much of the era. Regulation was perhaps most botched, however, in the financial sector.

The Great Recession. The Economic Crisis of 2008-2009, the second and more acute economic crisis of the global era, in which most developed countries lost 4 to 6 percent of their GDPs, was the worst downturn since the 1930s. From the first quarter of 2008 through the second quarter of 2009, the U.S. economy declined by 5.4 percent. Most less-developed economies underwent milder declines, although there was large variation in this. World GDP loss was 3.5 percent.

Like the Great Depression before it, the Great Recession encountered severe turbulence in the financial markets, and the global financial system began unraveling. Amid a decreasing supply of money, so many financial institutions had engaged in irresponsible lending and were facing bad debt that they were compelled to halt further lending and build up capital to bring balance sheets into compliance with regulatory requirements. Ominously, many large entities with vast and reverberating financial obligations were veering toward or falling into failure, creating ever-widening tsunamis of illiquidity. No financial institution felt secure lending to any other. Credit frequently being no longer available, many corporations could not pay their bills or invest, and many consumers could not spend. Businesses laid off workers, and unemployment began rising sharply.

Extremely costly government efforts to manhandle the ailing economies and cushion hardship brought a sharp increase in the already inordinately large national deficits and debts of most developed global-capitalist economies, aggravating the fiscal crisis. The Obama administration used the recession not as an opportunity to overhaul U.S. regulatory policy in a manner supportive of the markets, nor as one to address out-of-control entitlement or healthcare costs, nor to prime the Keynesian pump by setting up temporary programs – it used the recession as a free pass to permanently ramp up government spending, creating major additional drag on the economy. Ambiguous Congressional flailing at financial institutions delivered the Dodd-Frank Banking Act of 2010, further reducing lenders' willingness to extend credit. As developed economies underwent comparatively weak recoveries from late 2009 through early 2011, financial and economic disorder subsided in the United States but mounted in Europe.

Meanwhile, labor force participation in the United States declined from a peak of 67 percent in 2000 to 62.5 percent in November of 2015. Of that 4.5 percent decline, 3.5 percent occurred after 2008.[58] Of the decline, about half owed to changing demographics with the aging of the baby-boom generation. Just over half of the remaining portion stemmed from increased disability enrollment.

The European Economies under Global Capitalism. The major European economies again reached levels approaching America's by the early 1970s, levels they had not witnessed since the onset of World War II.[60] Their positive recoveries occurred with strong socialist legacies and bigger government than in the United States.

Through the 1970s, northern European countries consolidated many-faceted, cradle-to-grave systems of social protection, while southern European countries assembled less extensive ones, coexisting with greater economic corruption. Amid increased inflation and losses of manufacturing and mining jobs, growth rates in Europe settled back to a more modest pace during the 1970s, not unlike that in the United States.[61] Slow growth emanating from extensive welfare and regulatory states continued into the 1980s in much of Europe.

Some European countries encountered reaction against big government during the late 1970s that curtailed the nationalization of industries and began their privatization. Britain took the lead as Margaret Thatcher closed state-owned enterprises in the oil, coal mining, airline, telephone, automobile, shipbuilding, and other industries. She privatized public housing by selling units to their inhabitants on generous financial terms. She pursued deregulation on many fronts and encouraged entrepreneurship, most notably in banking and finance. Wherever she could, Thatcher sought to weaken labor unions.

A limited, somewhat analogous development occurred in France when Socialist President François Mitterand, in office since 1981, vigorously nationalizing banks and extending welfare benefits, underwent his historic pirouette in 1982 to endorse his chief opponent Raymond Barre's fiscal and monetary conservatism. In selling off France's inefficient, state-owned mines, albeit haltingly, Mitterand too signaled a tendency away from the traditional socialist element of the welfare state even in continental Europe, at least for a time. Although other countries followed to a degree, government in Europe kept growing in different ways and overall.

Europe's labor markets for the most part remained tightly regulated. Laying off workers has been extremely difficult and costly for employers in most of Europe. Jobs there, to a large extent, became and remained property rights whereas, despite some movement in that direction, they generally did not in the global-era United States. The professions in Europe, as in much of the world, also managed to retain more restrictive certification requirements and monopoly power than they did in the United States. British attorneys, for example, were long able to maintain special privileges that their American peers could not. Riddled with archaic regulations, Greek labor law was extreme, allowing 70 closed occupations, from attorneys to truck drivers, to retain monopolistic privileges.[62] Nevertheless, various European countries made strides toward opening their labor markets, including Ireland, the Netherlands, Denmark, Slovakia, Estonia, and even Greece, in addition to the United Kingdom.

Nor did Europe accommodate entrepreneurialism to the same degree as the United States. Critical Silicon Valley legal and financial arrangements were missing across the Atlantic. The United States' highly entrepreneurial start-up charters, great engines of efficiency, were illegal in many European countries. France did not allow the liquidity priority for preferred stock – through which founder and venture capitalist investments are protected against ruinous dilution of their early holdings by subsequent management. European law did not allow 20 percent of start-up companies' stock to be set aside for employee incentive plans as in the United States. American firms could, but European firms could not, allocate to a key executive, engineer, or idea-person 1 or 2 percent of the company, for which he then gave his all for modest pay and the chance to make millions in capital gains. European tax treatment of options was also generally unfavorable to entrepreneurialism. European equity markets were poorly developed, making it excessively difficult for companies to go public. Europe had no equivalent to the NASDAQ small-cap market for medium-sized companies. Consequently, European venture capitalists had no convenient way of selling their shares as start-ups began to mature. Since they could not easily liquidate their investments, they could not easily make new ones. The absence of a European high-yield debt market further hampered entrepreneurialism. Nor was there any European equivalent to the business-savvy, entrepreneurially-minded law firms willing to push the envelope in legal innovation that were found in the creative centers of the American economy. European financial law barred many efficient, enterprising ways of allocating money.

The European Sovereign Debt Crisis. Not surprisingly, given their uphill battle with big government, European financial institutions were under considerable pressure from unsustainable sovereign debt owed most notably by Greece, Italy, Belgium, Portugal, and Spain. European banks lent these predominantly Catholic and Mediterranean countries sums that they were going to have a difficult time mustering the political will to repay. In the irrational exuberance of the late 2000s in Europe, some of the borrowing governments, Ireland and Spain for example, poured funds into subsidized housing booms as did the United States. Greece, the most overextended of the five, devoted its resources largely to government pensions and other state benefits.[63] Greece resisted reforming a defunct tax system, trimming civil service rolls, and breaking guild and union strangleholds to make itself more competitive. European banks' lending, much of it for excessively leveraged sovereign debt, made them financially vulnerable. The greater scale of those banks than their American counterparts compounded the financial dangers.

Southern Europe in particular allowed its economic problems to worsen. Italy had no net GDP growth after 2001.[64] Its small business limped along in chaotic fashion, with highly creative small firms dotting the countryside of northern Italy, engaged in everything from furniture manufacturing to graphic design. But the country left these firms hardly any way around impossible burdens and restrictions other than via corruption. Italy's chronic political dysfunction led many of those businesses to an ambiguous, under-the-radar strategy that sharply limited their size, for if they grew larger, they encountered daunting fiscal and regulatory dis-economies of scale.[65] With public finance badly out of balance, the country was deeply in debt.

Although France tried for a time during the 1980s to curb the growth of its welfare state, the latter continued to grow. In order to pay part of the bill, income taxes were increased to 75 percent under President Hollande for those in the highest income bracket for the 2013 tax year. After poor results, the top tax rate was reduced to 45 percent two years later. A wealth tax was also instituted for those whose net worth exceeded €800,000 although it was soon rescinded. Where French labor was organized, companies and unions took a confrontational mode, working against rather than with each other, and often against the government as well. Exports languished, and the French economy had virtually no growth between 2008 and 2016.[66]

Northern European economic performance was much better than Southern and held down by the latter. From the 1990s, Germany presented an impressive example of how the North cooperatively coped. Germany's guiding philosophy was that the country needed to stay economically healthy, and that major economic interests should not harm the productive engine that made everything possible. This approach entailed reaching out on all sides and compromising. Germany pared down its welfare and regulatory excesses even as it was shouldering the weight of reintegrating East Germany and paying disproportionately into EU coffers. It weathered the 2008–2009 downturn while running only the thinnest of deficits, although it did allow its banks to become dangerously exposed.

Kurzarbeit, or working shorter hours during economic crises in return for a degree of job security, an approach that was not even thinkable in the United States, played a central role in Germany's economic success. Kurzarbeit was about retaining an exceptionally well-trained labor force in order to keep standards and productivity high. German management understood that holding onto a quality workforce was important because difficult to replace, and it wanted to be positioned to rebound at once and in top form when demand returned. Organized labor played a pivotal role in this commendable accord by exchanging flexibility in work hours for job security. Kurzarbeit was an unusual example of intelligent, win-win, productivity-enhancing restriction of the labor markets.

Although with hesitation and reservations, German unions negotiated cooperatively with business, also agreeing to relatively modest salaries, wages, pensions, and benefits, with an eye to the long term. Germany's exemplary training and apprenticeship programs developed out of long-established guild traditions, another case of cooperation on all sides.

Even recipients of unemployment or welfare benefits played their part. In order to retain government assistance, they were required to work for one euro per hour, which had the advantages of keeping those displaced close to the world of employment, but not overly content with their assistance.

They may have had other problems, but the Scandinavian countries also showed liberal societies how to address their economic ones. For example, as *The Economist* notes, "Sweden ... reduced public spending as a proportion of GDP from 67 percent in 1993 to 49 percent [in 2013]. Its public debt fell from 70 percent of GDP in 1993 to 37 percent in 2010, and its budget moved from an 11-percent deficit to a surplus of 0.3 percent over the same period," even as it was tightening its pension system.[67] Sweden also substantially cut its tax rate for those with the highest incomes, a reduced its corporate tax, and removed various taxes on wealth.[68]

The Japanese economy soared during the first half of the global era, surging to world leadership in steel, shipbuilding, automobiles, and consumer electronics. Its management techniques became as good as any in the world. Japan maintained a lean welfare state complemented by familial social obligations. By the late 1980s, Japanese firms were buying large amounts of commercial real estate in Los Angeles and other U.S. cities, striking fear in sections of the American business community. Japanese GDP growth averaged 10 percent annually during the 1960s, 5 percent during the 1970s, and 4 percent during the 1980s,[69] but only 0.9 percent from 1992 to 2016.[70] Japan's national debt was only a moderate 0.6 times GDP in 1990, but after greatly increased borrowing its debt reached a forbidding 2.5 times GDP by the mid-2010s.[71]

Liberalizing Third-World Economies under Global Capitalism. The spread of capitalism during the global era brought about the industrialization of most of the third-world economy. Drawing upon enormous foreign investment, third-world countries realigned with the global markets and greatly expanded their industrial production. Global industrial output increased sharply from 1965 and service-sector output even more sharply. Major efficiency gains occurred as complex services became concentrated in the first world and basic manufacturing and agriculture in the third world. As the third world increased its competitiveness in complex services in the 21st century, they too increasingly benefited from outsourcing.

Capitalism brought unprecedented growth to liberalizing third-world societies, but their economic ascent was arduous. Global markets upended a great deal of traditional economic protection before third-world societies had the resources, time, and orientation to temper the markets with any but minimal welfare and regulation. In the absence of welfare, third-world countries relied upon persisting communal and kinship ties that offered much but not all support in times of need. Although their traditional communal supports were much disturbed, they did not disintegrate to the degree they have in the West.

As special-interest giveaways, bloated welfare expenditures, and burdensome regulations weighed down most first-world economies, crony capitalism afflicted most third-world ones. In their crony capitalism, insiders embedded in strong communal, clientelist relationships worked closely with government officials, enabling them to operate in circumstances of legal ambiguity. Powerful patrons received favorable treatment from officials while patrons gave them direct and indirect stakes in their business dealings. The crony capitalism widespread today in Asia was prevalent in early modern Europe and continued in Mediterranean countries through the global period, albeit with reduced generality and force.

Cronyism is associated with the tendency of much third-world capitalism to operate top-down, providing another link to the hierarchical societies of recent centuries with their mercantilist policies. Accordingly, ambitious, rising Asian and other economies frequently dampened domestic demand, lowered currency values, erected import barriers, and ran trade surpluses with the world. Their governments often encouraged particular industries, as South Korea did with its push into semiconductors. That country's D-RAM business was built clumsily via heavy-handed government subsidy and leverage. Indonesia's project to manufacture jet planes was another top-down boondoggle. On the other hand, Brazil's aircraft industry was successful, though partly top-down. Despite the spectacular growth of the Asian economies, a great deal of resource misallocation occurred in them and in other developing economies. Popular concessions like food subsidies and energy price controls also hindered many third-world economies.

At the other end of the economic and geographic scale from the first-world centers of global capitalism were the least developed portions of Africa, Latin America, and Asia, which some termed the fourth world. There vast, chaotic slums teemed with millions of desperate hawkers of everything from dirty water to recycled plastic, sunglasses, and telephone cards.

Lagos, Nigeria largely made up a single gargantuan slum of 15 million or more out of a megalopolitan population of approximately 20 million, whose inhabitants survived as they were able among sprawling garbage heaps and whose daily hardship was gnawing and life expectancy short.[72] Such places existed as eddies removed from the main currents of third-world development. The street hustlers of fetid fourth-world slums and the executives and professionals of sleek office towers and business parks experienced the same hurricane-force winds of global economic markets, although worlds apart and with extremely differently preparation for them.

Hierarchical Economies under Global Capitalism. Although market economies became dominant in most third-world countries, hierarchical ones continued to exist in North Korea, Saudi Arabia, Iran, and numerous other oil-producing countries as well as in much of sub-Saharan Africa. The most important hierarchical economies were not in the third world but the second world, particularly in China and Russia. Their economies no longer manifested the hard opposition to capitalism that they had during the national era, but the dominant hierarchical sectors were controlled for state purposes by authoritarian regimes arrayed geopolitically against global-liberal ones. Moreover, the weighty, elite portions of their private sectors have close relationships with the government and tend to make decisions with an eye to regime approval.

Deng Xiaoping began boldly reforming the Chinese economy in 1979, from an almost entirely socialist one toward one with a rapidly growing capitalist sector. He began with limited return of rural land to peasants as private plots, transforming them into farmers producing for the markets. Where Mao was a poet and idealist, Deng and his successors were pragmatic managers. The Deng regime was devoted to development, emphasizing increased economic and military power. "The smashing of the iron rice bowl" was an early Deng policy and slogan repudiating society's paternalistic obligations to the people; there was to be no further state guarantee of subsistence. China's legal infrastructure for a market society lagged badly until about 2000 but then developed rapidly, with the help of a great deal of imported American business law. The regime supercharged economic development through such measures as keeping tax rates low and placing huge emphasis upon elite educational institutions. Nevertheless, having little ability to innovate because of the closedness their regime required, the Chinese rulers turned to the wholesale theft of intellectual property. Paradoxically, even as party leaders allowed the emergence of numerous billionaires and accorded them accolades, they continued to disparage and discriminate against former landowning families.[73]

As for the Soviet Union, when special access to import stores, shopping sprees to the West, and access to Western popular culture became prime rewards to the elite, as they did from the 1960s through the 1980s, it was only a matter of time before key sections of the society would openly advocate capitalism and support fundamental reform. In an era of jet travel and instant electronic communication, revolutionary socialism was no longer viable without enormous coercion to counter the appeal of the productive and charismatic markets. As communism began collapsing in Eastern Europe in 1989, its newly Western-oriented, formerly occupied countries turned to markets and swiftly joined to the first world. The other contiguous non-Russian dependencies floundered for the most part, some reverting from second- to third-world status.

Russia was able to make lurching first steps into the economic markets under Yeltsin and Yegor Gaidar in 1992. In the years afterward its economy opened more to the markets but came under domination by the secret police and billionaire oligarchs careful to stay in their favor. Amid political and legal menace, Russian business had to tread carefully around and defer to the privileged hierarchy prevalent in its upper reaches. As Hernando DeSoto says, "Russia and the more hierarchical former Soviet dependencies … look astonishingly similar" to Latin American countries like Mexico and Columbia, having "strong underground economies, glaring inequality, pervasive mafias, political instability, capital flight, and flagrant disregard for the law,"[74] but Russia was more developed than they. After a turbulent period of uncertainty, it settled back into second-world status with China.

Why Did Global Capitalism Triumph?

The Pax Americana as the Foundation of Global Capitalism. The Pax Americana was the sine qua non of the efflorescence and spread of global capitalism and all that flowed from it. Global capitalism owed everything to the allied victory in World War II that destroyed the Axis regimes and with them the world's most virulent sources of militarism and among its most virulent sources of vicious economic practice. The United States, Britain, and their liberal allies were in a position after the war to foster the international economic markets they valued. Had the Pax Americana or something similar to it not been established and maintained, the period would have witnessed a continuation of the wars of conquest and dog-eat-dog mercantilist practices of the 31-year crisis.

International trade had flourished under the Pax Britannica, and it flourished again under the Pax Americana. But it had stagnated as economies went through the 31-year crisis with the liberal international order under assault by powerful hierarchical societies and their ways and ideas. That it took until the early 1970s for international trade to again reach the levels of 1913 as a percentage of GDP is testimony to how devastating the international conflict of the 31-year crisis had been to economic markets.[75]

Throughout history, the master key to the blossoming and spread of capitalism has been outflanking the power of the state to pounce imperiously upon the conduct and profits of business. In order to thrive, business had to have a way out of the hierarchical straitjacket that inevitably stifled it. Prerequisite to the globalization of the economic markets was the prior globalization of a minimalist, hands-off, low-key international order, placing a reality check on authoritarian rulers and their cronies' ceaseless efforts to arrogate all things to themselves.[76]

Interests and the Demonstration Effect in the Spread of Capitalism. Once made safe from depredation, thanks to a liberal security regime, international economic markets reward regimes that embrace them and punish those that shun them. Under these circumstances, no rational state dare resist the economic markets for long without weakening itself in relation to other states. First-, second-, and third-world countries alike have faced the basic reality under the Pax Americana that avoiding the economic markets was contrary to reason of state and futile.

The demonstration effect of observing the success that capitalism brought to other countries played a pivotal role in the spread of capitalism after 1965. The striking initial examples were Germany and Japan's spectacular postwar recoveries, but their cases were unpersuasive because it was too easy to invoke special national-cultural explanations for their successes. More compelling were the robust recoveries of Britain and the United States from the doldrums of the 1970s under the free-market policies of Thatcher and Reagan. Their healthy growth through the 1980s was notable because it followed the disappointing results of both countries' anti-market policies of the 1960s and 1970s. Most compelling though were the "four tigers," Hong Kong, Singapore, South Korea, and Taiwan, all of which became third-world economic wonders by the 1980s through adherence to free-market principles. Their spectacular economic ascents caused a global sensation.

The Asian neighbors of the four tigers had bleacher seats from which to watch and emulate their development. Then there were the negative cases of the USSR, Cuba, North Korea, Albania, and Burma, among others at the time – all going nowhere with heavy-handed statist policies. The collapse of the Soviet Union boosted the spread of capitalism by further discrediting the hierarchical model, an event that was particularly consequential for India. The message that countries attentive to reality had to get with the capitalist program was amplified by their business communities whose experience in the markets and whose interests made them especially enthusiastic about the markets. Elites and whole nations absorbed the lessons around them and resolved to play catch-up and raise themselves to wealth and power.

Insofar as calculations of national interest coincided with the perceived interest of governing classes, they were crucial in the political contests over the expansion of the markets. Nearly all third-world countries were still traditional-hierarchical during the 1960s. Collectivist, possessing rich community, and able to count on natural sharing if the threat of destitution arose, nothing was more difficult and counterintuitive for them than to accept economic markets. Nevertheless, it got through to most third-world elites and leaders that adopting capitalism was the only way their countries could achieve sustainable growth and acquire prosperity and power. In numerous cases their adoptions of the markets were substantially defensive, undertaken in order that competing countries not get ahead of them. Although the results were plain to see, many Middle Eastern and sub-Saharan African countries and Cuba resisted, typically because their hierarchical rulers feared that they would not be able to retain control if they acted in their countries' best interests.

Why the Tech Revolution? The central cause of the continuing industrial revolution in the first world and the industrialization of the third world was capitalist economic growth. Market-derived economic growth brought the first industrial revolution of the late 18th and early 19th centuries, and further economic growth brought each subsequent wave of the industrial revolution. Industrialization spread to the third world because free markets and free trade preceded it and because technological progress in transportation and communication made large-scale global trade efficient. Container ships so sharply reduced transportation costs that it became profitable to move even bulky items all over the world when done on a sufficiently large scale. Internet and telephone technologies allowed nearly free instantaneous communication and distribution of digital products worldwide. The third world long had the potential for low-cost production, but other than Japan it only adopted the institutional means of bringing it about and became the beneficiary of the technological means of overcoming its geographical remoteness from the mid-1960s.

The Silicon Valley's bubbling creativity and hyper-entrepreneurialism were rooted in the distinctive Californian and especially northern Californian culture of rebellious questioning and experimentation. Its economic innovativeness was homologous with the beatnik and hippie movements and student revolt that began in the San Francisco Bay Area. The region's longstanding social and cultural boldness also manifested itself in economic boldness. An almost two-century-old tradition born of the experience of diversity, uprootedness, and unusual individualism lay behind this. Even the state's childrearing highlighted extreme freedom. California's market-savvy children grew up skeptical about authority, questioning tradition, and streetwise in economic and all other markets.

Participating in global markets was difficult for nearly everyone, but astonishingly many Californians took to it with gusto. In part, the Silicon Valley also depended upon its great universities, particularly Stanford and U.C. Berkeley. Europe and Asia's business-people grew up in more coherent, reassuring, and confining settings that did not lend themselves to all-out innovation. Californians' individualism arose from experience in many-sided markets, and it complemented and furthered them during the global era. Replicating the sociocultural conditions of their profound entrepreneurialism was a tall order.

The pace of technological change accelerated in part because the infrastructure of innovation was built out in the United States to make funding start-ups routine and inexpensive. An entire venture capital industry came into being to facilitate the flow of money to start-ups. The era's larger, more variegated, more flexible, and more efficient capital markets meant that the ideas of the most creative were able to gain funding in ways that had never before been possible. It was revolutionary that founding start-ups became inexpensive and routine. Technological change also accelerated because of the growing awareness that technological development was central to the capitalist economy and held enormous economic potential.

Why the Revolution in Finance? The global era's unparalleled innovations in finance drew upon outstanding innovation in the *theory* of finance. Just as natural science only began strongly contributing to engineering development and economic growth during the national era, economic science only began doing so in earnest during the global era. One of the most important means was through the new theory of finance with its brilliant series of discoveries about and prescriptions for the financial markets beginning in the 1960s.[77] Underlying the entire revolution was the work of ubiquitous arbitragers looking for and often quickly correcting price discrepancies. These financial innovations made possible the vast expansion of derivatives markets all over the world with their enormous efficiency gains (and negative externalities). One of the key ways in which they enhanced efficiency was by clarifying the logic and necessity of hedging.[78] The revolution in finance led to global capitalism's more financially driven economy.

Why the Revolution in Management? Corporate structures became flatter and more streamlined during the global era in part because under global markets' severe economic competition, it was no longer feasible to support the tall, unitary, bureaucratic pyramids of the early national era or often even the medium-height, semi-autonomous divisional pyramids of the later national era. They became too expensive and cumbersome. Corporate structures also became leaner and more dynamic because technological development helped enable them to become profitable. The extremely inexpensive communication available first allowed and then required decentralization. Businesses could no longer afford to provide the number of managers or stability of employment for them. Efficient new management tools and just-in-time inventory controls making use of the new technologies also reduced bureaucratic overhead. Part of what allowed the flatter structures were also the extraordinary skills and extreme commitment of the era's business executives, as is analyzed in chapter 4. Complementing the unparalleled skills of in-house managers, the widespread use of management consultants helped enable the customized, streamlined, exotic, new structures to work and spread.

The new pattern of corporate governance by the markets left greater room for discretion on the part of management. Such governance provided additional incentives for managers but also permitted abuses, as in the opportunistic recklessness at Enron and at various financial institutions leading up to the banking crisis of 2008-2009. Management was also able to use its new power to some extent to award itself unjustifiably high compensation packages.

Exponentially increasing organizational, managerial, and financial sophistication, aided by the explosion of information technologies, continued to generate higher returns to scale, contributing to growth in the size of business firms all over the world. Economies of scale were captured in retail through centralizing marketing decisions, building attractive product lines, and cutting costs. Increasing scale brought superior branding, advertising, and marketing. Larger retailers were able to drive down costs and out-compete smaller retailers by sedulously seeking products in the cheapest markets of the world. E-tailers like Amazon trounced competition and grew rapidly by eliminating retail space and employee overhead. Rapidly advancing knowledge of business practices was part of what made possible the global reach of corporations.

Increases in the scale of retailing in particular were also about the subtle exercise of monopoly power, where illegal actions were routinely carried out just below the thresholds of prosecutability and recoverability. It is illegal in the United States for a chain to put in a store near an existing independent, undercut it until it goes out of business, and then raise prices. Yet such conduct is also difficult to prosecute, a story that was repeated countless times. U.S. hesitancy to protect small business with European-, Japanese-, or Indian-style anti-chain regulations contributed to the process, as did a legislative political class eager to serve the special interests.

Why the More Competitive Labor Markets? As the wide-open labor markets of the global era eroded the many supports of the company men of the national era, and people were thrown onto their own resources, the circumstances of the working class changed radically. Large numbers of workers who once held secure jobs had scant choice but to become managers of their own careers and proprietors of their own labor, making the best of the discipline and savviness their circumstances conferred. Many of those tested by the markets, often in service jobs, were able to rise into the middle class, but many others were not. As workers were tossed about by the vagaries of corporate balance sheets, more of them also became wary and manipulative, feeling little beholden to employers and freely jumping between them when able. Increased outsourcing, advanced automation, and more competitive labor markets reduced industrial employment, dispersed the working class, gave it more varied experience, and rendered it less visible than during the previous era.

Labor unions greatly weakened in the private sector because international trade punished business as that allowed unions to use monopoly power to gain wages and salaries departing significantly from those of the free market. Industry after industry in which labor did not respect the fierce competition of robust international markets, and/or in which business did not successfully evade or fend it off, went under. The oligopolistic U.S. automobile industry went into a long, slow, agonizing death spiral in large part because it was not able to compete well internationally after having caved in to patently shortsighted and exploitative UAW demands. Neither management nor union bosses had the integrity and courage to correct what both long knew were unsustainable agreements.

Unions found abodes in the public sector under global capitalism where their monopolism latched onto that of the state, sapping not particular industries and businesses, but the strength of the nation, or in relatively monopolistic corners of the private economy like Boeing Aircraft, where they did something similar. Organized labor may have protested cheap competition from abroad, but it was able to do little about its plight other than divert some of the spoils of existing monopolies where possible. American unions – though not German ones – were different varieties of the same kudzu as the guild encrustation that throttled 15th-century Bruges, Ypres, and Ghent. In an amoral setting, only discipline forced upon unions by the global markets kept them cut back.

Much of the autonomy of the professions eroded under global capitalism for reasons similar to those behind the weakening of most unions, for they were often no longer able to protect themselves from competition. Growing government involvement was crowding the medical profession, as were its competitors. Voters were unwilling to tolerate many legal restrictions protecting professional privilege because of the strength of the markets and the culture supporting them. Were the global markets to recede, private-sector unions and professional privilege would return with a vengeance.

As labor markets became more competitive in many respects, the drumbeat of advertising was spreading consumerism, intensifying the powerful economic motivation already present. In the world of materialism, the "winners" were associated with symbols of success disseminated through the media and the "losers" with those of failure. Consumerism became so deeply imbedded as to displace other aspects of life.

Sociologist Daniel Bell, among others during the late 1960s, became concerned that the abundance and materialism accompanying advanced capitalism would erode the work discipline necessary to sustain the system, leading people to withdraw from the labor force into leisure.[79] Not to worry! Advertising and marketing achieved precisely the opposite, raising economic expectations and motivation to feverish levels, bringing a slavish new devotion to the material. Far from rendering people unfit for employment, global capitalism suspended mechanical rabbits of consumption in front of them, capturing their desires for its own purposes. The American dream and similar dreams all over the world were redefined in more materialistic ways. The era's extreme materialism was part of what made the labor markets highly competitive.

Advertising's seductive messages insinuated powerful wedges of desire into consumers, who longed for myriads of new objects and services without most of which they had long been perfectly content and frequently better off altogether. Living in a world of unreal images, people scurried about for the right clothes or electronic devices, arranged to frequent the right restaurants and shops, and exhausted themselves for housing at the right addresses – most of which represented withdrawal from reality and meaning to dwell in a noisy, distorted, this-worldly anti-nirvana. The world of objects became a generalized hysteria in which the symptom shifted from place to place.[80] Advertising fanned the flames of appetite, dangling sex, envy, hunger, and delusion, riveting attention to wants instead of needs, obligations, or service. On behalf of capitalist economic interests, advertising installed escalating material want and fleeting satisfaction as a false salvation. Money gave misplaced cultural power to the pretensions of the empty, undermining the ability of the full to stand their genuine ground.

What Drove the Continual Ratcheting Up of Government Expenditures and Regulatory Burdens? The seemingly inexorable growth of welfare expenses and regulatory burdens in the first world had three main causes, beginning with the interplay of economic interests.

The traditional progressive model of government as provider for the general interest and simple benefactor of the people is partly correct; government *did* achieve national and internal security, establish economic infrastructure, regulate monopolism, secure the rule of law, alleviate collective public health threats, and so forth. As a whole, however, it carried out these tasks poorly and inefficiently. Over and above patently necessary defense and regulatory endeavors, the bulk of the government's direct and indirect drain on the economy was made up of bureaucratic overhead, social programs, and regulatory impositions which only the beholden or naïve could accept as unambiguously answering genuine need rather than serving special interests.

Increasingly numerous and powerful special interests demanding government subsidies or regulations for their own purposes lay behind most growth of government during the global era. The special interests begin with those of the political class. Ever more baldly and systematically treating government policy as their personal capital, politicians, civil servants, and those around them produced continual accretions of interested, needless expenditure and regulation. The special interests bring formidable resources to the political table. As James Buchanan, Mancur Olson, and others have taught social scientists, it was much easier to organize special than general interests.[81] The general interest is at a particular disadvantage during times in which the interest of the whole is supported by neither a committed and engaged public nor by principled officials. Once a government program is in place, the special interests defending it become dug in, have resources in place, and are extremely difficult to dislodge.

Powerful special interests including politicians, bureaucracies, unions, and corporations with stakes in government policy, along with the recipients of disproportionate services, have held the country in a tightening vice. The result was the terminal sucking of resources into unsustainable and poorly managed entitlements together with the regulatory waste of private sector resources on a comparable scale. A telltale sign of the provenance of the Great Recession and following economic doldrums was that for the first time in the nation's history, more very high-income households were found in metropolitan Washington, DC than in New York, San Francisco, Los Angeles, Houston, or the other centers of the productive private economy.[82]

Growing government from 1965 onward drew importantly upon the anger and perceived interests of multiculturalist groups that were able to successfully argue claims of injustice against the society. It drew upon a social ethic that was no longer directed toward need in general but toward attempting to redress alleged collective injustice. Black discontent in particular was unmistakably the deepest concern of the American social programs of the 1960s and 1970s.[83]

The fundamental leanings of program recipients and protected employees, those with secure government and monopolistic corporate jobs and/or union membership, are the second major cause of the inexorably growing burden of government. For, apart from their interests, their experience of economic independence or dependence shapes the character of people and classes such that their basic ways of feeling, thinking, and acting bend in different directions. Those who depend upon government or monopoly become accustomed to economic security and favor hierarchical solutions to economic problems. By contrast, those who are independent and long immersed in the markets tend to support them. The experience of encountering and coming through reversals in the markets engenders toughness and resiliency; that of being spared market swings engenders the opposite. The unremitting discipline of the markets produces and hones a strong sense of personal efficacy, where the slackness of dependency erodes it. As Friedrich Hayek notes, "independence of mind or strength of character is rarely found among those who cannot be confident that they will make their way by their own effort."[84] Without the entrepreneurs' experience of high-stakes adaptation, the dependent tend to feel helpless. The longing of the dependent for security and succor contributed mightily to the expansion of the welfare and regulatory states. The more cushioned people are from the economic markets, the more they feel the need to be taken care of, and the more they sincerely impute similar needs in others. The individualist ethic is a celebration of human resourcefulness and self-reliance; the social ethic is a *cri de coeur* from the insecure for ministration.

The independent and dependent also have sharply different ways of thinking. Through constantly being pressured by the markets to consider how efficiently their firms or business units are conducting themselves as wholes, entrepreneurs develop facility at conceptualizing the overall productivity of collectivities. They understand that, if it is to fare well, society like their enterprises, must order its priorities, marshal its resources, and deal productively with the exigencies that arise. Insofar as people are shielded from the markets, they become oblivious to productivity. When problems arise on the job – trouble with the pace of workflow, reliability of inputs, or behavior of co-workers – dependent employees all too often request that higher-ups come to their aid. When challenges arise, aid recipients are even more likely to plea for others to take care of them. Absent the very notion of productivity, the protected sink into ad hoc moralism untethered by economic rationality. As spontaneously as those in business think of individual solutions to economic problems, the dependent think of government solutions. As governmental and corporate monopolies grow larger, every new protected position and welfare slot incrementally erodes the underpinnings of economic markets and strengthens those of hierarchy. Global capitalism works against the tendency of hierarchy and dependency to feed upon each other, but that tendency must ever be contended with. Economic ideas project from these fundamental leanings.

The third major cause of growing government involvement in the economy from 1965 on was the chorus of support from the elite media and academia for the expansion of government. Intellectuals attacked and blamed society rather than the individual for alleged poverty, while they ignored the economic burdens and moral hazards of welfare and regulation. They did so in large part because influential journalists and scholars of the period were usually dependent employees of large media or university bureaucracies, whose own feelings of economic helplessness and vulnerability blinded them to the comprehensive societal need for economic responsibility.[85] Never having run an enterprise or met a budget, they sank into narrow, idealistic, ad hoc moralism, emotionally recoiling against putative injustices, void of constraint by pragmatic concerns for societal productivity. PR and advertising by the intellectuals against the economic markets made a huge difference. A few influential intellectuals defended the economic markets, including Milton Friedman, Irving Kristol, William Buckley, George Will, and Victor Hanson, but it is fair to say that church and state, so to speak, were in virtual unison against the economic markets.

Why Did the Great Recession Occur? The central cause of the Great Recession was a set of regulatory failures. Like the Great Depression before it,[86] the Great Recession was in large part brought on by poor management of the money supply, again by the Federal Reserve Board but this time also by the European Central Bank (ECB). As during 1930 and 1931, the money supply was allowed to drop precipitously during 2006, 2007, 2008, and even into 2009. Fed chief Ben Bernanke, an academic economist, was misled by the increasing complexity and elusiveness of money in its proliferating new forms amid rapid financial and technological innovation – as he also was by the growing unreliability of official statistics. Thus, he was led to wrongly suppose that the money supply was increasing worrisomely. Primed since the 1970s to fear inflation, Bernanke, like most generals, was fighting the last war, that of 1966-1981 against inflation, rather than the current one; and he long missed the deflationary threat to the economy. Lacking Wall Street's attunement to the financial markets and savvy skepticism toward official numbers, Bernanke's Fed persisted in maintaining a dangerously tight money supply during the vulnerable period leading up to and into the recession.[87]

More reliably than the idealistic, politicized government econometric measures, the bond markets were long signaling the absence of inflationary worries. Wise judgment based upon long experience in finance and a palpable feel for the markets are always needed as a corrective to the official numbers. The Fed's sudden and panicky increase in banks' capital requirements in October of 2008 from 4 to 7 percent, forcing them to halt lending, was part of its regulatory mismanagement. During the following 24 months the volume of commercial and industrial loans declined from $1.6 to $1.2 trillion. The ensuing credit crisis reverberated through the U.S. and global economies.[88] The Fed's monetary policies put severe downward pressure on the financial markets – bad monetary policy sweeps all before it. European central bankers, prominently including German bureaucrats forever reliving their country's hyperinflation of 1923,[89] shared Bernanke's blindness and, if anything, exceeded in delusional vigor the Fed's efforts to quell the phantom inflationary tendencies. The Great Recession was in large part another "oops" occasion – "sorry for the mistake" – nearly eighty years after the one that misguidedly turned a recession into the Great Depression.

Derivatives brought great efficiency gains to the economy, but they also brought serious side effects. The vast increases in the magnitudes of financial obligations and leveraging created by their proliferating contractual mazes have significantly increased the vulnerability of the financial system and economy, requiring attentive, appropriate regulation. An ordinary downturn is one thing, but a financial meltdown is another, far more serious occurrence greatly needing to be protected against. Early in Alan Greenspan's chairmanship, the Fed farmed out or dropped most of its banking regulatory responsibilities.[90] It made another enormous mistake early on in allowing Lehman Brothers to go under, further shaking economic confidence all over the world.

Grossly deficient regulation of mortgage banking also contributed to the Great Recession. Mortgage-backed securities, large numbers of retail mortgages bundled into derivatives, greatly facilitated investors' wholesale buying and selling of mortgages. In and of themselves they were good examples of the efficiency of the new financial vehicles, but irresponsible, predatory, and – yes – avaricious lenders, borrowers, investment banks, ratings agencies, and quasi-governmental entities subjected mortgage-backed securities to horrible abuses. Fannie Mae and Freddie Mac corruptly utilized taxpayer money to lobby and strong-arm Congress into overlooking their thoroughly cynical, increasingly short-term and reckless practices. The government-sponsored behemoths knowingly underwrote the accumulation of more than a trillion dollars of dangerously leveraged obligations, guaranteeing millions of mortgages with perilously high debt-to-equity and income ratios in order to run up their own compensation and perks. Fannie Mae and Freddie Mac's lowered standards for granting loan guarantees in the housing market contributed to dangerous overextension by great numbers of naïve homeowners. Egregiously lax, interested, and corrupt oversight, ultimately by Congress, was no less reprehensible. Major investment banks' misrepresentations of the sound-

65

ness of their mortgage-backed securities were knowingly fraudulent, as were the ratings agencies' AAA evaluations of them. The Federal Reserve Board had the power to curb these practices but did nothing, owing partly to Alan Greenspan's selective laissez-faire blindness, partly to his deference to a changing Wall Street no longer worthy of it, and partly to his want of the courage to face down powerful interests.[91] The resulting mountain of bad mortgage debt presented a financial time bomb, given the stratospheric housing-price bubble driven by the unsustainably free and deceptive mortgage money available.

Fannie Mae's reckless misconduct from the early 1990s through the Great Recession and beyond – professedly to extend home ownership to more renters and especially those from minorities but actually for padding its executives' compensation – played a large role in bringing about the mortgage debacle.[92] Legislators and regulators jettisoned soundness because doing so was veiled by seemingly worthy surface considerations, and, well, they thought they could get away with it. Over and over again, the primary justification for the wholesale abandonment of lending standards and breaching of regulatory and industry safeguards was to increase rates of home ownership. Scoundrels of every description – Jim Johnson and his fellow Fannie Mae executives, members of Congress from both parties, Angelo Mozilo and his associates at Countrywide, duplicitous loan brokers, and many, many others whistled the same false tune. Of no concern to any of them was either the country's distress or the massive ensuing loss of wealth in minority communities, whose modest assets and hopes were disproportionately tied up and then dashed in mortgaged home ownership. The ways in which liberal guilt and the inclusion of difference, the leitmotifs of multiculturalism, resonated disturbingly through the entire sordid real-estate bubble and collapse warrant pondering and discussion.

The Basel Accords capital rules' pushing of banks into holding mortgage-backed securities by weighting them as having low risk and sovereign debt as having no risk at all, were also extremely ill advised. These regulatory actions helped draw banks en masse into dangerously exposed debt portfolios, first in the United States and then in Europe.[93]

Financial dysfunctionality was allowed to build in many other forms as regulators, stock exchanges, and accounting boards ceased their vigilance against accounting gimmickry, some of it outright fraudulent. Curiously, in 2003, only two years after the Enron collapse, the Financial Accounting Standards Board (FASB) loosened the rules for reporting "off-books," special purpose vehicles of the very sort that had brought down Enron.

This lapse further reduced transparency and undermined the soundness of the American banking system.[94]

The failures of regulation to keep pace with economic and financial change and of regulators to competently and honestly discharge their duties were primarily responsible for the depth and severity of the Great Recession. Complacently formulaic in opposing regulation, the Bush administration tended to give its Wall Street friends what they asked for and to assume that the financial system could mostly look after itself. The combination of the revolution in finance and poor financial oversight produced massive financial vulnerability in the United States, Europe, and around the world. The complexity of the economy and its new financial instruments required competence and responsibility of regulators but did not get them. As a result of the missing and bollixed regulation, immense disequilibria were allowed to build up in the economy, and once the downturn began, the threat of financial collapse arose.

Why Did the European Economies Have Somewhat Different Economic Structures than the American? Most of continental Europe, unlike the United States, Britain, The Netherlands, and a few other deeply liberal countries, was predominantly authoritarian during much of the 19th and early 20th centuries. Its relatively recent experience of economic hierarchy and prolonged exposure to powerful hierarchical culture tended to make Europeans less entrepreneurial, more restrictive of economic markets, and more receptive to the welfare and regulatory states. Often forced to keep redundant workers on the payroll, European businesses were hesitant to hire new ones. Slow growth and high unemployment long plagued most European countries largely because of strong labor laws.

Continental Europe's different economic structures were also due in part to the fact that its countries retained stronger community and consensus than did the United States. Until the last half of the global era, much of Europe had not for many centuries experienced as large migrations and mixing of sharply diverse peoples as had the United States. Only 2 percent of Europeans lived in European countries other than that of their birth. Europeans had a great deal of time to smooth edges and harmonize socio-cultural variations, unlike Americans whose country was formed more recently through large-scale movements of people and the mingling of stark differences. The resulting solidarity in Europe more easily supported curtailment of the markets and maintenance of fuller welfare states. Having stronger collectivism, social bonds, and senses of obligation among aid recipients, a well-integrated society may also be more generous with its less fortunate members. Moreover, stronger communal ties, as in Switzerland or Italy, allowed authorities to require the relatives of a needy single mother or elderly person to share in their support, lightening the burden on the state while increasing the moral pressure on the recipient to perform appropriately.[95]

Europe's comparative homogeneity and workedness were successfully drawn upon in Germany to forge difficult cooperation between government, business, and labor, cooperation that would never have been possible in a context of French or American discord. Germany brought its social programs into fiscal balance through a combination of intelligence, pragmatism, collectivism, hard work, and good will, enabling it to move early to trim the excesses of its welfare state. Nevertheless, European countries' stronger consensuses and citizen responsibility were declining through the era, in large part due to high levels of immigration.

Why the European Sovereign Debt Crisis? Like the Great Recession in the United States, Europe's sovereign debt crisis, beginning in 2011, was primarily government caused. As in this country, pressures from special interests representing those seeking benefits and regulations were strong for expanding the welfare and regulatory states but weak for fiscal and regulatory responsibility. In Europe too the force of the leanings of the dependent was added to that of the special interests. Yet those interests and leanings could have been better managed had the incompleteness of the Maastrict Treaty of 1992 bringing the European Union into being and of the arrangements establishing the euro currency not hobbled European effectiveness.

The tragedy was that monetary union could not work safely without fiscal union, but fisical union was not politically feasible. Europe's sovereign debt crisis was ultimately caused by the idealistic hope that the continent might in due course become a democratic unity, at once strengthening Europe, expiating guilt over the Third Reich, and making the continent a moral beacon to the world. Risks were taken, reservations set aside, and realistic accounting suspended regarding the dubious finances of several eurozone members because of this hope. The Germans and other northern Europeans paid out a great deal beginning in 2011 to hold onto the euro largely because, in their good European citizenship, they overestimated the willingness of marginal, southern member-states, to fulfill their promises in the absence of firm mechanisms to enforce fiscal compliance.

Given their moral resources, several weaker countries needed the possibility of depreciating their currencies to restore economic growth, but their doing so was not possible under the euro. Britain and Switzerland, with long histories of capitalism and reservoirs of financial realism and shrewdness, steered clear of the euro for just such reasons. The complex flaws of Europe's incomplete union allowed the vast underlying contradictions of unaffordable social benefits and economic regulations to build to dangerous levels. Exposure to global economic markets required that Europe open its markets, adapt to their rigors, and cut back unsustainably generous benefits and burdensome regulations, but the euro made such tightening greatly more difficult.

Why the Liberalizing Third World Began Sustained Economic Development Only in the Global Period. A new culture of capitalism played an important role in helping regimes and societies marshal the political resolve to undergo the wrenching transition into capitalism. The economic markets enjoyed outstanding PR during the 1980s and 1990s, and still excellent PR until 2008. Some of this popularity owed to the rhetoric and appeal of Thatcher and Reagan. The media glamorized entrepreneurialism, business, technology, and the Silicon Valley for decades. Nor did the culture around capitalism cease being generally positive after the Great Recession; it became mixed. The cultural force of the markets assuaged most fear of civil disorder that had helped forestall economic liberalization in earlier societies.

Sustained economic growth by less developed countries had seemed hopeless to those in developed countries during the national era (1885–1965). Little did Westerners know at the time that much of the problem was theirs. Under Harold Laski's influence, a generation of third-world leaders was educated at the London School of Economics (LSE) during the mid- 20th century, in top-down socialist planning not so different from the traditional hierarchical pattern they needed to overcome. Development specialists worked against the markets, recommending and sometimes building huge steel plants in India or grand infrastructure projects in Ghana that seldom had the hoped-for impact. Transition of third-world societies directly into national capitalist structures simply did not occur. Where approximately eight European authoritarian societies and four former European colonies had been able to climb to modernity during the early liberal period (1500-1885),[96] not one authoritarian society was able to do so during the national era, at least not on its own, that is, without going to war against the very idea of modernity and suffering military defeat at the hands of well-disposed opponents. Under Nehru and the Gandhis, India's post-independence Congress Party bought into the inappropriate Laski model. In an atmosphere of complacency and self-satisfaction, it long flirted with socialism and the Soviets, while going nowhere economically.

No single university had the kind of policy dominance during the global era that LSE had at mid-century, but aspiring third-world leaders tended to shift during the global era to universities in the more market-friendly United States. The most economically influential American institution of higher learning for the third world has been the University of Chicago, dominated by the free-market approach of Milton Friedman and his followers. What actually worked in the third world – opening up the economic markets – was quite different from the self-defeating statism that national-era development specialists and intellectuals touted. The transition of third-world countries directly into capitalism simply did not occur before the global-capitalist period because such a transition for a third-world country, without market-induced incentives and enterprise, was something like asking a person to climb from the peasantry directly into the upper-middle class, skipping the working and middle classes altogether. From Nehru to Nasser, many third-world leaders got nowhere fast. Laski offered a wobbly ladder missing its lower-middle rungs; it took middle-class self-control for granted. Friedman's ladder was secure, though unappealing to the genteel, because it went from the ground floor up, providing for third-world people's development of middle-class alertness and discipline along the way.

When formerly hierarchical, non-Western societies earnestly adopted the free markets, they began the sustained economic growth that had previously eluded them.

New technologies and adaptations developed in the first world tended to diffuse through much of the world due to advances in the technologies of transportation and communication. That much of the best management, accounting, technology, law, and finance quickly went global was free transfer of the productivity of the most developed economies to the ambitious newcomers, contributing mightily to their strong economic growth and unprecedented development. Much of this intellectual capital was not proprietary, but a good deal of it was pirated.

Advances in technology also made possible the elimination of a long-standing source of third-world resistance to the markets in their earlier contentment with the customary. It did so by providing the means to supplant traditional wants. Much of the third world adopted the economic markets and began sustained growth in part as a cumulative effect of capitalism's ubiquitous advertising, marketing, and merchandizing that created high demand for consumer products. As third-world peoples were flooded with material images via the media, new desires drew them into the cash economy and consumerist whirl.

Once transitions to capitalism were effected, rates of economic growth were higher in third-world countries than in first-world ones partly because they started at the bottom and had so much room to improve. Their peoples were determined to save and accumulate without delay and were unwilling to support costly government programs. The drive behind their herculean efforts to quickly rise allowed the burdens of the welfare and regulatory states to remain relatively light. As satisfaction with economic standing was achieved and settled in, their tension slowly fell back toward the norm, and economic structures and growth rates slowly converged toward those of relatively content first-world societies.

The rule of law progressed in most third-world countries during the global era, contributing to the spread of capitalism – but not as strongly as it might have. Those in privileged industries and professions with protection against the markets frequently resisted the rule of law, taking advantage of arcane practices from the hierarchical past to engage in rear-guard action opposing the clarification of ownership, for example.[97] Supporters of hierarchic backwardness exploited legal and bureaucratic opacity for every advantage. The third world long had a good deal of property, but this property was held in opaque, collectivist forms unsuitable for promoting exchange, such as houses built on land whose ownership rights were not adequately recorded or unincorporated businesses with undefined liability.

Since the rights to such possessions were not adequately documented, these assets could not readily be turned into capital, could not be traded outside of narrow local circles where people knew and trusted each other, and could not be used as collateral.[98] There was "too much room for misunderstanding, faulty recollection and reversal of agreement."[99] As property law takes hold, it "fixes and realizes capital," making certainty possible regarding the ownership and transfer of resources.[100] Property rights were clarified only with difficulty. Such structural differences between first- and third-world capitalist economies also resulted from the fact that the latter had little or no experience with open capitalist economic markets.

The waves of extra-legal migrants in the third world who squatted on underutilized land, traded where forbidden, and clashed with authorities enforcing the old, conflicted property rights constituted a major force for legal and economic renewal. Those moving into the extra-legal barrios and favelas of the third world were the analogs of the peasants who migrated illegally into the free, prospering cities of the Middle Ages, building early capitalism in Europe.[101] To the extent to which modern property law was adopted, it lowered transaction costs, enhanced calculability, and reduced cronyism.[102]

Why the Precariousness of the Era's Hierarchical Economies? Many of the period's authoritarian holdouts and backsliders against global capitalism were oil-producing countries. Despite the Middle East's long history of trade and some cultural support for the markets, many of its economies, such as those of Saudi Arabia, Iran, and Bahrain, remained predominantly hierarchical because authoritarian rulers retained control of their countries' petro-chemical resources. Russia was in a similar situation. Rulers' possession of large oil supplies has an effect similar to that conferred by aristocratic control of the land in traditional hierarchical societies. So long as rulers' oil and natural gas revenues continued to flow, true capitalism had little chance except subordinately and precariously. However, energy technology was developing rapidly by the end of the era, oil markets were extremely volatile, and power based upon petroleum reserves was becoming less secure.

China, with its dominant hierarchical economic sector and market-based secondary tier, sought to reap the economic benefits of capitalism while engaging in mercantilist, top down development and suppressing personal freedom. That profile conferred advantages in the short and middle runs, but it introduced colossal distortions and vulnerabilities in the long run. As China's economic markets intensify and a progressively larger, more capable, and more independent middle class arises, the regime's political monopoly will come under greater challenge. Insofar as economic and political controls are truculently intensified, the economic distortions will intensify and further jeopardize competitiveness. The Chinese economy became the world's second largest by the end of the era, but it was also vulnerable. This was evident in the continuing incompleteness of its rule of law. As James Fallows succinctly puts it, "in China ... law is one thing and reality is another."[103] The vulnerability of the Chinese economy was also evident in its massive debt and real estate bubbles tainted with corruption. The regime could run through its extensive foreign currency reserves rather quickly if those bubbles pop.

BROADER CONSIDERATIONS

Twelve hundred years after their humble beginnings during the early Middle Ages in Venice, Milan, Bari, and Amalfi and fifty-five after the end of World War II, relatively free markets had largely triumphed by the end of the 20th century, and the world had become predominantly capitalist. From Canada to Brazil, Norway to Indonesia, and Japan to Nigeria, integrated world markets delivered oil, cotton, computers, automobiles, jet planes, software, and money at whatever prices and quantities supply and demand would bear. Strewn by the wayside was the wreckage of the brutal tyrants, imperious officials, conspiring revolutionaries, starry-eyed utopians, and faint-hearted do-gooders who had sold short in the prolonged bull market.

As capitalism had long brought extraordinary benefits to the first world, it was now also bringing them to the third world. These benefits included the sustained economic growth that provided the means of solving many other problems, first and foremost those pertaining to national security. Capitalism's unsurpassed economic and technological productivity enabled market societies to defend themselves against the authoritarian murderers and thugs who forever seek to impose their wills by force upon their peaceful neighbors. The global markets lifted several billion human beings out of poverty and well over a billion into middle incomes around the world. They generated the means with which to educate as never before. To the extent to which third-world countries resolved to achieve growth, capitalism catapulted them toward first-world development and living standards. Global capitalism did not lock third-world countries into traps as peripheral suppliers of primary products – it released them from those traps. Whether the initial thrust was from textiles, bananas, copper, manganese, lumber, tourism, or anything else; where the global markets were accepted, prosperity and diversification followed. Socialism, not capitalism, locked third-world countries into the periphery.[104]

The lifting of the third world toward the productivity and living standards of the first at the same time represented a tremendous global economic equalization. As the third world grew at a faster clip than the first from 1987 and steeply so from 2007, inequality between countries decreased as considerable catching up went on globally. The 70-fold gulf between first- and third-world incomes of the late 1980s and early 1990s declined to a 42-fold gap by 2013.[105] Much of that convergence, soberingly, was a function of slow growth in the first world during and after the Great Recession. First-world citizens had no one but themselves to blame for the slide in growth rates from 2008 that was responsible for many of their complaints about globalization.

Yet income inequality within the United States increased during the global era to the highest levels it had reached since the early 20th century, more than in most other global-liberal societies. Real income rose considerably at the top in this country, stagnated for most others, and declined for those at the bottom. Some of that inequality occurred because as the third-world poor entered first-world countries and lived side-by-side with developed populations, inequality came closer and became more visible, the flip side of inclusion. The apparent increase in inequality from this source was only a matter of where it was located; it was perspectival. Some of it was also measurement error from federal income figures not including government benefits or unreported income. Nevertheless, the trend was real and concerning. Yet, as becomes apparent in the chapters to come, increased inequality of power was even more pronounced and more worrisome, not only suggesting that further increases of economic inequality may lie ahead but raising acute concerns about the political, social, and moral ramifications of that inequality of power.

Economic inequality rose in this country and others in part because as the economic arena became global, stupendous fortunes were to be made, for the larger the economic markets, the larger the disparities, all else equal. Such inequality in the United States and other global-liberal societies rose because of intense international competition in which third-world competitors relying on cheap labor were undercutting many first-world businesses. They were more successful in taking away working-class employment and less so in taking away middle- and upper-middle-class employment, but they were moving up the food chain, taking away progressively better jobs. An additional reason for the increased economic inequality of the era is treated in chapter 4.

The prospering of the third world should be recognized as a global equalization in part offsetting the harmful contribution of the larger scale of global markets to inequality. Since much of the increased economic inequality in the United States was in effect a provincial complaint about a larger process of globalization which was egalitarian in many respects, one would think that Americans, whose country played the decisive role in fostering the global markets, ought to be able to handle the relatively modest adjustments required of them. Some perspective should be kept regarding relative income slippages of a few percentage points here and

there when so many in the United States and around the world have greatly benefited from the global markets. Cheating on the rules of international trade is another matter.

Undeniably, the economic markets, like any others, are inseparable
from Schumpeterian destruction as well as creation.[106] Wherever there
are sunrise forms, there are also sunset forms: As new businesses, industries, technologies, and skills rise, old ones decline. Capitalism is a posi-
tive-sum game, but the markets inevitably require many adjustments that
are accompanied by hardship. The pain they inflict is sufficiently difficult
to accept when it strikes close to home that the economic markets have
few permanent friends, even among their avid supporters.

Nor are capitalism's challenges only economic, for when the markets
are as extremely powerful as they became during the global era, they also
skew priorities. Tocqueville spoke insightfully of "that craving for material well-being which leads the way to slavery."[107] During the national
era much book publishing, for example, was relatively dedicated and
self-sacrificing. Publishers, whose companies were frequently medium
sized and independent, often truly believed in what they were doing and
selected books on the basis of their lasting literary or intellectual value,
in effect subsidizing high-quality writing. Bennett Cerf was one of those
fine publishers. Under global capitalism, most publishing by far became
concentrated in the hands of a few large corporations for whom the earlier
commitment was replaced by the bottom line. Things were little different
in the media or business generally. The market economy so imperialized
American society and culture that they substantially became the inciden-
tal outcomes of powerful corporations' needs to maintain profitability.
Global capitalism played an important role in the large moral vacuum that
formed around it. Nevertheless, countries could not avoid the economic
markets without inviting vastly more trouble than any attending capitalism. Down the anti-market road lay closing themselves off from the rest
of the world, languishing economically, and inviting tyrants domestic or
foreign to run them into the ground.

The growing economic inequality of the last half century in the United States posed a major problem for the country, but that problem primarily had other sources than economic ones. Above all, it had political,
social, moral, and cultural sources. Since every social institution and aspect of personality has interacted with global capitalism, it is best to keep
assessments of the global economic markets somewhat provisional until
the wider circumstances have been examined. To commence this fuller

analysis let us turn to the ways in which the United States began coming apart in 1965, beginning with how large numbers of Americans ceased identifying with their country.

PART II
COMING APART IN FIVE DIMENSIONS

CHAPTER 3

THE ADVENT OF MULTICULTURALISM

THE CHANGING BREADTH OF ATTACHMENT

The breadth of Americans' identification narrowed during the late 1960s and early 1970s as attachment was redirected from the nation to racial, ethnic, gender, and lifestyle groups; not in everyone, but in enough that it firmed into a tacit consensus. Increased concern with the group went hand-in-hand with heightened sensitivity toward how society treated it and diminished concern with how it treated society. The United States was one of the earliest countries to make the transition, but many others went through it as well, including all in the West. This highly charged narrowing of attachment was as central to the global-liberal paradigm and era as was the opening of the many-sided markets, and it had profound consequences.

As identification shifted from the nation to the group, racial conflict began increasing during the civil-rights movement in which African Americans employed Gandhian language and tactics of nonviolence from the Indian independence movement to reject their second-class status and gain legal rights. The conflict sharply intensified with the Watts riot of 1965 and subsequent ghetto riots as the civil-rights movement abruptly metamorphosed into a movement of black power that expressed disaffection and pursued tangible and intangible benefits.

Group restiveness increased in other countries and along other lines, partly spread from the United States to racial and ethnic groups abroad and partly spread to gender and lifestyle groups in this country and elsewhere. After an era of relative quiescence, racial and ethnic antagonism flared in Northern Ireland, Quebec, Spain, and Belgium. Blacks began militantly opposing white domination in Rhodesia and South Africa, Tamils began increasingly contesting Sinhalese domination in Sri Lanka, and Slovenes, Croatians, Muslims, and others began systematically opposing Serbian domination in Yugoslavia. Factious sentiments held by a swirl of hostile and mutually suspicious ethnic groups in Eastern Europe and Central Asia helped strip the Soviet Union down to its Russian nucleus. The increased salience of the group and decreased salience of the nation were central to these conflicts.

Before examining the multiculturalism that underlay the new salience of the group and the upsurge of violence, let us examine the buildup to it in the United States.

The Holocaust and the Civil-Rights Movement

The single most shocking and horrifying event of the twentieth century was the Holocaust. Civilized human beings everywhere were left forlorn by the Third Reich's systematic slaughter of more than 6 million Jews. No ordinary word even sufficed to name the heinous event, and a new usage came into the language: *Holocaust* as a burnt offering in reference to an entire people in genocide. The anguish was particularly acute for survivors, who, traumatized by what had happened, resolved never to forget. Amid their profound sorrow, it stuck poignantly in their memories that, in all too many cases, when European Jews desperately needed refuge and flight was still possible, no country in the world had been willing to take them in. The Holocaust helped set the stage for global liberalism's preoccupation with groups.

The global-liberal focus on groups was anticipated and given impetus during the postwar decades as diffuse feelings of guilt and sympathy arose in thoughtful people regarding prejudice and discrimination. The combat participation of black soldiers in World War II (in segregated units) and labor of black workers side-by-side with white ones on the home front led to increased disquiet about racism and early support for civil rights. A growing and increasingly impassioned movement against racism and anti-Semitism began gaining momentum. Against this background, President Truman desegregated the U.S. military by executive order in 1948, to favorable reception in much of the country. The U.S. Supreme Court mandated public school desegregation in 1954 in its famous Brown versus Board of Education decision. By the postwar years, as Lemann says, "Race relations stood out nearly everywhere as the one thing most plainly wrong in America...."[108]

The civil-rights movement began in 1955 with the Montgomery bus boycott and raged on in lunch-counter sit-ins, boycotts, and protests over the following decade. From its onset, the movement was closely intertwined with action by the federal government, especially the judicial but also the executive and legislative branches.[109] As increasingly large and effective protests produced gains of consciousness in the South and throughout the country, a critical juncture arrived when President Kennedy was elected. An eloquent speaker, he helped persuade much of the

American middle class to acknowledge the justice and inevitability of civil-rights legislation. The accelerating movement reached an initial crescendo with the March on Washington and Martin Luther King's "I have a dream" speech of August 1963.

When Kennedy was assassinated in November of that year, the nation's grief at the loss of its inspiring young leader was followed by a desire to live up to his high ideals. In the eyes of many, he became a martyr to the causes of inclusion and tolerance that he had nobly espoused. The civil-rights bill, long mired in southern opposition, swiftly became law in early 1964 as a monument to the dead leader and main crescendo of the civil-rights movement. It was testimony as well to President Johnson's parliamentary genius.[110] Police brutality against peaceful protestors the following year in Selma, Alabama outraged Americans across the country and strengthened the national resolve to set things right. The Civil Rights Act of 1964 and Voting Rights Act of 1965 removed most remaining legal defenses of racial and ethnic discrimination in the United States. By the time of their passage most Americans accepted national responsibility for working toward overcoming racial and ethnic injustice, directing resources toward easing conditions for minorities, and strengthening norms and virtues toward overcoming prejudice and discrimination.

Almost as an aside amid surging respect for all peoples, the Immigration and Nationality Act passed against little opposition in 1965, opening U.S. borders that had been nearly closed by restrictive law since 1924. The new law introduced the quota system that, with modifications, has been in effect since. Where the earlier law had been heavily Eurocentric, the countries of the world were now assigned quotas in approximate proportion to their populations. Levels of legal and eventually illegal immigration were also allowed to rise steeply.

Although a relatively diverse society from its origins, the United States had possessed a national consensus in support of broad social unity from the country's origins through the early 1960s, except for the Civil War period; a consensus that had strengthened during the national era. That consensus carried moral force and charisma which drew large numbers of its citizens together, although it also left some out. It was presided over by the WASPS (White, Anglo-Saxon Protestants), the upper-, upper-middle-, and middle-class versions of whose culture were the esteemed norms through the national era. With varying degrees of ambivalence, many who were different, among them Catholics, Jews, blacks, Hispanics, and Asians, had accepted that consensus, paid respect to it, aspired to blend into it, and raised their children to do the same. The national-liberal paradigm and era held through the August 6, 1965 passage of the Voting Rights Act, the second civil rights law.

Multiculturalism in the United States

The national era ended and the global era began with the Watts riot that started five days later, on August 11th. "The 1960s turned as if on a hinge" during the summer of 1965, Nicholas Lemann says; the huge ghetto riot "instantly convinced the whole country that there was a severe crisis in the black slums."[111] The national era with its overriding sense of the country's unity ended, and the global era with its sense of disunity was under way. The focus turned from the nation to the group.[112]

The multiculturalism foundational to the global-liberal paradigm and era is the ideology of identity politics based upon the assumption that society is a set of racial, ethnic, gender, and lifestyle groups rather than a national unit. It holds that the focus should be upon the alienated, unjustly treated groups among them rather than upon the larger society.

Multiculturalism values the designated victim groups and disvalues the dominant majority. It assigns the moral high ground to the groups and the low ground to whites, Anglos, gentiles, men, and heterosexuals. Multiculturalism encourages difference and discourages assimilation. It blames and disparages the once celebrated larger society by associating it with the discredited white majority that had dominated in the past. It opposes attempts to strengthen or benefit society as a whole, both because it takes that notion to be meaningless and because its adherents feel allegiance to the groups rather than to society. Its globalism lies in its opposition to nations and support for international entities like the EU and UN that weaken them. Among its more remarkable effects, the multiculturalist framework transformed the national era social ethic of helping those who needed it on universal grounds, into the global era ethic of helping those who needed it as members of particular groups.[113] Émile Durkheim classifies societies structured by particularistic emphasis upon groups as blocks in such a manner, like imperial Austro-Hungary, the USSR, traditional India, or the Middle East, as segmentary rather than unitary.[114]

The multiculturalists' most explosive accusation against the earlier American order was of racism, that the country had acceded to slavery until the Civil War, tolerated Jim Crow (the Southern regime of segregation) from the Civil War through the early 1960s, and permitted major discriminatory economic, legal, social, and educational practices after that.

Shocking television clips of police violence against innocent protestors in an ostensibly free society deeply affected Americans and others around the world, sparking solidarity among and with group members and prompting widespread outrage that helped institute the reign of multiculturalism. News coverage of protestors' persuasive messages and heroic stands also marshaled support. As Americans came under the influence of multiculturalist action and rhetoric in the mid-1960s, deep discontent and rebelliousness swept over blacks – and, soon after, young people, Hispanics, women, and gays. The riots accelerated the tendency, as did the assassination of Martin Luther King.

As multiculturalist blame took hold and began generalizing, group identity was inflamed and national identity subdued. The members of multiple groups were becoming collectively self-conscious and demanding with great ethical force more respect and rights than they had been receiving. The perception was building in the American public of the contradiction between the nation's central values and the systematic exclusion and mistreatment of blacks and other groups. Most also came to feel that societal peace required understanding the groups' circumstances and accommodating their reasonable demands.

Among their targets, the multiculturalists and those allied with them mounted a withering critique of the American WASP establishment of the previous era that had permitted collective injustice to occur. Slammed with charges of racism, the old establishment's genial WASPs substantially capitulated. The horrors of violence against and mistreatment of blacks, Jews, Hispanics, women, gays, and members of other groups were the foundational memories that seared themselves into the mentalities of a generation, an era, and much of the world during the transition into global liberalism. The theme of negating the intolerant majority and struggling on behalf of the victim minority dominated the social imagination of the era. Its central domestic policy concern became seeking to define and redress sociocultural conditions as manifesting collective injustice.

A tacit consensus came to support some but not all of the basic assumptions of multiculturalism. The consensual core was that the country had to try its best to overcome prejudice and discrimination against blacks, Jews, Hispanics, Asians, women, and gays; in the society, culture, and law. That consensus did not extend to the movement's attempts to go beyond equal rights toward equal outcomes. Many such attempts were intensely opposed though others sometimes obtained majorities. Forced busing was extremely contentious locally around the country, often flaring into violence and disruption, as in south Boston, but it never emerged as a major political issue nationally because it was imposed by the courts.

Affirmative action too was widely opposed, but nor could that issue ever scale politically because judicially imposed. The public was willing to accept moderate political correctness with its norms protecting group members from communication or action that might give offense. Well before that rubric appeared, a consensus quickly and happily banned the offensive epithets referring to group members that had been in wide currency through the early 1960s, but there was little and vague consensus regarding political correctness beyond this initial case except in strongly liberal settings.

Highly charged from the onset, multiculturalism was accompanied by bitter struggles and a great deal of rancor. Many of the combatants were conflictualist, i.e., they considered conflict to be the normal state of affairs and broadly embraced and justified it.[115] Jean-Francois Lyotard, for one, urged people to take the offensive and struggle socioculturally. His first principle was, "To speak is to fight."[116] The contestation became compulsive and polarization the order of the day, with positions dug in and fortified. In a country that had long been accustomed to relative harmony, multiculturalism spawned continuing conflict when regularly going beyond its limited supporting consensus.

The change brought by half a century of multiculturalism was immensely consequential, but it was subtle. Most Americans were only partially aware of how deeply multiculturalism was changing the country although they were apprehensive about it. Many of them, including strong majorities of the pre-1960s generations, retained predominantly national references but acquiesced to a degree on multiculturalism in the hope that their doing so would help overcome collective injustice and promote amicable relations with the groups.

Multiculturalism Around the World

The victorious 1960s uprisings against authority in continental Europe bore resemblance to but differed in important ways from that in the United States. What was discredited across the Atlantic was above all anything associated with fascism. Early in the global era thoroughly anti-fascist, anti-colonial young, white radicals and their allies rather than aggrieved groups became ascendant in Europe. In an atmosphere of moral outrage and blame, the younger generation and its older sympathizers demanded that militarism and imperialism be halted, access to university education broadened, and the personal freedom extended with which to live their lives as they would. Except where it concerned regional sovereignty – as with Basques in Spain, Irish in Ulster, and Walloons in Belgium – Europeans were relatively unconcerned with minority relations for a quarter-century longer than were Americans, at least on the surface.

Many European countries had guest-worker programs, but they retained strict immigration controls through most of the 1980s. Near the end of the Cold War, immigration laws were relaxed and many guest workers were permitted to remain in their host countries. Following the collapse of the Soviet Union, immigration from Eastern Europe increased dramatically and became the focus for a time. When rejection of the West became more apparent in Muslim minorities after 9/11, Europe began paying more attention to the problems they posed. Immigration policies tightened during the 2000s but loosened again before long. Muslim immigration accelerated sharply as Syrian refugees began flooding into Europe in 2013, with more than a million arriving in 2015 alone. The Muslim populations of major Western European countries, including the United Kingdom, reached 5 to 8 percent by the end of the era, with France at the top of the list.

Europe had long had large variations among Christian and secular sociocultural patterns and harmonized them reasonably well; only from the 1990s did it encounter difference comparable to that in the United States, Canada, and Brazil.[117] Europe's new diversity was troubling because to a disconcerting degree its Muslim population formed a large, resistant bloc withholding allegiance from the deepest principles of its host countries. Some Muslim Europeans were practicing jihad in the radical sense of violent opposition to what is not Islamic and were mounting continual terrorist attacks against their Western hosts by the summer of 2016, but large numbers of Muslim Europeans were also profoundly dissenting in other ways. As Ayaan Hirsi Ali says, "We were taught that, as Muslims, we should oppose the West."[118] France, Belgium, Sweden, and other countries foundered in their response, allowing the formation of semi-sovereign *banlieues* or suburbs, ghettoes that authorities all but abandoned to Islamists, criminals, and shari'a law. Europe's Muslim uprising was frequently accompanied by an informal underground movement having some of the characteristics of organized crime, notably in the way in which it widely coerced its members and particularly women into resisting Western ways. Ali gives numerous examples evincing European multiculturalists' denial about and co-dependency regarding this coercion.[119]

India, one of the most heterogeneous societies in the world, inherited deeply entrenched sociocultural segmentation in its caste system. Although it achieved much of great value under Nehru, the country lost a fine chance to establish universal, caste-blind principles constitutionally and instead ratified many sorts of group rights.[120] In 1989 a Congress-Party-dominated coalition government instituted major affirmative-action set-asides of government jobs and higher education admissions for those of lower castes.[121] In 2011 Prime Minister Manmohan Singh's Congress Party government extended those set-asides to almost 50 percent of available positions. Affirmative action had the negative side effects of both reviving the caste system and promoting resentment between castes.[122] Tensions between India's 80 percent Hindu majority and 13 percent Muslim minority also increased somewhat from the early 1990s, thanks to the Islamic Resurgence, provocations by the Pakistani regime, and, reactively, intolerance by the Hindu-nationalist Bharatiya Janata Party (BJP). Like its affirmative action programs, India's partial recognition of Muslim communal shari'a law was multiculturalist.

Japan, in contrast to the West and India, had comparatively little diversity, sought to avoid increasing what it had, and refused multiculturalism, resolutely continuing to honor its homogeneous nation, society, culture, and history throughout the era. While not aggressive toward any country or group, it denied atrocities committed during World War II and avoided the topic of its small Korean and Ainu minorities. Japan had become an outstanding democratic country with its own rich and worthy tradition and values, and it was a vital ally of the United States.

The alarming disjoint of the global era was between liberal societies' respect for and solicitude toward others domestically and internationally amid the overcoming of injustice, and hierarchical societies' fundamental disrespect for others amid deliberate perpetration of injustice. The West, India, and their friends around the world were respectful of others while China, Russia, and most Muslim countries pointedly were not. Huntington's "fault-line" conflicts between civilizations emanated overwhelmingly from authoritarian rather than liberal societies, from tyrannical ruling classes that grind their people and their neighbors into the ground as they are able to, in part through aggressive nationalism.[123] In place of respecting difference, the Chinese regime, for example, filled prisons with political dissenters and extensively employed the death penalty against harmless Christians and Falun Gong. Putin and the FRS (Russia's secret police) consolidated their regime by bombing apartment buildings and killing hundreds of innocent Russians in order to scurrilously blame Chechnyan

separatists and scapegoat and suppress them with wanton violence to rally naïve Russians behind the reassertion of tyranny.[124] Without usually being as coldly efficient, Muslim tyrants were every bit as ruthless. Far from
embracing difference, authoritarian societies suppressed and exploited it.

THE SOCIAL SOURCES OF MULTICULTURALISM

Multiculturalism in the United States arose out of the experience
and leanings of minorities, especially Jewish and black Americans,
born of their sensitivity and anguish regarding discrimination and prejudice they had suffered individually and collectively and sometimes continued to suffer. Modern Jewish sympathies, particularly after the Holocaust, focused strongly on and embraced unjustly treated groups. Having
long experienced victimhood associated with *their* difference, the same
was true for blacks. Both remained collectively self-conscious, within but
to some extent apart from and resistant to the larger American society.[125]

Multiculturalism struck a special chord as well among the members
of other racial and ethnic groups and, subsequently, those of gender and
lifestyle groups. Hispanics, Asians, the LGBT community, and to some
extent women had sufficiently distinct experience and circumstances that
difference was relatively salient for them. Ascending group sensitivities
began shifting the focus toward race and ethnicity during the postwar
years but did so decisively during the mid-1960s and helped keep it there
for more than half a century. Young people were part of the original multiculturalist coalition as a distinct group, but their group-conciouness dissolved as the War in Vietnam and the draft wound down, they grew older,
and the youth movement was discredited. As multiculturalism took hold,
group identity increased and alienation intensified.

The comparatively homogeneous circumstances and Christian traditions of most Americans instead had affinities to unitary identities and
perspectives. Given their perennial experience of having been in the vast
majority protected by relative unity, white gentiles of the middle, upper-middle, and upper classes were shocked, disoriented, and said, *mea
culpa* as they encountered the powerful rhetoric, narrative, accusations,
and demands of multiculturalism. They allowed it considerable leeway in
the interests of social reconciliation despite its radicalism, splintering, and
conflictualism that went against their Christian grains of reconciliation.
The pall of socially constructed guilt long held the accused at bay.

From early on the groups found receptive ears and crucial support
from growing numbers of white liberal sympathizers especially numer-

ous and influential in the upper and upper-middle classes. Much of their influence emanated from their lopsided domination of the courts, the media, and higher education. As historian Richard Abrams says of the 1950s, early 1960s, and first decade of the new era, most of the major progressive changes of the time in United States were instituted by a well-intentioned "liberal elite fortuitously entrenched in key social, political, and especially judicial positions."[126] As the ground shook beneath them with the emergence of the new upper class to which we turn in the next chapter, ordinary Americans' background of earnest but sheltered Christian middle-class tradition little prepared them for the assault of multiculturalism.

The central pivot upon which the global-liberal paradigm and era turned was the multiculturalist blame of the United States, its heritage, and those who supported them. The talent, resources, and strong leanings of the groups and their powerful allies prevailed over traditional America. The ghetto riots may have damaged more black than white property, but they did effectively manipulate white guilt. Those uprisings morally discredited the country and its heritage while banking large reservoirs of guilt, conferring power upon the previously excluded and their allies. Their massive, one-sided culture war and PR campaign blaming and discrediting the United States, the West, and their traditions were decisive against the good will, educational limitations, and inexperience with cultural markets of average white Americans. The alienated groups and their upper- and upper-middle-class allies' forceful snapping at all who failed to agree helped enforce their consensus through the period. Together they became dominant in many ways during the global era. The national-liberal paradigm had buckled under their combined weight, making way for the new one.

Multiculturalism's discreditation of the country brought a cascade of harmful consequences, beginning with its impact upon black Americans. President Johnson conveyed the heart of the argument: "You do not take a person who for years has been hobbled by chains and liberate him, bring him up to the starting line in a race and then say, 'You are free to compete with all the others.'"[127] Multiculturalist blame absolved black Americans of responsibility for their condition in life. Shelby Steele sees multiculturalism's tarnishing of the country and its history as having tabooed application to black Americans of the very principle that had animated the American economic, political, and moral achievement, that of people taking individual responsibility for their lives. Why try, if the deck was supposedly stacked against you? Why bother if others were to blame? It became verboten under multiculturalism to ask that black Americans take responsibility for their lives like others. In place of the power of taking responsibility, they acquired "the power to shame, silence, and muscle concessions from the larger society on the basis of past victimization."[128] To Steele, "White guilt led black Americans to a great mistake: to talk themselves out of the individual freedom we had just won for no purpose whatsoever except to trigger white obligation."[129] As he sees it, our most basic power lies in our taking of full responsibility; no one benefits from the help of others without doing so.[130]

Another major consequence of multiculturalism is that, under it, Washington was conveniently marketed as the neutral arbiter and righter of past wrongs as agency was reallocated from individual persons to the federal government. It reinforced that allocation of the central role to the government by striving throughout the period to define justice as equal outcomes rather than equal rights to work hard and compete. At the same time, it sought to attribute group differences in performance or achievement to discrimination. Both stances helped cement the relationship between multiculturalism and growing government. As one of the founders of multiculturalism, Johnson knew what he was doing.

The era was unusually contentious in large part because the struggles for collective recognition and justice central to the experience of societies under multiculturalism involved matters about which people feel intensely, their very identities. Identity politics is inherently charged, tribal, and a negative-sum game. Its intense passions tend to banish reason and reconciliation. In their primal anger, the groups were neither aware of nor concerned with the destructiveness of their politics. Human beings are seldom naturally combative, but they may be made so by ceaseless, profound strife.

The resistance in Europe from the late 1980s occurred in part because the Muslim world accepted a virulent, anti-Western paradigm with the onset of the Islamic Resurgence. Turning away from domestic questioning and reform, large numbers of Muslims blamed their discontents on Israel, the West, or other Muslim sects. No less responsible for the resistance in Europe was its ineffectual response to the same. That response in turn owed largely to its belatedly coming under the influence of multiculturalism at the end of the 1980s, which led to evasively interpreting the threats posed by Muslim immigrants and their offspring as humanitarian concerns or group rights, rather than as the continuation of 1400 years of Muslim invasion by other means. The ineffectuality centered on the way in which multiculturalism played upon Europeans' sense of guilt over fascist atrocities. Amid declining leadership, some of the region's ineffectuality also arose from the organizational morass of being stranded between a fully operational, democratic EU and the autonomous nation-states of the past.

Even when Europeans thought about immigration in practical terms, it was mostly about the need for labor. The end of the Cold War further eased what realism there was in Europe as the lessening of Soviet-American tensions through the 1960s had eased it in the United States.

Generational change was extremely important in Europe as it was in the United States. As the World War II generation receded, the toughness, realism, and balance with which to refuse entry to those difficult to integrate also receded. Willy Brandt and Helmut Schmidt could manage it; Gerhard Schroeder and Angela Merkel could not. Like the Pax Americana and global capitalism, multiculturalism had deep and pervasive effects upon the societies under its sway as the focus of identification and attachment always does.

However necessary it was that the United States return to the problem of race during the global era, its doing so under multiculturalism carried a steep price, for the doctrine's accusations of grievous collective injustice against the country, its founding fathers, and its entire national heritage initiated a reverberating series of negative consequences that we shall see in multiple additional ways in which this country and the West began disintegrating during the global era. Multiculturalism represented the fundamental coming apart that drove the multiple other comings apart.

After taking a growing toll through its 51-year reign, multiculturalism itself became one of two fundamental issues most in contention by the end of the global era, both in the United States and in Europe. The next chapter introduces, describes, and analyzes the global era's new upper class of gamers that posed the other of those most contested issues. Each of the subsequent chapters will further characterize the effects of both multiculturalism and the gamers, for the two had enormous impacts upon how the United States and other advanced liberal societies fared during the global era.

CHAPTER 4

THE RISE OF THE GAMERS[1]

I f one is to profoundly understand a society and era, as Max Weber
superbly taught, one must grasp the character and spirit of their dominant class.[131] A great deal that was central to the United States from
1965 to 2016 was shaped by its new upper class of *gamers*.[132] I mean by
that term a gender-neutral synonym of *gamesmen*: Consummate competitors, many of whom cut corners. Their character-based ways of perceiving, thinking, feeling, and acting were stamped all over the society
and history of our time. The most successful executives and professionals
dominating all institutions were gamers. The proto-gamers of the 1960s
and the full-fledged ones of the 1970s largely displaced the WASP upper
class and the paradigm it bore, although that leading class and paradigm
continued to moderate the gamers until the early 1990s. As Heraclitus
says, "Character … is destiny."[133] The central role played by the gamers in
the United States has been among the less understood aspects of all that
has occurred since 1965.

THE CHARACTER OF THE GAMERS

E ssential to the gamers is that they possess not only the basic rational
self- consciousness and self-control of the middle-class superego but
higher-level versions of the same, with which they control the elementary versions. Instead of feeling bound by rules, they flexibly use, modify,
or discard them to further their individual goals.[134] Unlike the merchants
and shopkeepers of early modernity who held inner rules rigidly or the
white-collar workers of the national era who held them while attuned to
others' expectations, the gamers are self-directed but accept no binding
rules. By "higher" self-control, I mean self-determination that is one layer
more reflexive or aware in certain respects; not that it is more worthy or
more advanced, all things considered. The gamers' stock-in-trade is provisional, pragmatic policies that further their interests. Utterly immersed
in and adapted to markets of all kinds, the gamers analyze everything and
hold everything to be up for grabs. Committed to no particulars, they cannot be easily flustered; but nor are they grounded or anchored.

1   A shorter version of this chapter appeared under the title "The Rise of the 'Gamers,'" in
The Independet Review: A journal of Political Economy, Volume 25:1, Summer 2020, pp. 105-116.

The gamers arose early in the global period as higher-level, rational self-understanding and self-management became dominant in the character of many of the most able, especially among those entering business and the professions. They began habitually employing their higher self-control to game their careers and fast-forward their ascents. Utterly directed toward excelling at the game, they are highly adept at all things connected with their personal advancement. Systematically pursuing their rational interests as they understand them, the gamers deftly adjust and fine-tune their performance at school and at work, discipline and position themselves to get into great colleges and universities, maneuver their way into valuable internships, and garner outstanding early jobs. Intensely competitive and savvy, gamers think and talk incessantly about job and investment opportunities throughout their careers. The dexterity of their educational and career moves is one of the keys to their success.

Another key is that they hone their job performances to virtuosity. Highly capable and building upon impressive education and early experience, they specialize, work extremely long hours, and develop formidable repertoires of knowledge and skill. In time they become supremely proficient at what they do. Gamer executives adroitly vary management theories, marketing strategies, and corporate cultures. Those in marketing, advertising, and communications agilely and cleverly use media and public relations to their advantage. Gamer tax attorneys and accountants ingeniously interpret subtleties of law and accounting to solve clients' problems and build their practices. Drawing upon sophisticated understanding and remarkable entrepreneurialism, gamer executives evince a creative adaptability far greater and more astonishing than any the middle class has known. There have always been unusual business opportunities in liberal societies, but never before have such astonishing skills been available with which to exploit them.

Gamer drive pushes forward much more intensely and unremittingly than did middle-class discipline in its heyday, leading to far greater personal income and wealth. So single-mindedly rational and instrumentalist are the gamers that everything largely becomes a matter of economics to them. As they subject themselves to a higher inner despotism, even their manner of speech with its long and short bursts of rapid, mechanical utterance betrays the severity of their striving. Global-era management was no longer the low-key, jovial, secure experience it often was at mid-century.

Weber judged middle-class discipline, as primed by the Protestant ethic and spirit of capitalism, to have been the engine of the West's unparalleled development during the centuries of early capitalism.[135] In its economic aspects, the character of the gamers was the advanced engine of development helping drive the much more rapid economic growth of the entire world during the global era, but in its non-economic aspects, that character posed major problems, even for growth.

Whether venture capitalists, politicians, scholars, or intelligence analysts, the inquiry toward which gamers lean is technical, reflecting their intense instrumentalism. The gamers may know a lot, but they tend to know things narrowly and calculatedly rather than comprehensively and intuitively. Their eschewing of the big picture and over-reliance on formal models and under-processed data are among the reasons it is hard to get elected officials to think beyond their polling numbers. The gamers' penchant for losing themselves in technical detail is partly responsible for the great American intelligence fiascos of recent decades, such as failing to see 9/11 coming. A prime example of gamer one-sidedness is the character of Mark Zuckerberg as fictionally portrayed in the film *The Social Network*.[136] Mitt Romney's brilliance and his uneven sensitivity are quintessentially gamer. However gifted, knowledgeable, and proficient the gamers, their one-sidedness renders them particularly vulnerable to being outflanked by the complexity and elusiveness of human nature.

Realists through and through, the gamers tend to be interested in comparatively little in and of itself – they want results. In their driving ambition, they cashiered the well-intentioned but often loopy idealism of the 1960s for striving. Avoiding and even disparaging the ideal, the gamers appreciate higher education overwhelmingly for the doors it opens and the fungible adaptability, credentials, and connections it bestows, not for its humanistic value. More than most human beings, the gamers project their own mentality onto the actions of others, as in the way they impute everywhere the cynical realism that pervades their thinking.

More individualist in most respects than the early bourgeois and vastly more so than the company men of the 1950s, the gamers take to competition with a relish. They work horrendous hours as latter-day, secular monks, yet the gods to which they are dedicated are no longer spiritual or even societal but their own power, wealth, and prestige. An essential trait of the gamers is one-sided striving for self.

The arrival of the gamers was crucial in several ways to the flat, agile corporate structures of the global economy, beginning with the extraordinary organizational and managerial sophistication they brought. The entrepreneurialism of the gamers and long hours they are willing to work have been vital to the streamlined new structures that place great stress on top managers and staff. Their facility with flexibly assuming and delegating authority, which the other-directed employees of the 1950s could not begin to match, was well suited to the needs of global-capitalist business. The gamers have also been masters at creating and utilizing technology.

Where peasants wanted only enough for their modest, customary lives, the early middle class wanted a standard of living ample for economic security, and the other-directed organization men and women of the mid-20th century wanted indefinitely more for comfort and keeping up with the Joneses, the gamers "want all" – it must have been in the 1980s that I saw a Marin County Porsche with that exquisite California license plate. If the middle class of the 1950s was consumerist, the gamers are hyper-consumerist. The gamers in politics or culture may not be quite as materialistic as those in business or finance, but they undertake the same gaming toward goals of high office, prestigious professorships, or renown as artists, nor are they averse to making a lot of money along the way.

Overloaded by the outsized demands they place upon themselves and invite employers to place upon them, the gamers multi-task through large parts of their days, nervously checking their hand-held devices for instant messages, emails, and trade signals from investment apps or services while talking on the phone or listening to what someone is telling them from the office doorway. Their eyes intermittently glaze over in conversation through the day as their attention skips around among their diverse undertakings. Burdened and cluttered, their minds are easily distracted during personal interaction.[137] Their narrow focus on instrumental goals and multi-channel juggling of tasks displace attention to and understanding of the big picture, the larger meaning of what they are witnessing and doing.

The stress from the gamers' virtuoso participation in extremely complex, rapidly changing, high-stakes competition is so great that they need heavy "R&R" when off the job. During time off, they tend at first to manifest harried weariness from their chronic overwork, evoking the exhaustion of the dog-tired peasants of traditional hierarchical societies or exceedingly hard-working farmers of early liberal ones. Leisure for the well-educated and prosperous once meant time for reflection, leadership, and creative activity. The long hours of hyperrationality and discipline today are often followed by depleted, low energy "vegging" in complete relaxation, such as blanket consumption of popular culture.

When their energy revives – if they do not return at once to work – they tend to intensely pursue often obscure hobbies, amusements, or challenges, skillfully gaming such activities as wine connoisseurship, exotic travel, rock climbing, or collecting rarities, not infrequently to the point of distinction. For example, while unwinding from his furious publishing pace, a gamer professor of history might over many years put in place during off hours a perfect Renaissance Tuscan garden in his spacious yard. Or, as David Brooks says, gamers may "turn nature into an achievement course, a series of ordeals and obstacles they can conquer." In their compulsive striving, "they want to be a 'serious' walker, tennis player, skier or whatever it is that they are pursuing in leisure."[138]

The high new bar set by the gamers was responsible for more than a little of the increased inequality in first-world countries over the past few decades. People have been competing with economic prodigies some of whom had been on the fast track to success since they were three-year-olds in select, accelerated preschools. Just as the disciplined Puritans and Jews of the 17th-century Netherlands, England, Scotland, Switzerland, and American colonies pulled ahead with their capitalist-honed middle-class characters, the gamers were now doing so with their greatly more competitive, market-honed characters.

The gamer upper class comprises approximately the top 5 percent of the population in the most-developed societies, though smaller percentages in less-developed ones. The scale of this upper class is determined by the number whose character is dominated by individualistic higher self-management. Such reflexivity is ascendant only in the gamers but also present to a degree in the executive and professional upper-middle class, comprising the second to top 5 percent of the population, and to a lesser degree the broad upper-middle class of better-prepared college graduates, comprising the second to top decile. Gamer virtuosity tapers off into mere competence in the upper-middle class, which is hybrid, partly gamer and partly middle class. Applying the gamer criteria far more strictly limits the focus to the top gamers who make up the top 1 percent of the gamer class, or, setting aside their families, some 50,000 or 60,000 elite gamers who manifest the gamer type in sharpest relief and substantially own and run the United States.[139]

GAMING MORALITY

At its most developed, the universalism or orientation toward the whole that was relatively widespread during the national era in the United States was as self-aware as the perspective of the gamers, only it was collectively rather than individually directed. It may have had lacunae with respect to difference, but whether religious or secular, that universalism was oriented toward balancing and harmonizing all sides of society and life. Then came a turning point around 1970 when those on business and professional tracks began reacting against the low-key other-directedness and geniality of the 1950s as well as the naïve idealism of the 1960s. In their hubris they jettisoned concern with society and instead spurred themselves on for career advance. The moral collectivist service of the national era began ebbing, and the amoral individualist maneuvering of the global era began flowing. In school and during their early careers, many of the most able, best educated, and most ambitious began coming to the notion that they would neither reject nor reform the system but would game it for their own purposes. In the language of the time, they would "beat the system." When gamers, whether in business, law, politics, or civil service, notice something amiss in the social or regulatory policy of their country, for instance, they do not think, "How can I bring this condition to the attention of public officials to correct for us all?" but rather "How can I profit from it?"[140]

Gamers pride themselves above all on the smarts invested in their complex, high-level individual reflexivity; but they are in denial regarding the high-level collective reflexivity, the thoughtfulness, ingenuity, and care with which large numbers of their national-era predecessors watched over and nurtured society.[141] It does not fit with their cynical assumptions. The gamers' attainment of rarified personal awareness has come at the expense of a radical withdrawal of attention from their society, civilization, and aspects of the human not of immediate use to them in their marches to success. Their higher reflexivity represents massive diversion of moral attention and concern, from society to their personal quest for power and wealth.

With well-rounded moral codes, the national-era professionals and specialists of 60 years ago were "experts." In addition to denoting mastery of their field, the designation connoted reliability in making their knowledge or its fruits available to others. This expectation had ethical content and was wedded to a norm of service. Gamer professionals and specialists have instead been *virtuosi*. They have routinely mastered what they have done, to an even higher level, but their reliability has been open to question: In general, they cannot be counted upon to act in the interest of others, and for this reason they tend to be treated guardedly. There are no experts in the old sense – everyone has had to look out for themselves. This reality cuts both ways: Patients or clients have to be suspicious that medical or investment advice they receive may merely be making its sources money or protecting them legally, while the professionals have to be suspicious that patients or clients may just be setting them up for a lawsuit or leading them on for free service.

Just as the gamers pay little attention to rules of other sorts, they pay little attention to moral rules. They do what advances their aims and what they want to do. As George Friedman says, the gamers appear "brutally indifferent to any interests outside their own."[142] Their families often excepted, the gamers tend to believe in nothing beyond themselves. Charles Murray refers to them as a "hollow elite" because they have "no code of values that they feel they are living up to and that they think are important."[143]

With most of the stewardship and trust gone, the morality of the gamers, such as it is, has tended toward radical relativism. Hillary Clinton's repeated statements over the years to the effect that reality or the truth is what people socially construct it to be, breathtakingly reflect gamer skepticism and cynicism. So, tacitly, does Senator Mike Lee's whiplash-inducing U-turn on Google's exercise of monopoly power. For the most part, the gamers do not think in terms of personal right and wrong or virtue and vice. When self-conscious about morality, they tend to avoid moral judgment or absolutes altogether. In the spirit of the times, the gamers achieved considerable tolerance in many areas during the global era, but their otherwise habitual skepticism and even tolerance seldom extended to politics, where they easily slipped into divisive, partisan opinion.

Except for a rare few, the gamers have not been *leaders*, which is to say, moral and wise human beings whose high positions and formidable capabilities are directed toward the well-being of society and their fellow citizens.[144] Top institutions of higher education during the global era liked to think they were grooming leaders, but they were not, not in the true sense; they were batch-producing skilled but uncaring strivers. As the anonymous California congressman said in his recent tell-all book, "Rules don't apply to us, just [to] the rubes we represent."[145] What gamers give to and receive from friends and acquaintances in the nation's capital is the infamous "D.C. scalp stare," in which they constantly look over each other's heads at parties and public events, hoping to spot more powerful and prestigious connections toward whom to quickly move.[146] As Julius Krein says, "American meritocracy has been a sham for a long time."[147]

GAMING THE WORLD

First overwhelmingly American, the gamer phenomenon has spread through much of the world. The gamers have been less prominent in continental Europe than in the United States, while the U.K. pattern has been intermediate between the two, but closer to their American cousins. More Europeans than Americans have refused to be led into the one-sidedness of gaming. The phenomenon has been delayed, moderated, and partly sublimated on the continent by concern for society. Just as the bourgeois were less influential and less unabashed in Europe during the 19th century, so the gamers were during the global era. The gamers have been more concentrated in several third-world countries than in Europe; in Singapore, Taiwan, and South Korea for example. There have been few gamers in Islamic countries (although the few have been very influential) but many among the Muslims of the West and India.

Gamers have dominated the most developed authoritarian societies for the last two-to-four decades, including China, Russia, and to a lesser extent Iran, Saudi Arabia, and the Gulf States. Gamers assumed control of China when Deng Xiaoping took over the Communist Party and established his regime in 1978. The party's brazen cynicism in simultaneously selling Maoism and Maseratis by the early 21st century, was vintage gamer. So was Xi Jinping's announcement of major troop cuts immediately before the onset of a large military parade in 2015. China (much like Taiwan, Singapore, and Malaysia) has witnessed the gamer phenomenon but with a difference: Those with family connections have received the opportunities, such as permission to obtain the most sought-after credentials, get the best jobs, and move to the cities. Connections continued to make a much bigger difference in East Asia than in the West. Among less developed authoritarian societies, Syria under Bashar al-Assad, Venezuela under Hugo Chavez, and Nicaragua under Daniel Ortega have also been dominated by gamers.

Why the Gamers?

A key source of the rise of the gamers, as of much else during the global era, was the fast-moving rough and tumble of wide-open global capitalism. The world economic markets were so horrendously competitive that, under their pressure, corporate business demanded and elicited ever-higher levels of profit and performance from top executives. The most sought-after employers of the national era did not so single-mindedly demand such adeptness; they were looking as much for prospective employees' integrity and character. Gaming arose as growing numbers of the most talented, under strong new pressures and inducements, became so good at what they were doing and began so intensely striving to do still better that they attained higher individualistic self-control. As gamer executives responded with supreme effort and subtle insight, they also rose, in time, to virtuosity in their work.

In a similar way, when top law graduates were placed in large firms having the highest expectations and potential rewards, frequently with the same corporations as clients, their firms also demanded and drew forth sustained diligence and, in time, higher reflexivity and virtuosity. Being professionally engaged with the leading consulting and accounting firms where the stakes were no less high also promoted the gamers' higher-level self-consciousness and virtuoso performance. The stakes in politics, though different, were every bit as high. As I put it in my earlier book, "In addition to outstanding ability, preparation, and effort, only with higher reflexivity and nimbleness do [young people] flourish in investment banks, consulting firms, or the halls of Congress."[148] The gamers were the latest in the series of fundamental character types that for the most part emerged historically from business, including simple ego-dominant hagglers, superego-dominant bourgeois, and other-directed, early- and mid-20th-century white-collar employees.

Gaming was given additional impetus in the United States by sharp competition for promising employment during the 1970s, as the baby boomers moved into tight job markets, while global capitalism was undermining the national protections that had sustained the comparatively forgiving US business environment that held through the 1960s. It was becoming more difficult to retain a sense of unhurried ease or societal stewardship amid the intensifying competition.

Another major contribution to the advent of the gamers was that students of modest origins were given new opportunity by the opening of the best schools and colleges during the 1950s and 1960s to those objectively performing at high levels. An idea of what it meant for merit to be defined objectively may be gained by noting the ninety-five-point increase in Harvard's verbal SAT scores between 1950 and 1960.[149] Other top universities and colleges also witnessed sharp gains in test scores. Part of what enabled the ascent of the gamers was that the social democratization of top schools delivered unprecedented numbers of extremely bright, exceptionally well educated young people, "injecting a massive jolt of human capital into the American economy," as Murray puts it.[150] The qualitative leaps in performance brought by the gamers would never have been possible without this democratic talent pool. As ambitious, capable students were increasingly allowed entrance into elite colleges and universities irrespective of class, culture, and group origins, the clubby

WASP establishment with its genteel manners and traditions of moderation and service was largely displaced. This opening helped change the American upper class from one of inherited and taken-for-granted privilege and responsibility into one of talent, credentials, and willingness to give all for personal advancement.

The growing sophistication of the most selective schools and universities went hand-in-hand with and greatly facilitated the emergence of gaming. Advanced education of budding gamers in mathematics, logic, law, economics, engineering, and other rigorous disciplines strongly channeled their lives into the molds of rationality and instrumentalism. At the best business schools, sophisticated, self-conscious knowledge of management, finance, and corporate culture was conveyed as students were groomed in the subtle teamwork skills that form much of the real payoff of MBA programs. So much of such subtlety had been learned about management, marketing, and finance by the 1970s that rising to the level of performance newly demanded by the corporate world increasingly required both higher reflexivity and professional education of those who would approach its upper ranks. In their internships and early positions, gamers-in-training subsequently acquired invaluable experience as they applied themselves for long hours to high-level tasks, involving real business problems.

Noting the changing circumstances as they themselves were changing, ambitious parents began gaming their children's experience and development for admission to and success in elite educational institutions and careers. As fast-track high-school and university students gamed their coursework and extracurricular activities with growing proficiency, they learned the deft, modulated ways that would increasingly mark their careers and lives.

The gamers became what they are through exposure not only to economic markets and educational opportunities but also through exposure to sociocultural markets. The most sophisticated elements of the 1960s uprising in the United States raised themselves to higher self-consciousness and self-control as had some of the great modernist philosophers and social thinkers upon whom they drew, including Marx, Nietzsche, Freud, and Marcuse. When influential figures of that decade did the same, they negated in all directions from their new redoubt of higher criticism. Carrying on the bohemian alienation of many cultural luminaries of the national era, the rebels of the 1960s were still idealist and collectivist, disdaining and taking for granted the economy. The die was cast as many of the rebels' younger peers attained the same reflexivity during the early 1970s while emphatically rejecting the collectivism, idealism, and anti-capitalism of the previous decade. But the gamers retained the earlier decade's radical relativism and more than a little of its proclivity to conflict. At work and in life, they too began taking most of their own and others' assumptions as limited in place and time and no better or worse than any others. Partly underlying the gamers' course has been a feeling of superiority to and rejection of the middle class and the society and civilization it has shaped. Their bohemian legacy helped bring them to gaming in sociocultural as well as in economic arenas.

Yet the crucial source of the gamers' withdrawal from leadership and responsibility was not their support for the sociocultural markets but their adoption already during the 1960s of the multiculturalism that shaped what they brought into those markets. For that doctrine's attacks upon and smearing of the United States and nearly everything American, Christian, and Western stripped the new upper class of concern for its country, fellow citizens, traditions, and civilization. Multiculturalist alienation left the gamers bereft of a sense of responsibility with which to lead the country or to restrain their private interests and desires on its behalf. As multiculturalists attacked and besmirched the country, its citizens, and Western Civilization, the young of talent increasingly turned their backs upon this society and smugly devoted their abilities and energy to furthering their own interests without regard to others. A wise, respectful, and constructive ideology would have nourished leadership and responsibility in a new upper class. Character is strongly conditioned by whether young people are brought up to respect their country, tradition, and fellow citizens. When they are not, many of them are going to withhold what is due to society and to others.

The separation of the gamers and to a degree the upper-middle class from the rest that Charles Murray beautifully sketches in his book *Coming Apart* was also crucial in facilitating the rise of the gamers, for geographical concentration provided the hothouse setting within which they could rapidly develop a distinct sociocultural matrix that fostered gaming. We may happily note that segregation by race has considerably diminished since 1965, but we must also note that segregation by education and income has increased even more. The gamers' attainment of critical mass around the centers of the economy, government, media, and higher education provided them the sociocultural support with which to homogenize and boldly go their own way. Their stark new difference of character, class, culture, and geography helped dissolve their sense of larger community and purpose, as did their endemic hubris, multiculturalism, and obliviousness to the whole.

The gamers' radical one-sidedness and alienation have also been products of the newness of their higher self-control. Their way has been in keeping with Hegel's dictum that those newly aware on a given level tend first to negate difference, with others and within themselves, before turning toward reconciliation. Since they are powerful and exhilarating, higher perspectives tend initially to imperiousness and negativism.[151] It takes time to work the rough edges from unfolding character types, allowing balanced versions of them to come to the fore. When middle-class discipline first emerged on a large scale in the Reformation, it too was severe and one-sided. It began moderating in the Enlightenment and by the early and mid-20th century had been worked into the mature form that was impressive in the American and British upper-middle and middle classes of the time. Just as the basic self-control of most in the middle class had been harsh in the 16th and early 17th centuries, the higher self-control of most gamers has been harsh for more than half a century. Under the turbulent economic growth and sociocultural differentiation of the global era, few were able to achieve the distance, tranquility, and senses of gratitude and responsibility from which leadership emanates.

Europe's greater restriction of capitalism than the United States contributed to its lesser prevalence of gaming. That hierarchical societies were dominant until recently across much of the continent meant the persistence of humanistic culture valuing leisure and the ideal but disparaging the economic and material. Relatively balanced upper and upper-middle classes have somewhat reduced gaming in Europe as they have the wide-open capitalism out of which it in good part emerged. Yet, as the global markets have forced Europeans to make concessions, they too have found themselves with more gamers, particularly in the younger generations.

Europeans have also gotten more gamers than they otherwise would have by opening elite institutions and weakening upper-class standards of distinction in the wake of the late 1960s uprisings such as that of May 1968 in France. The third world witnessed the rise of its gamers as it has encountered the same global economic markets as the first world and become prosperous enough to send more of its most talented to study at world-class universities and to build excellent educational systems of its own.

The gamers' power in our society has come in large part from the fact that there are so many of them. A 5 percent upper class may sound like a small one, but where most upper classes historically have made up only about 1 percent of their societies, American gamers number more than 16 million, including dependents, contributing greatly to their enormous power and influence. Their great ability, single-mindedness, and remarkable sociocultural homogeneity following decades of self-segregation have also strengthened their position, drawing most of the upper-middle class to their side, for example. The ultimate threat they pose comes equally from their strength and their hubris; in particular their advanced inability to acknowledge the humanity of, and recognize themselves in, the more than 160 million fellow Americans who are middle class.

The gamers may be different in manner and style from the brash upper class of the Gilded Age, but the decisive differences are circumstantial, including the degree to which they have cemented themselves into positions of dominance across all institutions and the degree to which they have alienated themselves from the middle class and the society they associate with it. That and their increasing segregation invited the narcissism and hubris of their profound alienation from the middle class and the liberal society with which they associate it. No larger percentage of them may be evil than the percentage of their late 19th-century predecessors, but the degree to which they are filled with themselves, the intensity with which their will-to-power asserts itself, the way in which they shrink from the middle class, and above all the lockstep way in which they dismiss the universal in religion, philosophy, politics, and life pose distinctly greater threats to this society than did the likes of Jay Gould, Henry Frick, and Boss Tweed.

GAMING AS OPPOSED TO LEADING

The ascent of the gamers has been beneficial in some respects, especially in the productivity flowing from their prodigious preparation and application. Think for example of the great economic value of what Bill Gates, Steve Jobs, Elon Musk, Jack Welch, and Sam Walton have accomplished, gamers one and all. On the other hand, grievous, offsetting collateral damage to society has resulted from the gamers' indifference toward the effects of their actions upon others and upon society, as is painfully apparent through the chapters to follow.

The very best of the global era, overcame gaming and instead embraced their fellow citizens and the larger society.[152] They became statesmen and wise counselors, carrying out missions rather than games. Among the most dedicated and exemplary of the era, leaders one and all, have been King Abdullah of Jordan, Tony Blair, Bill Bradley, Willy Brandt, William

Bratton, Tom Coburn, the Dalai Lama, Bob Gates, Billy Graham, John Paul II, Bob Kerrey, Henry Kissinger, Irving Kristol, Heather MacDonald, George Mitchell, Charles Murray, David Petraeus, Colin Powell, Ronald Reagan, Helmut Schmidt, Eric Sevareid, George Shultz, Thomas Sowell, Margaret Thatcher, Paul Volcker, James Woolsey, and Lee Kwan Yew. These men and women may have agreed with each other on little more than that we ought to attempt to overcome oppositions and work together for the common good, but that is all we need. They have brilliantly directed their extraordinary talents in different ways toward the long-term well-being of the whole. Such leaders have been all too few since 1965. On a more modest level, although hardly less important cumulatively, gamers could remain what they are in other respects but balance their stellar careers with moral restraint, community involvement, and great families, and some have done so. Most of them by far, however, have instead been feverishly milling about for personal gain while leaving society adrift. Average citizens will follow leaders, but they will not follow amoral, cynical, and frequently conflictual elites; they will defer to a universalistic upper class but not to an indifferent, manipulative, and self-dealing one.

The metaphor of the game with regard to the pace-setting new upper class of the global era is apt not only for its focus on their single-minded competitiveness but also for the light it casts upon their ultimate unseriousness. The pure gamers climb more ladders and take more exotic vacations to nowhere. The 60-, 80-, and even 100-hour weeks of so many supremely talented men and women represent the clear-cutting of old-growth forests. The gamers could contribute so much more if they only cared. All but a few have instead been making Faustian bargains, the devastating consequences of which we will be encountering for a long time. Yet, since each of their institutions and character types sheds crucial independent light upon a society and time, let us next consider the democratic political institutions that gamers were increasingly subverting during the global era, also with major detrimental consequences

CHAPTER 5

DEMOCRACY EMBRACED, CONTESTED, AND EXPLOITED

THE FLOW AND EBB OF DEMOCRATIZATION AROUND THE WORLD

The Flow of Democratization, 1974–2000. The key advances of modernity were confined almost entirely to the West until the global era, although not all Western countries had fully participated in them. Democracy[153] diffused rapidly during the late 20th century, beginning with southern Europe. In 1974 Portugal initiated what became a great wave of democratization. After the death of General Franco in Spain the following year, Prime Minister Adolfo Suarez adroitly brokered a series of pacts between opposing forces to ground his country's new democracy upon reconciliation, balance, guarantees, security, and trust. Spain's democracy also required the wise, courageous defense of King Juan Carlos in facing down a coup attempt in 1981. Its "pacted" approach was particularly influential in Latin American democratic transitions, which were frequently negotiated between a hierarchical regime and its democratic opposition such that a balance of power was maintained between multiple forces.[154] Greece too became democratic during the 1970s.

Latin America went from minimally to overwhelmingly democratic during the last quarter of the 20th century. The Philippines became democratic in 1986, Taiwan in 1987, Indonesia in 1998, and South Korea in steps through the late 1980s and 1990s. Dramatic democratization occurred among the formerly Soviet-dominated Eastern European countries when, after decades of oppression, most of their authoritarian regimes imploded following the collapse of the Berlin Wall in 1989. The Balkans became predominantly democratic in the aftermath of Yugoslavia's disintegration, beginning in 1992. South Africa, Nigeria, and Ghana became predominantly democratic during the 1990s.

Already established in the mid-20th century soon after independence and partition, India's parliamentary democracy has been fragmented and disjointed; but, like much else in that country, it has performed reasonably well under the circumstances, even considering its interruption for a year and a half of dictatorship by Indira Gandhi. The two largest parties, Congress and the BJP, primarily represent secular elites and Hindu nationalists respectively.

The Congress Party, long the stronger of the two, was closely aligned with entrenched bureaucratic and economic interests but sought to form coalitions with lower-caste parties, in part via the country's huge affirmative action program. In opposition to the elites, the BJP sought bold reforms, opportunity, and more responsive government, gaining relatively consistent support from the middle class and notable support across the caste and Dalit spectrum. India has been, by far, the world's largest democracy.

The formation of many new democracies during the late 20th century was a most important achievement. The world had only 12 democracies in 1941 when the United States entered World War II, but it had 120 by the year 2000.[155] In late 1973, fewer than a quarter of the world's countries were democratic. "Of the 110 *nondemocratic* states in 1974, 63 (or 57 percent) subsequently made a transition to democracy," joining those already democratic.[156] Forty authoritarian countries became democratic following the collapse of the Soviet Union and Yugoslavia. As late as 1988, only 40 percent of the world's regimes were democratic, but by 1994, 60 percent were.[157] The extent of global democratization remains significant when populations are considered instead of the numbers of countries: In 1973, 36 percent of the world's population lived in democratic countries, 64 percent in authoritarian ones.[158] By the year 2000, the population in democratic countries had risen to 57 percent while that in authoritarian countries had declined to 43 percent.[159]

The Persistence of Authoritarianism in the Core Hierarchical Societies, 1974–2000. Although most third-world and Eastern European countries were becoming democratic, the core hierarchical states remained authoritarian.[160] Boris Yeltsin repudiated authoritarianism, took steps toward democratizing Russia between 1991 and 1993, and cultivated the appearance of democracy, but ruled autocratically almost from the beginning and suppressed parliament and the constitutional court already in 1993. He sharply reduced the security services for a time but was immersed in and surrounded by corruption throughout and kept the FRS close to him.

Complicit with the secret police in the planning of high crime, and needful of their protection for himself and his family from multiple charges of corruption, the blustery campaigner for Russian democratization was, finally, unserious about it.

Mao's communist regime, after crushing opposition and concentrating power on the mainland, reviled and suppressed the well-educated, former property owners, moderates, and others with independence for nearly three decades. As Mao purged China of traditional and liberal elements, he willfully curtailed the country's development, leaving it weak and impoverished by the time of his death in 1976. The Deng regime remained strictly authoritarian while rapidly introducing economic markets. It long maintained the ruse of political liberalization by slowly and partially opening local government to competitive democratic contests during the 1990s and early 2000s, but the regime's true colors were evident in its forceful suppression of the democracy movement at Tiananmen Square in 1989 and its ongoing suppression of even such distant threats to party control as those from mild Falun Gong and independent Christians.

The Islamic world intensified its perennial authoritarianism during the global era, Indonesia and a few other countries excepted. Large numbers of Muslim states were tyrannical, including the Assad's Syria and Saddam Hussein's Iraq. Robust coercive apparatuses were prominent features of most Muslim regimes. Their security forces were often formed largely of conservative rural elements whose ethnicity was selected to help ensure loyalty. Some Muslim regimes remained monarchical, though, and a few of these, such as Morocco under King Hassan, were comparatively moderate and more accepted by their populations than the dictatorships.

Politics, the Media, and Citizen Involvement in the United States. The politics of the global era was intimately associated with the explosion of the mass media. Public life was increasingly carried on via them, with the predominant influence increasingly exercised by organized interests over a distracted and passively consuming, if irritable and skittish, electorate. Politicians were acutely aware of the need to market themselves in a complex and subtle media environment and became highly skilled at doing so. Sensitive to a fault to changes in opinion polls, they relied upon operatives adept at public relations to staff their offices and campaigns as media savviness became the analog to the sophism and rhetoric of old – those with it tended to win and those without it, to lose. PR skills comprised a good deal of what registered as charisma. Fiercely fought, many-sided PR campaigns deluged citizens with political information but fragmented and decontextualized it in barrages of 10-second sound-bytes and 30-second ads. Political careers were made and broken through the media.

The news played a central role in media politics. During the national era, norms of journalistic responsibility had supported the hallowed notion that the press and broadcasters were to carry important but distant news as a matter of civic obligation, despite its limited commercial value. U.S. television networks, although private, had regularly supported money-losing news divisions while the governments of many other developed democracies had publicly funded news broadcasting. Networks and newspapers had frequently maintained larger staffs of correspondents and reporters and supported higher-caliber news and analysis than was justifiable in stark terms of profit and loss. Owning a television network, newspaper, newsmagazine, or publishing house was often regarded as a public trust. During the global period, by contrast, the news media were increasingly owned by large corporations whose callings were no more exalted than their quarterly profits. Fewer news bureaus were maintained, and news content was mingled with entertainment. Orientation toward large audiences and profitability led toward fluff, violence, sensationalism, and negativism to grab attention, draw coveted audiences, and game revenues while displacing substantive news.

Much of the most prominent journalism of the first postwar decades had trained its eye on how well society as a whole was faring, but journalism rarely noticed it during the global era; it instead tended to report on the game, who was spinning and socially constructing what, when, how, and why. Tacit in this focus was the assumed relativism of good and bad or right and wrong – for the individual, the country, and the world. Paradoxically, global-era journalism did acknowledge that there *was* such a thing as what was truly better for the interests of this or that class, group, party, or person. The focus was redirected from the whole toward the part.

Mid-century journalists, in a spirit of public service and professional pride, had also taken norms of value neutrality seriously when presenting the news. When their successors describe, interpret, or explain – insofar as they are insulated from economic constraints – they far more often impart a political slant to the news. As the influence of the 1960s generation slowly wound its way through the media, the *New York Times* went from relatively neutral news reporting to reporting what advanced its publisher, editors, and journalists' political agendas in the early 1990s. Pieces of reportage often became smirking political blows delivered underhandedly. *Times* photographs of the two presidential candidates during the closing weeks of the 1992 U.S. elections presented an amusing example. The photos selected of Bill Clinton tended to be commanding and presidential, while those selected of President G. H. W. Bush were awkward and silly. Journalists went from being citizen-soldiers of the truth to being scrappy participants in partisan politics. Journalists, like other intellectuals, became overwhelmingly liberal in orientation. Each cause, issue, and candidate they supported had the home-court advantage; each they opposed played its games on the road. By the end of the period, journalism had been reduced to politics. Much as bureaucrats exercised considerable political power, although their doing so was neither fully acknowledged nor approved, so did journalists. Those in the media became an important part of the political class, the fourth branch of government, as some put it.

Yet much of the citizenry ignored at least the elite media and went elsewhere to find independent views. Cable television brought greater variety, populism, and shrillness to the news. The rise of the Internet brought a kaleidoscopic proliferation of media sites and blogs, providing astonishingly abundant and varied news and commentary, if still skewed. As newspapers were in economic freefall and the elite media in relative decline, citizens faced a greatly more open, if uneven and challenging, news market from which to draw in forming their opinions.

Into this journalistic hall of mirrors flowed the exceedingly subtle issue- and image-management of the gamer participants in the news, for whom the truth was socially constructed and in quotation marks. Whoever's narratives and definitions of the situation captured the news set the agenda of public discourse and muted the opposition. The result was many levels of sophistication combined in myriads of diverse standpoints and interests in the media's swirling bricolage. As politics became a struggle over controlling media attention in which rhetorical virtuosi engaged in no-holds-barred PR combat, journalists were well positioned to play a prominent role. Amid the deft feints and interpretations, it became difficult for anyone to maintain steadiness of perspective, not least the politicians and journalists themselves. Average citizens were at a severe disadvantage.

Political knowledge, interest, and participation by the public declined amid the overwhelming complexity. According to Robert D. Putnam, "voting in America [was] down by about a quarter, and interest in public affairs by about one-fifth" during the last quarter of the to a 20th century.[161] Greater participation returned episodically, as in the 2008, 2012, and 2016 presidential elections, but involvement tended to fall back to the new norm soon after. The oversight of many having been withdrawn from the political markets, the governing class narrowed, and political inequality increased, to an even greater degree than did economic inequality.

The Triumph of the Special Interests. American political parties slightly loosened and weakened overall in the global era from what they had been in the national era. Party conventions yielded most of their power to nominate candidates to primary elections during the 1960s and 1970s, but those primaries made room for other political actors and entities to move in. Power-brokers became even more significant players than they had been, but they operated in a more roundabout fashion by arranging a great deal of the context, while no longer directly providing the main event.

As the parties receded, the special interests became larger, better organized, and more entrenched, lavishly pumping money into politics. Particularly after the Supreme Court rulings of the 1970s that spending money on political campaigns was a first amendment right and of 2010 in the Citizens United case that corporations had free-speech rights comparable to those of individual citizens, the American political system was awash in money and cynicism. Politicians became increasingly free to auction their services to the highest bidders in campaign contributions, political support, stock tips, and offers of lucrative employment or business opportunities after leaving office. Plenty of calculated self-dealing had been witnessed before in American politics, but its nearly general practice with only the barest moral limits became an increasingly striking feature. Peggy Noonan rightly characterized the Obama administration as "all-politics-all-the-time," although the label applies to the gamers of both parties.[162]

Typical of what happened during the global era in U.S. politics, even at the local level, occurred in a Boston suburb when longstanding mutual respect and consensus-building yielded to organized interest-group maneuvers (by teachers in this instance, often police, fire, other public employees, or developers elsewhere) to stack meetings and force through agendas in their narrow interest while disregarding the needs of the larger community.[163] All too many politicians alternately made craven deals and pandered to the thoughtless whims of distracted and frequently self-centered citizens.

The New Polarization in the United States. The national-liberal upper class played a lead role in formulating federal, state, and local policy through its clubs and informal social networks as well as by setting the tone of morals and manners.[164] During the 1950s and early 1960s, Congressional "disputes were mediated by a culture that encouraged a kind of heterogeneous civility."[165] Robert Byrd embodied that culture throughout his long career; few did after him. The atmosphere of boosterism, courtesy, and trust began falling away in the United States during the 1960s.

Following the collapse of the national-liberal establishment and political consensus during the mid-1960s, American society became increasingly polarized. Amid conflictualist political melees, division and acrimony became the order of the day. Politics became an unrestrained, amoral exercise in gonzo attacks, smear campaigns, and gotcha journalism. When in the Congressional minority, each party, as politically advantageous, sabotaged needed legislation on many occasions in order to attempt to undermine the majority. Not surprisingly, elected officials from the two parties frequently came to loathe each other. Nowhere was the contentiousness more apparent than in skirmishes over Supreme Court nominations. The confrontational mode of the 1960s and early 1970s came to dominate many aspects of the era as political combat prevailed. Raw partisanship in the forms of hardball politics, negative campaigning, and shrill personal attacks increasingly became the norm. The bitter late-1960s standoffs on some university campuses between radical leftist students and conservative Young Americans for Freedom (YAF) members foreshadowed the divisions that began making their appearance a decade later at the national level.[166] Taking rancorous dispute to be the normal way of treating oppositions, the 1960s generation was a conflictualist one, many of whose basics were passed on to subsequent generations.

The global-era generations having been badly divided internally, polarization understandably occurred between the gamers and those with the audacity to oppose them. The greatly outnumbered Christian conservatives of the 1960s, precursors of the Christian Right of the 1980s, adopted their own mildly contentious manner in response. The mutual hostility, personal attacks, and character assaults between the Clinton White House and press on the one side and Newt Gingrich and the Congressional Republicans on the other during the 1990s represented the standard, divisive conflict between political opponents of the new generation and era. The combat waged by the Obama administration, whose declared policy was total political war against conservatives, intensified the pattern. Although the general public seldom punished the many flagrant offenders in vicious politics, it was nowhere near as polarized as the politicians and activists through the era.

The key underlying problem in American politics from the 1990s on was a moral one. As Joan Didion says in *Political Fictions*, "Those inside the process ... congealed into a political class, the defining characteristic of which ... [was] its readiness to abandon those not inside the process."[167] According to Mark Leibovich, the constant refrain to each other by the self-referential members of the gamer political elite about what Washington had become was the cynical shrug, "It is what it is."[168] Moral decline hit American politics with force during the 1990s as the World War II and 1950s generations were leaving the arena, and the 1960s generation was taking over. Insofar as it affected politics, this decline was concentrated among the gamers and, above all, the elites among them.

The growing power and declining morality of elites and public officials directing large interests rendered the American political system increasingly dysfunctional. For example, Senate tradition and rules long hallowed the filibuster. After the loosening of requirements for ending a filibuster in 1975, a 60-vote majority was required to halt floor debate and proceed to a vote on an ordinary bill. The device had been used before on rare occasions when a few Senators or the minority party were extremely opposed to a piece of legislation, but it became standard partisan procedure during the global era. From the late 1960s, both parties when in opposition increasingly used the filibuster, and from the 1990s, they did so systematically to block the will of the majority. Amid amorality and division, the filibuster that had relied upon consensual restraint and convention in earlier eras brought gridlock. Even with changes in the law in 2013, allowing a simple majority to prevail for executive and judicial nominations other than those to the Supreme Court, the filibuster became a powerful obstruction.

The Growing Political Stagnation of Other First-World Democracies. Democracy was improved in some respects in other first-world countries during the late 20th century. The secret ballot spread, election monitoring strengthened, vote counting became more reliable, and the freedom to communicate and organize on behalf of diverse political persuasions was better ensured. Italy made progress toward overcoming lingering hierarchical influence during the 1970s. It introduced higher standards of public accountability and reduced political corruption during the 1990s. Minorities, from the Irish in England to Roma (Gypsies) in Hungary, gained political rights. Women in all developed democracies strengthened their rights to participate and hold office during the global era. Even in Switzerland, where women were not allowed to vote until 1971, they won a majority of governing cabinet positions in 2010. These democracies showed universalism in recognizing, adjusting to, and compromising with new entrants to the democratic marketplace and coaxing them into accepting democratic give and take. When, from time to time, a small, implacable, terrorist opposition was encountered, with whom neither ingenious flexibility nor supreme tolerance availed, as in the cases of Germany's Rote Armee Faktion (RAF), Italy's Brigate Rosse, and Spain's ETA (the Basque Homeland and Freedom organization), persuasion was augmented by necessary force.

Yet most other first-world democracies declined in performance overall during the global era, as did the American. Political paralysis spread in Europe during the later decades of the global era, overshadowing improvements. Its democracies were growing sclerotic and less able to register and deal with major problems; witness the contradictions of the Eurozone, the denial by a majority of Swedish voters of the ruin advancing around them in connection with immigration, and the trailing off of defense budgets and military preparedness to dangerously low levels. European political parties had better subordinated the special interests and their disparate demands during the postwar decades and early global period than American parties;[169] but much of that ability was lost as parties were overmatched by interest groups, and politicians became freer to wheel and deal. European voters may not have undergone the decline in political knowledge, interest, and participation that American voters did, but they often blithely ignored reality. The exceptional countries whose democracies were performing better by the end of the era than they had half a century earlier included Norway, Denmark, and Finland, countries with unusually high sociocultural coherence.

Japanese democracy showed signs of regime vitality throughout the global era but was worrisomely constricted from the late 1980s through the end of the global era, unable to successfully address its economic problems. It did further open its political markets in 2009 as the victory of a new coalition led by that country's Democratic Party seemed to be a milestone for its democracy.

Until then, except for a brief interlude, Japan's center-right Liberal Democratic Party had governed continuously since the 1950s with power shifting between changing coalitions of relatively enduring party factions, instead of the usual democratic oscillation between parties of the left and right. The party factions were built upon networks of personal bonds emanating from powerful patrons. In earlier times, as Seymour Lipset says, "Japan was an extremely hierarchical society, which placed a tremendous emphasis on obligation to those higher up as well as to those down below,"[170] a pattern that continued to exert a good deal of influence. Japan's democracy was advanced, but, like the Swedish capitalism that coexisted with a large public sector, its political markets retained subordinate elements of hierarchy. Its national bureaucracy long exercised inordinate power, often treating legislation as though it were just recommendation. Government agencies in Japan were marked by strong clientelism and loyalty.

The Reversal of Democratization and Strengthening of Authoritarianism in the Early 21st Century. After its stunning progress during the late 20th century, net democratization ceased early in the 21st century and began slightly reversing from about 2005. By the year 2000, 63 percent of countries were democratic, 37 percent authoritarian. That held through 2014, but more refined measures were showing a weakening in the third world.[171] Moreover, as third-world democracies were slipping, and first-world ones were languishing, authoritarian regimes were upgrading and strengthening their rule.

Vladimir Putin's Russia exemplified the new authoritarianism. He was the President of Russia, not its First Secretary or Führer. He abided by the constitution when doing so was not too inconvenient, even to the extent of formally shifting to prime minister for four years when term limited. Under Putin, the Russian parliament met and passed laws, opposition parties seemed to flourish, representatives gave public speeches, and courts regularly heard cases and rendered judgments. Some relatively independent newspapers operated, though few if any independent television stations. Early 21st century Russia, unlike the USSR, allowed a good deal of personal freedom. People had access to the Internet and came and went much more freely across borders.

All of these apparently democratic features were, in reality, window dressing, not permitted to impinge upon the regime's monopoly of power. Russia under Putin remained thoroughly autocratic. Public utterance or action that was anything more than innocuous was likely to bring the regime down hard upon its source, albeit in deceptive and surprising ways. Suppression could arrive, for example, in the form of arbitrary trouble with tax authorities, fire marshals, building inspectors, licensing authorities, or other regulatory officials. If the political threat were significant or persistent enough, the offender or those near and dear to him could expect to be badly beaten or murdered, again almost always under ambiguous and confusing conditions. The trappings of democracy were present, but, as described by William Dobson in *The Dictator's Learning Curve,* artifice and guile mooted them in Putin's gamer dictatorship.[172]

Cunningly, the Russian regime was highly aware that a major inherent weakness of hierarchical systems is their increasing tendency to suppress and distort the information getting to their rulers, with the result that governance tends to lose effectiveness. Accordingly, the Putin regime went out of its way to develop politically safe ways to keep in touch with popular knowledge, attitudes, and sentiments. One means by which it did so was via a large network of public-reception offices where citizens could lodge complaints against the government. The intent was that these be taken seriously, meticulously registered, and followed up. Another internal reality check was the Public Chamber, a large consultative body selected and convened as needed by the regime. It was drawn from people of many regions, social classes, sorts of expertise, and vantage points, to whom the regime could turn for information and advice, although it had neither independence nor authority.[173] Putin remained quite popular.

The Chinese upgraded their hierarchical rule with the Deng Xiaoping regime in 1978. Protected by Zhou Enlai through the perils of the Mao era, Deng founded his dynasty upon assembling a talented elite capable of working together and maintaining a relatively long-term time horizon, and placing limits on how elites and masses could involve themselves politically and conduct their lives, while maintaining illusions about continuing communism and engaging in democratization. The regime abandoned the latter charade in 2007. Amid intensifying censorship, China's authoritarianism began tightening in the years afterward. After formally granting Hong Kong special civil liberties and limited democratic features for a period of 50 years when accepting its sovereignty from the United Kingdom in 1997, the regime increasingly reneged on that grant, provoking the protests of 2014. The rule of law might have gained force in the Chinese economy during the early 21st century, but none of it translated to political rights. The Chinese regime was resourceful but vulnerable, because faced with the daunting challenge of staying ahead of the deep contradictions and tensions in its vast, rapidly changing country.

Turkey followed a trajectory parallel in important ways to Russia and China over the last twenty years, first extending the appearances and some of the substance of democratization and then withdrawing them when safely in control. President Recep Tayyip Erdoğan and his Islamist Justice Party exercised power over a prolonged period, for the most part deftly. In office as prime minister from 2003 and as president from 2014, his first great political challenge was easing the military out of the veto it had held in Turkish politics since the reign of Ataturk in the 1920s. His doing so appeared to be a democratic objective, in that while Turkey had established a democracy in 1945, it had been suspended four times by military intervention, the last occasion in 1997. Erdoğan and his associates' painstaking restraint while pursuing effective economic policies enabled them to suppress the Turkish military's limited, secular, tolerant, and stabilizing, though hierarchical, veto. In order to maintain the guise of democratization, Erdoğan and his Justice Party conveyed the impression of being dependable stewards of the country. After long presenting themselves as democratic, they broke the independent power of the military in 2011. Erdoğan and his party then immediately began acting autocratically and cracking down on critical news media and journalists, for Turkey's unusual military had posed a check on misrule. Erdoğan made use of a failed coup attempt in 2016 to further consolidate his authoritarian rule.

Although Egypt remained authoritarian throughout, its transient partial democratization from 2011 to 2013 also prominently involved the military. The Egyptian military cooperated with pro-democracy young people in the toppling of the Hosni Mubarak regime but was unwilling to step back from its dominant position or relinquish its control of up to one-third of the economy. What it was willing to do was allow some voice to the people, especially on matters of less concern. The Islamist Muslim Brotherhood's election victory in 2012 and Mohamed Morsi's accession to the presidency offered hope for a time, but Morsi was incorrigibly dictatorial, bullying his way in numerous directions and attempting to take more power than the generals were prepared to grant him. They ousted him in July of 2013 with popular support. Egypt was again governed by its military from 2014 under the leadership of the thoughtful, pragmatic President Abdel al-Sissi.

Thailand's Prime Minister Thaksin Shinawatra, a personally authoritarian, multimillionaire crony capitalist with a police background, mounted successful populist appeals to the countryside and began consolidating power extra-constitutionally in the early 2000s, impairing the democratic regime that had been established in 1997. According to Larry Diamond, "Thaksin was undermining the rule of law, dismantling constitutional checks and balances, stifling dissent, delegitimizing opposition, and dividing the country."[174] Charges of disclosure violations and corruption hung over him until he was ousted by a liberal-minded military coup in 2006 supported by Thailand's urban middle class and respected king. The polarization was ratcheted up when, with Thaksin in exile, his sister won election as prime minister in 2011. After prolonged turmoil, the military again took over in 2014.

Hugo Chavez, elected president of Venezuela in 1999, craftily subverted a troubled democratic regime to govern dictatorially. Bolivia lapsed toward hierarchy under Evo Morales' leftist populism beginning in 2005, while

Ecuador took a similar turn under Rafael Correa in 2007. Cristina Kirchner moved Argentina in an autocratic direction following her election as president in 2007. She undermined the independence of the central bank, appropriated private property, looted social security, manipulated government statistics,[175] and in 2015 gave every appearance of having murdered the courageous prosecutor who was on the verge of indicting her for complicity in covering up the 1994 Iranian bombing of the Jewish center in Buenos Aires. Kirchner was ousted in the elections of November 2015 by the center-right Mauricio Macri. The *Chavistas* were defeated in Venezuelan legislative elections the following month, but forces of democracy had a considerable distance to go in Argentina and were routed in Venezuela.

Some gains for democracy partly offset the numerous setbacks. For example, against a background of military dictatorship since 1962, President Thein Sein of Burma began easing his country's authoritarianism and ending its seclusion in 2011. Far-reaching civil liberties were instituted, and the parliament was allowed to become independent and assertive. Relatively free elections were held in November 2015, and the opposition National League for Democracy (NLD) under Aung San Suu Kyi won a resounding victory, but the relationship between the parliamentary majority and the military was still to be resolved. Tunisia became partly democratic following its popular uprising, initiating the Arab Spring in 2011. Predominantly hierarchical Morocco also took steps toward democracy as did Singapore and Peru.

The hierarchical regimes of the global era, weak or strong and from all traditions, were mostly bad ones with immoral, violent elites. Their rulers often fought their way to the top amid chaos and brutality and were eager to reap the precarious benefits of their literal or figurative coups. Democratic regimes may have declined only a little in the early 21st century, but those that became more authoritarian, including Russia, China, and Turkey, were much more important than the few becoming more democratic.

WHY DEMOCRACY FARED AS IT DID DURING THE GLOBAL ERA

What Caused the Spread of Democracy? The Roles of Capitalism and Character. A master source of the remarkable spread of democracy around the world during the late 20th century, as in earlier periods, was the extraordinary spread of capitalism. Much of this influence came through the global shift to more rational-instrumental and less emotional-traditional ways of thinking and acting that accompanied the thriving economic markets. Global capitalism habituated vast numbers of people to intense problem solving in everyday life, preparing them for and inclining them toward democratic decision-making. After one long copes with countless, varied instrumental challenges on a small scale in business, one is ready to cope with similar challenges on a large scale in politics. Becoming more tough-minded and critical as a result of exposure to capitalism's ceaseless buying, selling, haggling, and taking of consequences from the same also predisposes citizens to democracy's mechanical approach to collective decision-making and law enforcement. People new to the markets instead expect strong communal and consensual relations in their collective undertakings and recoil from the self-assertion, negotiation, and impersonalism of political markets. Such basic features of democracy feel unnatural to those with little exposure to capitalism.

The experience of conducting business fosters alertness to and involvement in politics. Capitalism furthered the late 20th-century democratization by contributing to the spread of political consciousness, in both its ideal and real forms, respectively political awareness and readiness to participate. Whether gained through experience in business or education, or to a lesser degree through the media or communal involvement, political awareness brings people within the range of democracy. Acquisition of the shrewdness, discipline, and disposition to act that capitalist experience confers also enables citizens to be steady when engaging in political action and efficacious about being heard. Political involvement by unaware and undisciplined recent migrants from rural areas tends to be episodic and inconsequent. Without more than intermittent political consciousness and weak competence, the third-world poor tended to be largely oblivious to politics, hopelessly out-maneuvered, and easily frustrated, unreliable supporters of democracy.

Growing realism flowing from the economic markets also contributed to democratization. Without capitalist experience, the more or less unreconstructed aristocracies still influential in early 20th-century hierarchical societies tended to be relatively idealist, as did their dependents. The old-style, ideologically oriented intellectuals[176] numerous in those societies and the liberal societies of the time were idealist as well. As aristocracies and such intellectuals faded from the picture, idealism diminished. Global capitalism banished the leisure and contemplation that nourished those classes, leaving people riveted to the bottom line and here-and-now, nervously watchful and eminently practical. This realism promoted incrementalism and attention to feasibility helpful to democracy, while it discouraged flights of fancy and utopian visions dangerous to it. Realism was particularly helpful for democratic leaders, enabling them to fluently modulate policy as changing political conditions required.

Capitalist realism undercut support for the chimerical goals that easily appealed to peasants, as in the Cuban Revolution, Chavez's Venezuela, the Shining Path in Peru, and Maoist insurgents in rural India and Nepal. Although eschewing the radical schemes of intellectuals is vital to democracy, moderate idealism balanced by pragmatism and restraint may be refreshing and inspirational for it.

Increased individualism was another capitalist-derived source of democratization around the world. Where *individuals* have an affinity to democracy, *members* have an affinity to authoritarianism. Shedding collectivism in the course of coping with challenges in the economic markets helps prepare citizens for the political markets. As populations become more individualist, they acquire a greater need for autonomy, begin forming their own opinions, become more confident, and act more assertively. Being dictated to grates on those with long experience in business. As people engage in markets of all kinds, they break out of patron-client relationships and participate independently.[177] The individualist, critical, take-charge monitoring of and participation in politics that are created and sustained by capitalist experience are vital to democracy. By contrast, the economic hierarchy in many parts of the third world and growing economic hierarchy in much of the first world militate toward collectivism, fatalism, and passivity, favoring authoritarianism.

Even the democratic Japanese have retained enough collectivism to feel that they cannot make a personal difference politically. This is part of why democracy in Japan, although genuine, has been somewhat hampered and its political markets less than fully competitive. Japanese voters embedded in persisting informal structures require a long time and many reversals before they turn to another political faction, much less to a different party from the one in power. This hesitancy helped impart sluggishness to their democratic politics. The tendency was to fall in with the consensus rather than stand up to authority and assert oneself. The elements of authoritarianism carried into Japan's democracy have largely been functions of the unusual workedness and homogeneity of traditional Japanese society, and therefore of its continuing strength of community and consensus. Westerners, with longer capitalist experience, have tended instead to be highly individualist and to feel relatively socially and politically empowered. The stormy opposite to Japanese politics in these respects would be Israeli politics with its turbulent groupings and loyalties amid deep individualism and frayed consensus. More perfect political competition, freer political markets, and the formation and dissolution of political factions readily take place in Israel, Palestinian participation aside.

The shift from authoritarian toward democratic personalities going on in much of the world during the late 20th century also contributed to democratization. Whether a society's modal character is authoritarian or democratic makes a major difference in what political regime it gets. A democratic or open personality leans toward relationships involving give and take with others, where an authoritarian or closed personality leans toward imperiously giving orders or, when subordinate, toward unquestioningly following them. Those whose character is democratic are tentative and critical, leaving room for others. Those whose character is authoritarian leave little room for others and expect little themselves. A democratic personality goes with tolerance and an authoritarian one with intolerance. Where the personalities of Americans, British, Canadians, Australians, Netherlanders, Swiss, and Israelis tend to be democratic, those in Muslim countries tend to be authoritarian, variations in propensity that are largely produced by exposure to markets as opposed to hierarchies, including political and religious ones. Part of what occurs in democratization is that democratic personalities slowly supersede authoritarian ones. As this transformation takes place, individual persons change comparatively little, and most of what occurs happens by generational succession. Democratization is messy and takes time to consolidate in part because character change leads, accompanies, and confirms regime change.

Another important route by which capitalism promotes democratization is through increased prosperity, enabling countries to expand and upgrade their educational systems. Improved education contributes additional rationality, critical facility, awareness, discipline, and experience with which people lean more strongly toward and participate more fruitfully in democracy. Like greater experience in economic markets, increased education makes people bristle at being censored, interfered with, and dictated to. Education consists in large part of exposure to the cultural markets, familiarizing its beneficiaries with the give and take of ideas, aesthetics, and values, fostering tolerance. Lack of education was traditionally associated with proneness to personalistic/tribal ties, rigid expectations, absolute commitments, and dissatisfaction with democratic processes and outcomes. Without sufficient knowledge and critical facility, even the most dedicated citizens cannot become perspicacious regarding what their country, region, class, or group truly needs and cannot know how to contribute to it effectively. Without education, people have too little ability to get what they need, too much conflict along the way, and too little capacity to forestall would-be tyrants. Directly and indirectly, spreading capitalism equipped large numbers all over the world with the basic competence with which to participate in political markets, while growing government and economic monopolism have been countering the effect globally in this century.

The Role of Universalism. Growing universalism also played a role in the democratization of the late 20th century, though a mixed one. The more developed a people's orientation toward the whole and the greater its wisdom and balance, the more likely their society is to democratize and the more successful the democracy. Universalism is particularly crucial in political leaders and seldom more so than with regard to their reasonableness and flexibility in accepting new entrants. When new classes demand inclusion in the collective conversation of democracy, established political classes may accede or attempt to suppress them. Increased universalism, breadth, and sensitivity, together with norms of inclusion, underlay the acceptance of the middle and lower classes, women, and ethnic and religious minorities into democratic political systems all over the world. Brazil's recent history exemplifies the pivotal role of statesmanship in consolidating and developing democracy. Presidents Fernando Cardoso and Luiz Lula da Silva, of the right and left respectively, generally proved good stewards of their country from 1994 through 2010, following responsible economic policies and pragmatic, conciliatory social ones.

The bulwark against special interests is stronger and corruption (in the weak sense of official self-dealing) reduced when a relatively universalistic leadership predominates, as in the United States during the national era. The bulwark is weaker and corruption increased when less universalistic politicians dominate as they did (with important exceptions) in this country from the late 1960s and especially from the early 1990s. Democracies shine in settings of moral strength and disappoint in settings of moral weakness.

A key manifestation of universalism favoring democratic development is attainment of morally assertive respect for self and other, such that citizens courageously stand up for themselves and their fellows, demand high ethical standards in politics, and expect the same of others. Insofar as this moral assertiveness is developed, citizens become attuned to the moral status of their regime and firm in dealing with it. The more ethically developed are citizens, the more outraged they become at illegitimate authoritarian rule, and the more they strive to obtain self-determination for the basic self-respect it brings. Corazon Aquino's 1986 uprising in the Philippines was largely fueled by outrage at Ferdinand Marcos' reprehensible acts as dictator and by refusal to put up any longer with the corruption rampant under his regime. Freedom of all kinds promotes such moral courage.

Another manifestation of universalism important to democracy is elementary tolerance. Spared the ravages of economic markets, traditional community tends to be accompanied by strong identification with the group and intolerance toward other groups. Those immersed in such community easily take the acceptance of difference as betrayal and fall into conflict in its presence, jeopardizing democracy. As groupbound peasants and villagers are transformed into rulebound bourgeois whose commitments are abstract and who learn to distinguish law and morality from the somewhat arbitrary ways of their community, the prospects for democracy greatly improve. Tolerance facilitates the airing of difference in a spirit of working together rather than of division. At the lower end of prospects for democracy are found narrow, irascible, resentful, little-developed peoples for whom tolerance is anathema, as in Pashtun Afghanistan and the tribal areas of Pakistan. As John Stuart Mill says, "a rude people, though in some degree alive to the benefits of civilized society, may be unable to practice the forbearances which it demands: their passions may be too violent, or their personal pride too exacting, to forego private conflict, and leave to the laws the avenging of their real or supposed wrongs."[178] Democracy fails when hatreds and divisions are too intense. Hence, the rarity of democratization under the Islamic Resurgence. Democracy did not get far in Egypt in large part because the Muslim Brotherhood showed no inclination to grant recognition to Muslims of liberal faith, much less to adherents of other faiths. Most such deficiencies of tolerance stem from inexperience in economic, social, and cultural markets, but they also may from elite hubris.

Whether provoked by radicalism, intolerance, personal authoritarianism, or elite arrogance, high levels of conflict and violence inflame divisions and intensify group identification. Peace and prosperity, to the contrary, ordinarily foster tolerance and reconciliation. Poorly developed countries without clear sovereignty or effective central administration often encounter such widespread turmoil and insecurity that democracy is difficult to sustain. People who might otherwise be disposed toward democracy may become desperate enough in the face of intimidation and fear that they are willing to throw themselves into the arms of strong men who promise the restoration of security, however objectionable their rule might be on other counts.

India's traditional universalism, tolerance, and relative peacefulness made it a comparatively strong candidate for democracy even though until recently its low levels of development and literacy worked against democracy. India's caste system long reduced class conflict by splintering most possible social bases of large, threatening division,[179] although conflict with Muslims and Sikhs outside the Hindu system was an ongoing concern. India's long colonial relationship with Britain also favored its democratization. India learned a great deal from the British and benefitted from the relative mildness of their colonial administration overall.

The Roles of the Demonstration Effect and Democratic Culture. A key draw of democracy around the world during the late 20th century was that its performance politically, economically, and in terms of self-respect gained, was in many cases compelling. Open-minded people everywhere plainly observed the effectiveness of the United Kingdom and United States' strong economic and political recoveries from the doldrums of the 1970s and of their military buildups in response to the Soviet invasion of Afghanistan. Neither the Soviet nor the Cuban dictatorship was able to come close to matching those Anglo-American achievements. America's enviable economic performance continued through the 1990s. People were concluding even in authoritarian societies that democracy was efficacious, civilized, and attainable if citizens would stand up collectively against and overthrow the hierarchies stifling them. Much of the strength of democracy's demonstration effect at the time hinged upon the leadership of Margaret Thatcher and Ronald Reagan, backed by the moral strength of the peoples who had formed and elected them. It was noticed as well in looking around the world that democracies do not suffer famines, even when they are poor.[180]

Democracy also gained charisma and won wide acceptance through the creation and dissemination of richly developed pro-democratic ideas along with an entire culture of democratic thought, slogans, and images via the mass media. This supporting culture emphasizing freedom and human rights facilitated the spread of democracy as its economic analog facilitated the spread of capitalism. The cachet of democracy played a large role in freeing the Eastern European Soviet dependencies for self-determination and helping most become solidly democratic. Democracy trounced dictatorship in the war of ideas and images during the late 20th century. For a time, democratic culture shamed most of the world's brooding corporals, crime bosses, larcenous gamers, and other actual and potential tyrants. For a time, authoritarian regimes nearly all had the same central problem as did the Soviet Union: How to survive politically in opposition to a world dominated by economic, political, social, and cultural markets, given the many-sided development and strength flowing from these markets, when under responsible leadership. However, both the demonstration effect and the culture became distinctly less favorable to democracy during the 1990s, as the great generation was being displaced by the 1960s generation.

The Roles of the Pax Americana and NGOs. Another master source of democratization was the Pax Americana, directly through the United States' wielding of power and the prestige drawn from its successful exercise and indirectly through the global capitalism the security regime made possible. It is not a coincidence that there were ten times more democracies in the world in the year 2000 than there had been in 1941. Over and above its exercise of soft power, the United States interceded overtly and/or covertly to help bring about a good deal of the democratization that took place. It intervened in Chile, the Philippines, Nicaragua, El Salvador, Iraq, Ukraine, and Libya, among many other countries. It also blocked numerous military coups against democratic regimes.[181] That Great Britain had not been in a sufficiently strong position under the Pax Britannica to intervene much in continental Europe during the 19th century is part of the reason democratization had been slow to nonexistent then.[182] Insofar as democracies are more powerful militarily than autocracies, democratization occurs; insofar as the opposite holds, democratization reverses.

An additional source of democratization was the building of civil society during the late 20th century. The greater the public involvement in independent political organizations, the better prepared a country is for democratization. Political organizations, whether interest groups, neighborhood bodies, or movements and organizations of the concerned, represent empowered, engaged collectivities of democratic citizens. One of the secrets to India's vibrant democracy was its rich civil society, which at the turn of the 21st century consisted of a panoply of more than a million NGOs (non-governmental organizations).[183] As Diamond argues, "A spirited civil society plays a vital role in checking and limiting the potential abuse of state power, but it also sustains and enriches democracy. Civil society organizations provide channels, beyond political parties and electoral campaigns, for citizens to participate in politics and governance, to air their grievances, and to secure their interests."[184]

From the 1990s, a subset of NGOs matured whose purpose was to promote democratization internationally, much of it through the nurturing of civil society. Staffed by revolutionaries with velvet gloves, these NGOs formed an infrastructure for democratization that moved from country to country. As in funding by USAID (the U.S. Agency for International Development), "international assistance to civil society is helping to build the civic architecture of free and pluralistic society" in many countries.[185] NGOs worked effectively in the Balkans during the 1990s and spectacularly so in Ukraine's Orange Revolution of 2004. International NGOs' maturing technology for nurturing civil society around the world significantly assisted in bringing about democratization between 1989 and 2004.

Why Did Authoritarianism Falter in Late-20th-Century in Russia and China? Many authoritarian regimes faltered during the late 20th century because democracy decisively won the contest for acceptance. At the apogees of the USSR during the mid-1930s and following the Allied victory in World War II, there was great loyalty to the Soviet regime within the Communist Party, if considerably less in the general public. Had that level of commitment been maintained within the party, communist rule would have continued irrespective of changes in public opinion. But by the late 1960s, the nuclear physicist Andrei Sakharov, in *Progress, Coexistence, and Intellectual Freedom,*[186] offered the hope of convergence and harmony between East and West. I listened to visiting delegations of Soviet scholars at the time privately tell their American peers that communism was "stale bread" which no one any longer took seriously. By the 1980s, the Soviet regime had almost no legitimacy left in anyone's eyes, even those of the apparatchiki running it.

The Communist Party's inability to halt the increasing awareness of the appeals of a Western way of life was a growing problem for the post-Stalinist Soviet regime. Its peoples were exposed to the power of liberal Western culture through contacts with Westerners and through the media, cumulatively eroding acceptance of the totalitarian regime. The

West's freedom of movement and expression, its restraint and decency, its movies and music, not to mention its endless supplies of housing and automobiles and shimmering images of Levi's jeans, Pepsi, and the beach were simply overpowering to a system that could offer little beyond the fulfillment of basic subsistence. The unhindered debate and give and take of democracy were more and more appealing to those under Soviet tyranny. Just as democratic culture overpowered most third world hierarchical traditions, it overpowered Soviet cynicism. The East Bloc's empty department stores, sterile apartment towers, and menacing border guards stood for the despair of a captive way of life.

The regime crisis in the USSR began in part as the newly capitalist Asian countries' huge economic success sank in.[187] It was one thing when Soviet subjects struggled while the West flourished, but the disappointment hit home once the West was joined in economic, political, social, and cultural vibrancy by any number of Asian upstarts. The collapse in Afghanistan put enormous additional pressure on the already widely detested and brittle Soviet regime by further discrediting it, although that alone was not sufficient to bring down the regime. Through his policies of glasnost and perestroika, Gorbachev introduced the Soviet Union and its dependencies to political freedoms they had never known, leading to an exhilarating but volatile release of hopes, to movement toward free elections in Russia and Eastern Europe, and collapse of the Soviet regime.

Yet the strength of anti-democratic elements militated against democratization in Russia. Serious political reform, while it maintained coercive control over a hostile empire, had to begin with the freedom of Eastern Europe and domestic republics whose citizens were unwilling participants in the Soviet empire. Only once the USSR shrank toward its natural political community could there be much cutting back of coercive control agencies and allowing of free discussion and free association. Absent either the rule of law or mutual respect and trust among Russians in the wake of Soviet demoralization, the hope for democratization proved unfounded, even with security forces reduced. Russia's turbulent gesture in the direction of democracy under Yeltsin soon abandoned all but transparent pretense and reverted to full authoritarianism and kleptocracy under Putin following the FRS coup in 2000. Putin and the secret police have ruled Russia since, curtailing civil liberties and coercing opposition.[188]

China's authoritarianism was challenged in 1989 because there was considerable support for the democratic movement among the upper and middle classes and urbanites, including some in the Communist Party. It was nevertheless suppressed, primarily because decisive elements within the party have had no intention at any point to abandon hierarchical rule unless forced to do so. They included hardliners in the Red Army and other security forces, a mostly invisible element within the regime at the time of Tiananmen. They grew stronger, more confident, and less invisible later. The democracy movement was suppressed as well because some in the ruling class, who might otherwise have been sympathetic, felt the students' democratic thrust to be premature given the large percentage of the country still rural. Problems were also raised by the student movement's association with popular concern for social justice in a manner that threatened to reverse the country's economic liberalization.[189] As David Ignatius says, "among the elite in China's wealthy cities, fear of the peasants in the hinterlands seems to be a bigger concern than the opaque Communist Party rulers."[190]

Why Did Authoritarianism Not Falter in the Late 20th Century Muslim World? Of the world's major religions, Islam has been the most authoritarian from the beginning, due to its origins in nomadic, warlike herding societies and early domination by warrior ruling classes. Conquering those in or near deserts and steppes set Muslim societies up for invasion, depredation, and the same in turn by others. Ibn Khaldun describes the continual churning of the Maghreb through centuries of conquest and reconquest.[191] Living in dangerous neighborhoods, so to speak, meant comparatively little experience of peaceful reconciliation and its fruits.

Islamic civilization has had relatively little chance to work through difference and develop traditions of trust, harmony and tolerance characteristic of the more settled civilizations. The Middle East's multiple impediments to democracy bear more than a little resemblance to Russia's, rooted alike in deep legacies of desert and steppe vulnerability, devastation, and demoralization, including shared experience of terrible despoliation by the Mongols. Neither has been fertile ground for reasonableness. Islam's authoritarianism has moderated to a degree in some places and times, as in most of Indonesia during the global era, but these have been exceptional.

Islam's deep authoritarianism has made it exceptionally difficult for Muslims to oust tyrants. Moreover, unlike the West, the Islamic world has never allowed a place for autonomous, secular culture, aside from confined technical knowledge. It has minimal acceptance of difference, no tradition of independent, secular criticism, women's rights, and virtually no history of democracy. Not surprisingly given its comprehensive closedness, traditions of misrule go back many centuries in the Islamic world. It has long produced and continues to produce disproportionately much of the world's tyranny.

Out of this background, Muslim populations achieved their dangerous initial, mass political awareness during the global era amid the hubris of newfound literacy and limited education. Wearing religious blinders, tolerance was difficult to achieve.[192] King Faruq's hierarchical Egypt of the mid-20th century, moderated by traditional rule and *fedayeen* quiescence, showed much more tolerance of Coptic Christians, who were even allowed to hold high government posts, than do today's Egyptians. Such arrangements were possible prior to the attainment of political consciousness by more than a few. As Arabs began leaving the fields (for, after the conquests most were peasants) and gaining basic education steeped in the Muslim faith, their popular fervor and harsh ethnic-religious intolerance set the tone. The *street* was born.

Uganda's President Yoweri Museveni rightly says that democracy requires a sufficient middle class that has developed beyond a sole preoccupation with matters of ethnicity, which in the Muslim world is bound up with religion.[193] Without much experience of economic or any other form of independence, no more than a small middle class could form. Among other things, the Islamic Resurgence expressed the birth cry of a people's first political consciousness. Its arresting howl lies at the foundation of their coeval paradigm diametrically opposing every aspect of Western liberalism.

Oil has also been central to contemporary Muslim authoritarianism, for Middle Eastern petroleum reserves have directly empowered autocratic rulers. As Diamond says, "When oil is a country's dominant export ... its people become clients, not real citizens."[194] When political elites control oil revenues, they need not consult with citizens on the use of government revenues. International aid often subsidizes authoritarian regimes and impedes democratization in a similar way. Nor do people have as much concern with how revenues are spent if they are not being taxed. As Samuel Huntington says, "no representation without taxation."[195] Eight hundred years ago, the framers of the Magna Carta understood that rulers are unchallengeable when financially independent.

Muslim rulers' oil industries have at the same time constituted dominant government sectors within their economies, subordinating the private sectors and containing their liberalizing effects. As is common in entrenched hierarchical economies, relatively few liberal and moderate rulers arose in the Muslim world during the global era because its upper-middle and solid middle classes were small and weak while its marginal middle and working classes were large and gaining in power. State-controlled oil pushes aside the free markets and curtails the human development that could help bring about a free and critical public. By strengthening bad hierarchical regimes and subsidizing economic dependency, Middle Eastern oil has been a curse for political development as it also has been for economic development. Of the 23 economies in the world most dependent upon oil production in 2010, not one was democratic.[196]

Deliberate manipulation of ethnic-religious sentiments to sidetrack publics and secure a false, shallow, partial acceptance was also central to the Islamic political authoritarianism of the global era. A great many Muslim countries are undemocratic today because their threatened elites were able to scapegoat outsiders, domestic and international, subsidizing hatred and intolerance to retain power. Muslim hierarchical regimes long milked the goat of the Arab-Israeli conflict to inflame religious bigotry and deflect attention from domestic devastation and toward Israel and the West. Middle Eastern autocrats' manipulation of radical Islam resembles fascist dictators' manipulation of nationalism in early 20th-century Europe. It also resembles the Chinese regime's increasing reliance upon nationalism for support, which it intermittently wields with intensity when it wishes to growl at the United States or its neighbors. Playing viciously on nationalist sentiments has been a standard gambit of hierarchical ruling classes since the French Revolution.

The Saudi regime survived with comparatively little overt repression by liberally and strategically spreading its oil money around and frequently invoking its special status as protector of the Muslim holy sites and benefactor of Islam. Gerontocratic Saudi rulers put this policy in sharp relief by cynically sponsoring fundamentalist Wahabism, giving their regime favorable domestic PR while quietly propagating and supporting jihad around the world. The Saudi monarchy long bought the silence of its coopted subjects even though most of them failed to accept the regime for decades.

As the Islamic Resurgence gained force from the 1970s and 1980s, many relatively secular Muslim regimes worked out modi vivendi with fundamentalists resembling those of the Saudis. Egypt's Mubarak regime, for example, jailed fundamentalists who worked against it while tolerating and even supporting those who curtailed their domestic political activities. Such contortions long kept the regime relatively secure while enabling the Muslim Brotherhood to grow in strength. Syria's Assad regime coldly employed a similar strategy until its citizens began trying to take matters into their own hands in 2011. The Jordanian monarchy, an exceptionally good regime, has been balanced and restrained overall; but it has been unable to fully include or win much acceptance from the restive, conflictual Palestinian community making up most of its population.

The Dynamics of Democratic Performance in the Third World. When the ability and determination of pro-democracy forces reach a high pitch, people become ready to stand up to authoritarianism. Once prepared, they tend to rise up when hierarchical regimes falter and reel, discredited in times of crisis. This occurred early in the Arab Spring. The Tunisian uprising, for example, was sparked when an official wrongfully destroyed the livelihood of a simple peddler, who then immolated himself in protest. In such cases the new order fights to liberalize, and the old order resists. The balance often tips from hierarchy to democracy in dramatic regime crunches in which popular indignation and empowerment surge past barriers and topple the old structures. These lurches have frequently been comparatively peaceful transformations in which portions of the hierarchical elite defect to democracy. Yet there is no easy and entirely gradualist route into democracy, nor is there usually an entirely peaceful one. A whole society or substantial part of it becomes self-governing all at once when restrictive rule yields to inclusive participation that is inherently less practiced. Inevitably the transition to self-determination is a bumpy one in which steps are taken both forward and backward, as is the case when a child comes of age or employees buy out a corporation. Nor was the path easy when democracy was being established in Europe and the United States in past centuries. Both sides make mistakes, small and large.

Sometimes, as in Taiwan, the transition is decisive, with the old regime's resolution shattered and the new structures sufficiently serviceable that no large reversals followed. In other cases, as in Ukraine, there were reversals in which the authoritarians in turn were able to discredit the nascent democratic structures, often by channeling frustration about mistakes and corruption, sometimes by exploiting nationalist sentiment, and not infrequently by outside interference.

Once citizens gain liberty and democracy, they must be continually vigilant and ready to defend them with their lives and property if they wish to keep them. Societies whose citizens are ever prepared to take at once to the streets in outrage and overwhelming numbers to decisively face down usurpers are societies whose democracies are secure. That requires the tough-minded, confident populations which only capitalism delivers and education confirms.

Malaysia, during the global era, presented an example of a mixed, partly free regime. Its citizens, though in many respects ready for democracy, were not yet able to reliably stand up to and remove high-handed, overbearing officeholders. Unscrupulous, majority Barisan Nasional (BN) party politicians played upon the insecurities of majority ethnic Malays in competing with minority Chinese and Indians, enabling the party to subvert the rule of law and govern continuously for more than five decades. Malaysia's long-serving Prime Minister Mahathir bin Mohamad, although doing some constructive things for the country, fomented division and suppressed opposition. He viciously traduced reformist Deputy Prime Minister Anwar Ibrahim and imprisoned him for years. Police violence toward peaceful protestors demanding fair election procedures took place in 2011 amid continued baseless legal persecution of Anwar and his opposition party supporters. Although incomes and education greatly improved in Malaysia, an unevenly critical and independent voting public struggled to govern itself amid salient ethnic and Muslim religious identification.[197]

Democracy may also be jeopardized when security forces have high levels of corruption. Mexico achieved important democratization while undergoing respectable economic development for more than three decades, but it bore a major burden of corruption, one that particularly plagued law enforcement and increasingly the military as the latter became more involved in maintaining domestic order. Overcoming official lawlessness was central to Mexico's halting democratization. The spread of large-scale narcotics trafficking was a major setback as vast sums of drug cartel money corrupted elected and appointed officials at all levels. Rogue elements in and associated with the government sanctioned violence and hobbled Mexican democracy by the 21st century. The incorruptible few among elected representatives, administrators, judges, police, and journalists risked their lives, and many were assassinated. Reducing intimidation of and by corrupt security forces, officeholders, and union bosses was crucial to building trust and empowering democratic elements.

Unlike the Mexican democracy, the Costa Rican democracy was one of the most robust in Latin America, in part because it had no military for most of the last century and developed under the umbrella of U.S. security. Flourishing capitalist relations and limited coercion by the state promoted a peaceful way of life favorable to democratization in Costa Rica.

A key political challenge in Latin American democracies, as in most others, was a shortage of the critical facility to notice corrupt elements and of the moral fiber to stand up to them. When voting publics are insufficiently critical, informed, or engaged, and public outrage is ill focused and vulnerable to manipulation, such arbitrary decisions may be forthcoming that democracy becomes untenable. The burden of corruption, demagoguery, or strife may become so great and unremitting in an ineffectual democracy that people are better off under authoritarian rule, at least insofar as a good hierarchical elite is available. Turkey benefited from its last military intervention and would have benefited from another during the 2010s. Cruder forms of official self-dealing may be found in most third-world democracies than people would be willing to put up with in the first world, but no citizens are one hundred percent vigilant.

Westerners have a difficult time understanding that more people around the world believe they are ready for democracy than actually are. Thinking that one's compatriots or group ought to be allowed to participate politically does not guarantee the wisdom of that appraisal, for there is such a thing as false political consciousness in which a people or group judges itself better prepared to participate constructively than it is. This was the case with many third-world peoples when they gained autonomy from colonial states, as it is when many thirteen-year-olds believe that they are prepared for independence. Those who are less developed may sometimes be thrown off by the culture of the more developed within a society, and people of less developed societies may sometimes be thrown off by the political or social ways of more developed societies. Having picked up fragments of democratic culture for which they are not ready, it is difficult for many who need good traditional elites to any longer accept them, sometimes with tragic consequences.

Why the Decline of Democratic Performance in the United States? Congressional restriction of the executive branch following Watergate was a major structural change that weakened American democratic performance. Under the circumstances, as John Marini says, a Democratic Congressional majority was able to infringe upon the authority of the presidency and increasingly reappropriate portions of the executive branch to itself. Since regulated companies were motivated to influence their regulation, Congress acquired a large pipeline to the special interests from its new authority. Its encroachment into the executive led to Congress's redefinition of its purview from legislation to the executive oversight of regulatory activity.

Democratic members of Congress gained the major benefit, but Republican members were included in the benefits and went along with the change.[198] Congress formed a tacit coalition with the courts by offering them an expanded role in interpreting the often deliberately vague associated laws. Under the new system, according to Marini, "Congress controls the administrative details of politics through the bureaucracy it created, and the judiciary reigns supreme in the realm of politics or regarding general policy matters…"[199] Yet the hobbling of the executive weakened that branch's ability to bring coherence and discipline to national politics as well as the power of voters to monitor and shape politics through presidential elections. This topic comes up again in chapter 8.

Whether in the first or third world, democratic performance tends to be high to the extent to which public oversight and access are strong. The growing scale and remove of government in the United States made it increasingly difficult for its citizens to control. Some of the effect arose from the increased complexity accompanying large government and some of it from the geometrically increased density and strength of the special interests accompanying the increased scale. The media conferred additional advantage upon large, well-organized, well-funded special interests.

The relatively high political interest and involvement of the national era declined because political gamers were running circles around average citizens, weakening their oversight and effectiveness. Many of the latter lost confidence that they could make a difference. Middle- and working-class voters often found political competition with the gamers and special interests too fruitless and exasperating to keep trying. The lowering of educational standards also considerably weakened public oversight. More than a little of the decline in participation was also simple refusal of the obligations of democratic citizenship, presenting self-dealing analogous to that carried on by unworthy public officials.

The gamers' moral decline was also alienating. Increasingly blatant manifestations of contempt by gamer officials, political operatives, and staffers toward their fellow Americans – as in egregious expressions of it by Angelo Mozilo, Jim Johnson, Rod Blagojevich, Jonathan Gruber, Benjamin Rhodes, and the Clintons – inflamed public ire. Those in and around politics became slipperier as well as smarter, and they wore down larger numbers of voters who hoped for better.[200] It became more difficult to compete successfully in the political markets as it became more difficult to do so in the financial and labor markets.

In the absence of effective oversight or morality, politicians and officials mostly became brokers for the special interests, seeking personal benefits rather than looking out for society or their constituents.[201] Since few who gained political power during the global era were concerned with the well-being of society, the quality of American governance declined steeply. Poor democratic performance lay behind the Great Recession as the public well knows, and there was frequent grumbling and sporadic outrage by good but overmatched citizens about the fact. When democratic citizens lack the resources or stamina needed to exercise oversight, and elites abandon their morality, special interests weasel into the expanding areas of opacity.

Decreasing citizen alertness and grasp of society were punished with parasitism.

The Etiology of a Class Struggle. The political division of the second half of the global era arose in large part because factionalized, paradigm-bearing cohorts were marching their way through the age structure. A revolutionary generation became politically engaged during the 1960s. The baby-boomers and their successors began coming to power in the 1980s but especially the 1990s. The 1960s generation had no recollection of the teamwork and sacrifice that were general during World War II, or of the postwar swell of gratitude for the many who had served their country. Having come of age fighting entrenched societal norms over civil rights, elders over moral restrictions, the government over Vietnam, and draft boards over conscription, its formative experience was of domestic rather than international conflict.

Two social classes and character types, gamers and the middle class, vied for political and sociocultural preeminence in considerable tension with each other during the global era: A large majority of gamers, over-represented in the upper reaches of government, the professions, the media, and among intellectuals, was at war with the middle class. A minority of gamers, over-represented in business and the clergy, was supportive of the middle class. Although somewhat split vis-à-vis economic markets, the gamers were radically libertarian vis-à-vis sociocultural markets. The cultural content they thrust into the media offended and disturbed many in the middle class and corrosively affected young people. Led by the few sympathetic conservative gamers, many in the middle class responded to the frontal assault on their character and way of life by rejecting their liberal gamer tormentors and a great deal that was associated with them.

A bitter, asymmetric class struggle took place during the global era over which of the two classes should set the sociocultural parameters. The gamers' self-centeredness and provocativeness aggressively challenged the middle class. Socio-culturally naïve, outflanked, and treated mercilessly, many in the middle class found no other way to defend themselves than via populist, know-nothing anti-intellectualism carried over from fundamentalist Christianity, some of it overtly aggressive, some merely passive-aggressive. With powerful and threatening new elites arrayed against them, precarious members of the middle class had to grit their teeth and willfully push ahead against the tide. Amid the sociocultural combat more than a few conservative gamers, whose characters were not usually as complex as those of their liberal counterparts,[202] adopted some of the know-nothingism and rigidity of their bourgeois allies and constituents. The frequent failure of top conservatives to match the nimbleness of top liberals was partly responsible for conservatives falling behind liberals in American political competition from the early 1990s.

The global-capitalist economy was not only a central source of the gamers' higher discipline but also strengthened the middle class's basic discipline, as had the early-capitalist economy. The arrival of global economic markets and departure of protected national ones exposed to sharp competition most of those who were once cushioned from capitalism by industrial and professional associations, unions, tariffs, and fair-trade laws. The icy waters of the global markets forced people to hustle unremittingly to find work, obtain clients, sell services, and perform myriads of adaptive chores amid gnawing uncertainty, which was just the prescription for instilling and strengthening discipline. The immersion of workers in the global markets swiftly rendered many of them middle class and conservative on economic issues although they remained less educated, resistant to the sociocultural markets, and relatively conservative on social issues.

On the other hand, a great deal of global-liberal culture undermined discipline. Adults' superegos were reinforced in the economic markets, but children were largely sequestered from these, while being dropped into the sociocultural markets. Other than through the effects of the market economy, American society was not good at lifting people into the middle class or keeping them there.

One of the two elite bastions of the radical relativism anathematic to the character of the middle class was the culture industry of intellectuals, artists, and the media, which was dominated by gamers whose attacks upon the superego and animus toward the conservative reaction undermined the middle class. Many in the therapy community were especially antagonistic toward middle-class discipline. As the therapy community waxed, its gamers' higher reflexivity leagued together with the id, celebrating release and denouncing restraint. The cosmopolitan, liberal gamers far outpaced the provincial middle class, while the latter plodded along as well as they could, mostly on their own. Some of the delay of the conservative reaction was because of the perennial lag in the supply of conservative ideas owing to the dearth of conservative intellectuals.

The other elite-dominated institution anathematic to the middle-class discipline was the judiciary. The courts introduced sociocultural laissez faire the likes of which the modern world had never before witnessed. The judiciary legalized homosexuality, abortion, and nearly all nonviolent forms of lifestyle or expression: It removed a great many restrictions from public school curricula. It nearly dissolved the earlier relatively mild censorship of pornography and the grossly offensive in magazines and books, and it greatly relaxed restrictions on movie and television content while reversing the traditional protections for Christianity. This judicial liberalization sowed confusion and consternation in the middle class. The reaction was unable to halt libertarian judicial rulings or counter the era's sociocultural corrosion.

The Democratic Party of the era was dominated by progressive gamers dissembling to group-member, single-women, aid-recipient, and protected, dependent-employee constituents such as those in government and monopolistic business. The Republican Party was dominated by conservative gamers representing middle- and working-class constituents. They dissembled as well to some degree, as in listening and nodding to Christian conservatives talking gibberish about evolution or stem-cell research. Gamers closer to the cultural than the economic markets – mostly those in and around the media and academia who were overwhelmingly progressive – tended to be skeptical and anti-middle class. These cultural gamers were for the most part employees of large organizations and buffered from economic competition. Gamers closer to the economic markets tended to be less skeptical and less unsympathetic to the bourgeois than their cultural counterparts, or sometimes sympathetic to them. Republican elites yielded to a degree to the party's harried, middle-class rank and file.

The relatively unified and concentrated liberal gamers of the two coasts were able to consolidate regional support from other classes for their leanings, but liberal gamers elsewhere in the country were able to do so only in pockets, albeit influential ones. Since most of the country was not sufficiently acclimated to the wide-open sociocultural markets to feel comfortable with extreme tolerance, much of it was fertile ground for the conservative reaction. In many parts of the country, the middle class pulled back from and opposed the liberal gamers, insulating themselves and going their middle-class way in opposition to them.

Men were more likely than women to vote Republican during the later decades of the era largely because they were more likely to be close to the economic markets and less likely to be dependent employees. Their different occupational settings, together with the facts that women were less likely to follow their husbands' political leads than they had been at mid-century, explain most of the gender gap.

Why the political stagnation of other first-world democracies? Like American democracy, European democracies became less able to make needed policy reforms through the global era because inherently monopolistic government was becoming larger, stronger, more bureaucratic, more entrenched, and more opaque; removing more and more areas of policy-making from parliamentary authority. Much of the problem in Europe derived from growth of the EU bureaucracy. The EU took control in many areas without fully operational and unified executive or legislative branches. The EU bureaucracy exuded an atmosphere of entitlement even stronger than that increasingly found in Washington. European citizens lagged in informing themselves and becoming engaged as government grew and became more complex and distant. Much as the rise of the nation-state displaced the estates of the Middle Ages through the 15th, 16th, and 17th centuries by exceeding the range of their democratic resources, the rise of the EU has displaced national European democracies by exceeding their range.

Amid stronger persistence of high culture and liberal education, continental Europe's leading classes remained somewhat more universalistic and in better harmony with their societies than those of the United States. Left-leaning European elites and upper and upper-middle classes triumphed socioculturally in a way they did not in the United States except on the two coasts, but those classes were less gamer, better integrated, more restrained, less provocative, and did not press their advantages as harshly and divisively as did their American counterparts. The European middle class for those reasons was less agitated and inflamed overall than the American and not as vehemently opposed to their elites. The aristocratic ridicule Molière once directed toward the bourgeois was still forthcoming in Europe, if often from convoluted, Marxist-influenced sources; but it tended to be relatively mild. There was less bludgeoning of the middle class with multiculturalism until the last decade of the global era.

The continental middle class was long awed or lulled into modesty and silence. Unabashed, unsublimated, superego dominants may have been numerous in the United States or Britain but were less frequently found on the continent. However, the prolonged political paralysis, euro crisis, refugee crisis, and challenge of Islamism in Europe began awakening the middle classes and discrediting the elites.

Japan's robust, relatively hierarchical consensus thwarted efforts at democratic political reform, including those to modernize administration, instill responsiveness, and overcome corruption. Should Japan's national security or economy suffer major reversal as a consequence of poor democratic performance, that consensus could be positioned to attack and discredit democracy. The force and recency of Japanese hierarchy and the continuing collectivism of its national character underlie this vulnerability.

More developed democracies may have had less blatant and crude corruption than less developed ones, but subtle, refined corruption could be comparably debilitating. The global-era first world's interested business subsidies, tax loopholes, regulatory lapses, unsustainable retirement programs, albatross medical systems, and burdensome monopoly grants to business and labor presented a vast swindling of populations by their politicians and the special interests swarming about them. The orchestrated lobbying, advertising, and PR services of the special interests were powerful indeed. To a considerable extent, what Aristotle said of demagogues applied to the engineers of mass opinion: "While the people rule over all, *they* rule over people's opinion."[203]

Why the Reversal of Democratization in the Early 21st Century? The central cause of the cessation and slight reversal of democratization around the world during the early 21st century was the declining political performance of first-world democracies from the 1990s. The world's leading democracies performed effectively from the 1940s through the 1980s and inspired emulation, but they did not during the second half of the global period. The deterioration of democratic governance patently lay behind their mounting national security and economic troubles. When the flagship American democracy was severely short of leadership, and most of its governing class had come to brazenly disserve the American public, when the French, Italian, and Japanese democracies were paralyzed and British democracy was doing no better than so-so, who in the second or third world would think that becoming or remaining democratic was neccessarily advantageous? Opinion leaders around the world instead began paying new attention to the rising authoritarian countries of the time.

A good deal of the late 20th-century surge in democratization had come from the great generation, that of World War II, prominently including Ronald Reagan. George H. W. Bush, of the same generation, reaped much of the harvest and helped keep the momentum going. Bill Clinton, although of the new generation, reaped some of the accolades because of his global popularity. A changing of the guard occurred in all social classes. Those bearing the national-liberal paradigm cared about how the country fared, gave generously of themselves, and prided themselves in leadership and involvement. As the leavening presence of the World War II generation more rapidly receded by the end of the century, democratization plateaued and soon reversed.

Democratization also halted because the relatively easy and likely countries had already become democratic. When the Soviet Union collapsed, most of Eastern Europe was ready to democratize. Many of the remaining authoritarian countries were not, including nearly all Muslim countries. Democratization halted as well because while first-world democracies were hitting developmental walls under global liberalism, authoritarian regimes were innovating and upgrading.

Why the 21st-Century Strengthening of Authoritarianism? Much of the strengthening of authoritarianism during the later decades of the era occurred because rulers learned how to counter democratization, as is insightfully argued by Dobson.[204] They were able to do so in part by camouflaging their regimes' authoritarianism through subtle public relations to foil their domestic and international opposition. National-era dictatorships obtusely proclaimed what they were with fanfare and bluster. They trumpeted the superiority of authoritarian systems with propaganda based upon rigid ideology and ponderous, neo-classical symbolism. Everyone knew which regimes were democratic and which were authoritarian through the 1980s, with the exception of the Deng-regime China, but it soon became difficult to tell.

Dictatorships that wanted to survive amid the global-era headwinds had to adopt a new modus operandi and PR strategy. Supporters of democracy now had to expend much effort in order to determine whether and to what extent elections, legislatures, and courts were shams. Dictators learned that if they veiled their rule and made it difficult for first-world citizens and their own subjects to grasp the nature of their regimes, they hardened those regimes against their democratic adversaries. Doing so was an especially useful strategy when the authoritarian regime was new and more vulnerable. Such veiling played an important role in turning the political tide against democracy.[205]

The new authoritarianism also strengthened itself by upgrading its subversion. Putin's Russia, for example, extensively subverted democratization in Ukraine, Belarus, Kazakhstan, Georgia, and other former Soviet dependencies, using secret agents to corrupt, defame, intimidate, or murder leaders. It used PR specialists to confuse publics, erode trust, poison sociocultural milieux, and sow discord. Putin and his agents brought about much of the terrible performance of Ukraine's nascent democracy in the years following the Orange Revolution of 2004 – how much, may never be known.

After losing Ukraine to democracy, Putin also began more vigorously countering the NGOs in that country and elsewhere. He severely restricted the international NGOs within Russia, as China also did. While these NGOs made and continued to make large impacts around the world, their maturing social technology of democratization was now being contested and blocked in many countries. Since the Soviet Union had obstructed democratization on a global scale, ending its global subversion was one more way in which the Soviet collapse furthered democratization around the world. Russia's aggressive interference in most of its former dependencies, as well as in Syria, Cyprus, Nicaragua, and many other countries, including even the United States, speaks of Putin's resumption during the Obama presidency of his country's global efforts to combat democratization. China, Saudi Arabia, and Pakistan also obstructed democratization internationally. Both the new veiling and the new subversion were effects of gamers reaching the top ranks in the major contemporary hierarchical societies, for gaming undercuts democracy and strengthens authoritarianism.

Russia pioneered in the new treachery because that country came under the rule of a shrewd, wily, and dangerous gamer when Putin took over in 2000. Yeltsin was clever but volatile, erratic, and only partly gamer. Putin was a gamer through and through, one of the most sophisticated yet to rule an authoritarian society. Dismayed as he watched the East German and Soviet regimes collapse from his positions in the KGB, he contemplated the fundamental circumstances of authoritarian societies in the global era. Where the Soviet regime was bureaucratic, turgid, and cumbersome, and paid for it in economic lethargy, regime rejection, and collapse, the Putin regime was tactically nimble in many respects and strategically so in others. Putin was mindful of the need to stay lean and solvent in order to grow economically and increase state power. In his regime's thinking, micro-management of its subjects went beyond the point of marginal return, needlessly running up costs. That was part of its logic in leaving the Internet relatively unrestricted. Doing so also had PR advantages. There were other, less expensive ways of handling the Internet, including the massive presence of regime trolls, propagandists spewing out terabytes of disinformation, slyly rendering it useless for democratization while discharging additional sinister regime assignments.[206] Putin's adept PR management was eminently gamer. Other less bold and cagey contemporary authoritarian regimes tended to be less gamer.

China did not democratize in large part because of the lingering effects of the country's long history of hierarchicalism, including deep-rooted collectivism and strong community and consensus. China was able to liberalize economic markets while keeping its political markets closed because the weight of its past left deficits of tolerance and restraint, especially among the rural masses who made up nearly half the population. As part of their authoritarian sociocultural legacy, the Chinese, like the Japanese, continued to take critical questioning to be a sign of personal disrespect.[207] Individualism remained anathema.[208] A diminishing but still profound and widespread fatalism also hindered democratization. China's experience with the economic markets was eroding the effects of millennia of hierarchy, and its young people increasingly felt indignant about censorship and hungered for democracy, but large numbers of Chinese remained manipulable by the nationalist appeals and sleight-of-hand of the determined, capable gamers in control of the levers of state power.

Singapore enjoyed the rare good fortune of gifted, benevolent hierarchical rule. The Lee regime's combination of unabashed autocracy and capitalism brought remarkable prosperity and a well-ordered society to Singapore. Yet the Lees' extensive accommodations to the economic and social markets and excellent educational system argued for the transitional nature of their benevolent despotism, for they prepared a capable and prosperous population that would increasingly yearn for collective self-determination. The rarity of the Lees' talent and benevolence also did. When less wise and less well-disposed successors arrive, as they must, so will increased pressure to democratize.

The force of the liberal democratic society and culture to which young and urban Muslims were increasingly exposed was a major cause of the Arab Spring uprisings. Nearly all of the protesters were concerned about economic suffocation and injustice under corrupt and inefficient hierarchical regimes. Turkey's economic growth from 1997 and democratization for a time helped inspire the Arab Spring. The Internet, cell phones, and other new forms of communication opened the insurgents to diverse cosmopolitan influences while enabling them to coordinate with each other and organize politically. The uprisings were suppressed, except in Tunisia, partly because the insurgents were relatively few in number and vulnerable to the machinations of brutal rulers. The larger problem was that the young freedom fighters were immersed in the sea of anger and intolerance of the Islamic Resurgence with its extreme nationalism. Even seeming moderates in the Muslim world overwhelmingly took for granted the assumptions of the reigning Muslim paradigm of the era. Not until that paradigm and its jihad were decisively defeated in hearts and on the ground could there be anything more than niche democracy in the Muslim world.

Addressing the Challenges to Democracy

The global era's developed democracies were, in many respects, impressive human achievements. More than bare political mechanisms, they were to varying degrees balanced institutions ensconced in intricate legal, social, moral, and cultural frameworks. It had taken sustained effort over centuries for their citizens to become able to carry on prolonged peaceful, democratic conversations across wide, deeply felt divisions and abide by the electoral outcomes. Patterns of tolerance and civility and bonds of respect and trust had been built up in advanced democracies as difficult political oppositions were overcome, even as new ones continued to arise. Where many utterly ruinous regimes had ruled historically, many comparatively good ones existed during the global era. Nevertheless, much of this hard-won legacy eroded during the last quarter century of the period.

The global era witnessed the gamers' rise to political domination and the middle class's political marginalization. The growing imbalance of power was strikingly evident in the way in which the gamers became part and parcel of the reign of the special interests. It also was in the consistency with which the gamers prevailed on the crucial issue of immigration. As Huntington says, the American public overwhelmingly supported tough enforcement of immigration laws, and only a small minority of

Americans opposed such enforcement. But that minority was substantially made up of gamers who got what they wanted through presidential decree, Congressional maneuvering, judicial ruling, administrative action, culture industry spin, or any tactic they found useful.[209] The changing power balance between the upper and middle classes presented a serious, many-sided challenge to American democracy.

Many promising ways of strengthening democracy were available, including restricting money in politics. Competing in the wide-open political markets, the special interests had become too well organized, too big, too strong, too cynical, and too destructive, precisely as large corporations had in the unregulated economic markets of the late 19th century.

Under Citizens United and related rulings, neither party was able to overcome the large interests lying at the source of many of the country's most serious problems. The Supreme Court was ready to go to the mat for economic laissez faire during the progressive era and again in the 1930s. From the late 20th century it was ready to do so for political laissez faire. The principle of free speech for large economic interests was not without appeal, but look at the consequences! The large interests that undermined American democracy lacked all feeling and judgment, and their horizons were disastrously narrow. Hayek says that individual human beings have some decency, but organized interests do not.[210] Large organized interests may be legal persons, but they do not pass the test of citizenship.

A second promising political reform was ending the obstructionist Senate filibuster. Abolishing it was a potential major step away from a gridlocked, bought-and-paid-for mechanism toward one again able to resolve the country's problems. An anachronism from a bygone era of national and Congressional consensus, the filibuster was as inappropriate and destructive during the global era as had been the empowered British House of Lords prior to passage of the Reform Bill in 1832. The British were in a crisis of democracy then, and we were near one by the early 21st century.[211] Partisans should not have clasped onto the filibuster out of misplaced fear of what the other party might do when it was their turn to govern. They should have relished the challenge. Each party needs to be able to enact much of its program when it has the mantle and be judged by the results. Extricating itself from its many problems was going to be exceedingly difficult for the United States without reforming the political markets.

All modern democracy has been founded upon alert, capable, numerous, and strong middle classes. The United States' predecessors in modern democracy, the Netherlands and Great Britain, were so founded. The vibrant American democracy of the 18th, 19th, and first two-thirds of the 20th century was founded upon such a middle class. As middle classes ascended economically and socioculturally, they first checked their aristocracies, then substantially drew them toward middle-class political notions and leanings, and then consolidated their democracies. Even the proto-democratic estates and free cities of the Middle Ages were founded upon strengthening middle classes. The United States fought its bloodiest war to force the aristocratic, ante-bellum South into the middle-class world of liberty and democracy. Sadly, this country for the first time witnessed its middle class eclipsed during the global era and, not only unable to influence the new upper class of gamers, but encountering its contempt.

As democratic citizens become more aware of their opportunities and mistakes, the tools are at hand with which to take advantage of the one and turn away from the other. So long as citizens are capable, engaged, and have the freedom to speak, hear, organize, and act politically, they may be confident that they shall eventually understand their unfolding circumstances and make the necessary adjustments. The mechanism with which to reform is always available in developed democracies. Governments, parties, and paradigms may be changed under democracies, but not under dictatorships, for they shoot the messengers. Only when citizens are incapable, indifferent, or suppressed do they have reason to despair over their futures. Authoritarian rulers may perform tolerably well for a time when uncorrected by critical opposition, but they eventually succumb to hubris and venality and bring down their societies. The wise embrace democracy, not thinking that it is a panacea but that it offers responsibility, dignity, and the use of a supple and authentic mechanism, if frequently slow and disorderly, for managing self-determination.

Let us leave now the rational-instrumental facets of society and turn to the emotional ones where many of the penultimate sources of our problems lie. I will first take up changes in community that took place during the global era and then those in morality.

CHAPTER 6

DEVASTATED COMMUNITY

THE SOCIAL MARKETS AND COMMUNAL DEVASTATION

The Social Marketplace. Community from 1965 to 2016 largely took the form of wide-open social markets in which many different patterns coexisted side-by-side, vying for supremacy. Spouses, partners, friends, neighbors, coreligionists, and even fellow citizens were increasingly selected in competitive social markets resembling their economic counterparts.

Never had community been more market-based and less hierarchical on such a scale than it was in global-liberal societies. Kinship ties had played a far greater role in people's lives in earlier societies when clan leaders, the extended family, or parents had chosen young people's spouses; or, during the national era, when young people had selected them on their own but usually from restricted pools. Communal relations were freely sought and freely offered during the global era. The social markets became enormous – much thicker, in economic parlance – with free choices being made from among vast numbers and kinds offered.

Community also frequently became global in reach with families and friendships extending beyond national boundaries and across the world. In earlier centuries, if a relative or friend migrated to another region, country, or continent, they were effectively lost to the group – not so during the global era. Those far apart were able to remain in close contact via relatively inexpensive means of swift transportation and communication. People traveled frequently and were more easily able make long-distance moves even as an increasingly large part of informal social life became bound up in the Internet's universal transcendence of geography.

As all of the traditions, subcultures, and ways of the world were brought into proximity with each other, tremendous local difference arose, and rapid mixing of groups occurred. First- and third-world peoples, Christians and Muslims, seculars and believers, hipsters and traditionalists had once been insulated from each other but were now cheek by jowl. Not only did the burgeoning real and virtual megalopolises of global-liberal societies mingle the peoples of the world, they also celebrated diversity. In a wonderfully apt expression, Williams termed the style of such diversity *chaotic-exotic.*[212]

From Community to Economy. Community was weakening and thinning almost everywhere during the global era as part of broader overall shifts from community to economy and from the emotional to the rational. As the instrumental and rational were entering into and mingling with community, they were both displacing it and marking that which remained with the rational signs of economy. More and more of the available community became embedded in or auxiliary to the economy. As people spend more time on the job, according to Putnam, community more often arises from work and among co-workers than in the past.[213]

Indeed, community was increasingly often incubated by economic entities such as corporations, nonprofits, and governmental agencies. Neither inherited from the past nor built by its members, such greenhouse community was spawned by entities having instrumental reasons for what they did. The elaborately orchestrated social activities within many large business firms, the industrially engineered informal groups in offices and manufacturing facilities, the internal marriages arranged by Japanese firms to facilitate solidarity, and the officially sponsored newcomers' groups on U.S. military bases were all examples of such community. Matchmaking increasingly often took place via the Internet or meetings arranged by corporations for a fee rather than via relatives, friends, or churches.

Group therapy was another form of artificial but useful community, one in which mental health clinics brought patients together to share their struggles and listen sensitively to each other. Hospitals sponsored similar support groups for cancer patients, their families, and survivors. Such arranged community may have been less spontaneous and less durable than the voluntary community in decline, but it was often both helpful and all that was left. What traditional community survived often grew up amid economy where it could, as living testimony to its displacement, like grass sprouting between slabs of concrete. Although adaptable and resilient, community, like nature, was severely strained.

The Decline of Face-to-Face Community. The flourishing face-to-face community of national-liberal societies had provided a setting within which conviviality could enjoy a resurgence, one that in retrospect seems like a quaint luxuriance. Informal sociality of many traditional kinds receded rapidly during the global period. As Putnam says, "active involvement in face-to-face organizations ... plummeted."[214] Social clubs were ubiquitous in the United States during the national era, and many people belonged to several of them.

From the mid-1970s to the late 1990s Americans went from almost two-thirds going to club meetings, to two-thirds never doing so. Many kinds of social clubs once worked mightily alongside other institutions to weave good will into the fabric of society. Elite civic clubs, Masonic lodges, and Rotary, Kiwanis, and Lions community organizations of the national-era had such a purpose. Between 1975 and 1999, those who attended one or more club meetings per month declined by 58 percent. Between 1965 and 1995, those who spent any time in a community organization declined by 57 percent. Participation in league bowling collapsed during the late 20th century, and with it a great deal of wholesome middle- and working-class camaraderie.[215] Steep decline of civic life continued throughout the period.

Shared public space became noticeably less comfortable than it had been through the early 1960s. Casual chatting largely ceased between strangers on the street in cities and even in many towns as Americans were no longer able to enjoy the easy rapport with each other they once had. The automatic camaraderie of the national era among theatergoers lined up to purchase tickets disappeared.[216] So jumpy did Americans become with each other that they often defensively said, "No problem," when responding to a stranger's "Thank you," in place of the generous and open traditional, "You're welcome."

Not surprisingly, friendship weakened during the global era and tended to become shallower, more reserved, and more easily let go. Americans spent less time visiting friends and more time alone. In 1985 only 10 percent of respondents reported that they had no one with whom to confide about personal troubles; by 2004, almost 25 percent did.[217] Circles of closest confidants declined by approximately one-third. The numbers of those who could confide in no one but a spouse increased by almost 50 percent.[218] Those who could confide in a neighbor fell more sharply, from about 19 percent to 8 percent during that nineteen-year period.[219] Neighborhood ties fell by about 50 percent all together. By 1999 Americans were going on picnics about 60 percent less often than they had in 1975.[220] Correspondingly, settings where people could easily socialize, like full-service restaurants and luncheonettes or taverns, bars, and nightclubs, decreased markedly in availability, while those where people could not easily socialize, like fast-food restaurants, increased markedly.[221] The relatively lush sociality of the national era had largely collapsed by the turn of the century, though the more educated were much less socially isolated than the less educated throughout the period.[222]

Religious community is a master source of involvement from which many other kinds of involvement spring, "Religious Americans [being] … up to twice as active civically as secular Americans."[223] Indeed, "nearly half of all associational memberships in America were church related, half of all personal philanthropy is religious in character, and half of all volunteering … [is] in a religious context."[224] This social involvement carried over into personal life, for "regular church attendees reported talking with 40 percent more people than others in the course of the day."[225] Many of the socially beneficial effects of religiosity arose through "religiously based social networks."[226] Like club membership, league bowling, and spontaneous public sociality, religious community greatly weakened from 1965. From a late 1950s peak, church attendance had fallen about 25 percent by the late 1990s.[227] Involvement in church-related activities other than mere attendance fell even more, by about 50 percent.[228]

Community was uprooted and shocked to a far greater extent during the global era than it had been during the early- and national-liberal eras. By this century, the ravaging of community reached the point at which vital civic organizations and concerned citizens' groups that monitor and correct important problems in government and society were sapped by alienation and apathy, resulting in markedly reduced effectiveness of American democracy.

The Rise of Mediated Community. A great deal of community was also radically reformatted during the global era as strikingly new forms of community arose and proliferated. Instead of being heavily involved in face-to-face relations with families and friends, people became immersed in mediated relations. Relations with families and friends were increasingly carried on via mobile phone, Skyping, and instant messaging, sometimes in long-distance partnerships or marriages and often in other family relationships and friendships. A veritable bouquet of new informal sociality grew up around a rapidly evolving set of technologies, including email, Internet chatrooms, blogs, and social websites like Facebook and Twitter. People found partners and reconnected with lost friends through social websites. They interacted breezily in email communication, unconcerned about grammar, spelling, or typos, skipping words and whole phrases, confident that they were understood. They retreated from public spaces to their homes and apartments where they spent more time physically alone but wired into virtual space, encompassing those with whom they wanted to be connected. Or they were alone with others at bistros or on subways as electronic messages flowed in and out of their devices. As virtual reality became more salient, great cities become neighborhood portals to the Internet's all-encompassing presence.

These changes in informal sociality were related to others in game playing. The games of the past, like cards, darts, board games, Ping-Pong, pool, and badminton were unmediated electronically. Now they became mediated, like Hitman, Grand Theft Auto III, Super Mario Galaxy, and GoldenEye 64. Although face-to-face sociality often accompanied video game–playing in such locations as crowded dorm rooms or large convention halls where all kinds of hooting and kibitzing transpired,[229] many forms of face-to-face relations were rendered obsolete and rare, displaced by technology. Poker playing had taken place earlier around tables in smoke-filled rooms. Now it most often took place over the Internet between strangers scattered across the globe. Video games allowed physical solitaries to engage actively with others via technology. The transformation of community echoed the way in which retail stores were closing as people more often shopped via the Internet.

The rise of virtual community partly – but by no means fully – offset the decline in face-to-face community. Even as new technologies increased the ease of communication, the community resulting from them was comparatively remote, and people were less interested in those around them, kept more to themselves, and felt lonelier. Three-quarters of a century after its arrival, television also still absorbed (or partly did) four and a half hours of American adults' time per day as it droned on in one-way, often solitary communication.[230] The widespread mediation of sociality compounded the sense of social alienation.

Those woefully short of satisfying relationships with their fellow human beings turned increasingly to relationships with pets, directing sensitive perspicacity, deep emotion, subtle humanity, and formidable resources to them. Never had so many dogs received so much loving care and attention from women spurned by trolling men, singles ensconced in tomb-like apartments, and seniors abandoned by grown offspring – while so many children were left unattended, prey to all too many dulling or disruptive influences. Video security proliferated to protect the unattended child or pet, but it hardly lessened the isolation. The era's increasingly tattered, minimalist, evanescent, and often mediated community left many feeling sad.

The Disintegration of the Family. Change in community was nowhere more dramatic or profound in the United States than in the family. The love and giving of husband and wife to each other and mother and father to their children were often no longer as unqualified as they once had been. Parents spent less time physically interacting with each other and their children, as the latter did with everyone else. The role of fathers in their children's lives receded across most family types during the global era.[231] Regular dining together of family members fell precipitously.[232] Nor did children give back as they once had. Seniors could look forward to bureaucratic holding facilities in their last years. Asian immigrants to the United States were often shocked at the very existence of such facilities, much less their number and sometimes revolting conditions.

During the 1950s the vast majority of families had been intact, divorce rare, fertility high, unmarried men and women seldom cohabiting, nonmarital births almost unheard of, and a large majority of children living with both biological parents. Sixty years later, most families were no longer traditional, divorce was widespread, fertility low, unmarried men and women often cohabiting, nonmarital births common, and a majority of children no longer living with both biological parents. In 1960, only 17 percent of American children lived away from their biological fathers; by 2013, 37 percent did.[233] Women headed 14 percent of white families in 1983;[234] they headed 25 percent by 2010.[235] Nonmarital births soared from 5 percent to 41 percent overall between 1960 and 2012.[236] Fifty-three percent of births to women under age 30 were outside marriage, a harbinger of things to come.[237]

Blacks underwent earlier and more extreme family disintegration than other Americans. Eighty-four percent of New York City black children had lived with both parents in 1925.[238] Even during the Eisenhower years only 20 percent of black births had been nonmarital; in 1964 only 25 percent had been.[239] By 2012, 73 percent of black births were nonmarital, while 53 percent of Hispanic and 29 percent of non-Hispanic white births also were.[240] Blacks led the way, but family instability increased rapidly in all racial and ethnic groups throughout the period.

If family disorganization was strongly conditioned by race and ethnicity, it was even more strongly conditioned by education. In 1960, 94 percent of white college graduates aged 30 to 49 and 84 percent of those with no more than high school diplomas had married. By 2010, 83 percent of college graduates had married but only 48 percent of the low education group. The percentage of divorced or separated among white college graduates aged 30 to 49 who had ever married increased between 1960 and the early 1980s but held steady afterward at about 7 percent. Among the corresponding group with no more than high-school education, those divorced or separated had already reached that level by 1970 and soared afterward, reaching 33 percent by 2010.[241]

The nonmarital birthrates of college graduates diverged sharply from those of high-school dropouts. In 1971, the rates were approximately 1 percent for college graduates and 9 percent for high-school dropouts. By 2008, they were 5 percent for college graduates but more than 60 percent for high-school dropouts, with intermediate levels for those with some college and those with only high-school graduation.[242] Americans of all education levels witnessed much increased family disorder from the beginning of the global era, but the disorder stabilized at relatively low levels for college graduates after 1980, while it continued to rise for the less well educated and reached catastrophic levels for those with no more than high-school education by the end of the era.

That the United States had a higher divorce rate than other developed liberal societies, is well known.[243] That it also had a higher marriage rate than they is not well known. More telling about the American family of the global era than either its comparatively high marriage or high divorce rate was the combination of the two. As Andrew Chernin said near the end of the era, "People partner, unpartner, and repartner faster [in the United States] than do people in any other Western nation. They form cohabiting relationships easily, but they end them after a shorter time.... In other words, having several partnerships is more common in the United States not just because people exit intimate partnerships faster but also because they enter them faster and after a breakup reenter them faster."[244]

Women streamed into the labor force under global capitalism, moving from community into the economy. Only 15 percent of married women had been in the labor force in 1940, but 41 percent were by 1970, 58 percent by 1990, and 61 percent by 2010, as the phenomenon plateaued.[245] At the same time, society peeled away most of women's traditional activities by monetizing and/or mechanizing them. A variety of relatively dispensable food preparation and household chores were ceded to professionals or labor-saving appliances, but many vital social-emotional and moral sustenance tasks that women had traditionally performed in the family were also abandoned. Many household tasks also remained, unpaid, upon the shoulders of women, typically in addition to full-time jobs; while many others were curtailed.

The substantial displacement of homemakers during the global era presented the second of the two most profound instances of the displacement of community by economy in all of history. (The first had come in traditional hierarchical societies as serfs abandoned subsistence farming to take paying jobs or start businesses in free cities or societies that welcomed them.) Women's full-time homemaking constituted valuable communal activity outside the formal economy. Large numbers of national-era homemakers had also been able to devote considerable time to community outside the family, including its oversight. That too was substantially abandoned.

Two different family patterns contended for dominance from the 1960s. The first was the nuclear family in which there were committed marriages, and, especially in Europe, committed, long-term, nonmarital relationships – for they were rare in the United States.

Many such informal pairings were lifelong. Where children were present in this nuclear-family pattern, mothers of young offspring tended to stay home and care for them for a time and to return to work when able. A considerable number of mothers in this pattern remained outside the labor force for longer periods, some through most of their children's school-age years. The committed nuclear family became one in which both partners tended to work full time, whether or not they had children.

A variation of the committed nuclear family during the global era was the gamer family. Amid strong instrumentalism and high rationality, the tone of spousal interaction in such families was often more that of a fast-moving executive committee than of traditional community. Both spouses having had formative experience in extremely competitive employment, a high degree of calculation and negotiation often also came into these relationships. Yet the great majority of the era's gamer marriages were not only stable but productive and caring relationships in which highly developed human beings helped bring out the best in each other while sharing life's ambitions, joys, and sorrows. When they had children, to the extent to which these alarmingly busy parents were able to spend time with them, they tended to hover over them, ambitiously guiding and instructing them in mature ways while nervously leading them through carefully arranged developmental experiences.

Having abundant resources, nannies, tutors, caterers, gardeners, and other paid service providers gave such families major assistance. Unfortunately, the gamers often postponed childbearing in the interests of career advancement for so long that only a brief window of fertility remained, as a consequence of which, along with their intense consumerism, these talented, accomplished young people tended to have low fertility rates.

Another overlapping version of the global era's committed nuclear family was the blended family in which each partner brought children from previous marriages or relationships into the new union. These compound families could present dynamic mixes that offered rich opportunities to everyone, but they could also be undermined by tensions with former spouses or frictions with stepchildren. Another overlapping variant was the rise of the non-traditional family of committed gay or lesbian partners who lived and sometimes raised children together. These and other non-traditional family types could be loving, fruitful, and challenging.

For increasingly many in global-liberal societies and especially in the United States, a second basic family pattern arose in which relationships were uncommitted, haphazard temporary pairings. Where children were present in them, the pattern comprised female-headed families. This alternative family type was typically characterized by overworked, fully employed mothers who partly ceded child raising to daycare and public schools and partly left it to chance. These parents could give considerably less time and care to their children than parents in committed nuclear families. The distribution of the uncommitted family pattern had a strong inverse correlation with education, overwhelmingly found in the United States among those without college degrees and especially among those with no more than high-school education. As the nontraditional family was on the rise, so was the "nonfamily" of unrelated adults living together. As the square footage of homes went up, they all too often became empty and barren.

The family was so disrupted and weakened in the United States that child-raising suffered dramatically. With less time, energy, care, and supervision devoted to them, most children were less well socialized. The socialization of self-control particularly suffered. Many studies show the presence of the father in the family to be especially vital to the socialization of boys.[246] Boys acutely need male role models and the weight of two-parent authority in the family. So much undercutting of the American nuclear family took place during the global era that the nuclear family could be said to have been slowly disintegrating as the extended family disintegrated during the early- and into the national-liberal era.

153

From Dating to Hooking-up. Relations changed between unmarried men and women every bit as much as they did in the family. The dominant pattern in the United States during the national era had been one in which dating led to courtship and relatively early marriage and childbearing. The global-era pattern during college years became one in which pools of young men and women socializing together while forming sexual unions predominantly within the group, sometimes leading to long-term relationships and marriage but far more often not. Within these groups, young people were often direct and nonchalant about arranging no-strings sexual encounters referred to as "hooking-up." These liaisons reflected no commitment between partners.[247] Addressing the matter of caring for the other in sexual relationships, Natalie Krinsky asked in her autobiographical novel *Chloe Does Yale,* "When was the last time you hooked up with someone who respected you, much less loved you? High school?"[248] In Kathleen Bogle's research, young women in particular, who usually preferred relationships with substance and commitment, were often distressed at the pattern. Some on campuses dated, but they were outside the mainstream.[249] After college graduation the dominant pattern shifted to dating, although hooking-up in fleeting encounters continued for some.[250]

The prevalent pattern of interaction between unmarried men and women with no more than high-school education was also hanging out and hooking-up. These encounters sometimes led to continuing relationships and marriages, but progressively fewer of the relationships or the marriages were committed and stable. Relationships among the unmarried with less than college graduation became more like the pattern of underclass meaninglessness that comes up below. Hooking-up and adult-singles scenes at both ends of the social scale were among other things manifestations of impoverished community. The extent of premarital sex on U.S. campuses or elsewhere was not what struck one but rather its casualness and how soaked it often needed to be in alcohol. Hooking-up was not a prescription for stability of subsequent family life.

The Gamers Apart. American society became sharply more segregated by class and especially educational class during the global era. Even as racial and ethnic segregation declined, the segregation of college graduates from non-graduates nearly doubled.[251] Robert Reich referred to the phenomenon as "the secession of the successful."[252] Led by the gamers, the well-educated and affluent were pulling away from the middle class to live among like-minded others in cities like New York, Washington, Los Angeles, San Francisco, Houston, Austin, Seattle, and Raleigh-Durham. They were segregating themselves into regional, metropolitan, and neighborhood lifestyle enclaves, clustering "in communities of sameness, among people with similar ways of life, beliefs, and in the end, politics."[253] Any middle-class visitor to Manhattan, Georgetown, Bethesda, Palo Alto, or Beverly Hills who was able to put aside the obvious signs of wealth would know immediately that he or she was separated from much that they saw by a sociocultural chasm. This phenomenon paralleled the retreat to like-minded others that had occurred in the social media. In separating geographically, the gamers and to a degree the upper-middle class became increasingly isolated from and began knowing less about their fellow citizens.[254] As people became estranged from each other, their communities balkanized, and vice-versa.[255]

The Underclass Apart. Another social class also began sharply differentiating and separating itself from the middle class from the mid-1960s – the underclass. The underclass is comprised of those without discipline and order who overwhelmingly made up the bottom of the U.S. population by income, occupation, and education. Banfield describes the members of the underclass as "radically improvident."[256] They have short-term time horizons, and their work habits are sketchy. At the other end of the spectrum from savvy gamers, those in the underclass stumble from crisis to crisis with nothing more than the schemes or whims of the moment to guide them. Finances, housekeeping, and nutrition are chaotic in the underclass while substance abuse is rampant, and neglect and mistreatment of children are widespread. Only the most haphazard discipline exists around underclass children, who may or may not attend school and may or may not return home at a reasonable hour. Friendship is shallow and fleeting in the underclass – indeed the haphazard, episodic relationship might better be termed *companionship.*[257] "The only cement for personal relationships" in the underclass "is the need and desire of the moment, and nothing is stronger but more fickle than need and desire unshackled by obligation."[258] As Murray puts it, "Underclass is not a synonym for poor or even for disadvantaged.... [It is] millions of people cut off from mainstream American life. They are not cut off from its trappings (television and consumer goods penetrate everywhere) but are living a life in which the elemental building blocks – productive work, family, community – exist in fragmented and corrupted forms."[259]

Adults who fail to acquire self-consciousness and self-control dwell predominantly in their short-term interests or desires, which is to say, these least-developed character types in global-liberal societies became members of the underclass.[260] The ego-dominant wing of the underclass are incessant, amoral hustlers on behalf of their interests, as continually conceived and reconceived ad hoc. Without presence of the superego, the autonomous ego has a free reign of grabbing and cheating. Where the ego dominant hustle incessantly, the id dominant are more subject to the emotions and desires of the moment. Where the ego dominant tend to be streetwise and manipulative, the id dominant tend to be feckless and lazy. The former are drawn toward a life of crime, while the latter are drawn more to a life of dependency on one form or another of welfare. Increasingly many men (but not as many women) were turning to casual employment, indolence, and lives of irresponsibility in place of sustained work and family life during the era, their egos or ids respectively

Even as a great deal of economic progress was being achieved in the United States, the underclass tripled in size to approximately 10 percent of the population between 1960 and 2016,[261] while the two deciles above it, those in the working class, were increasingly touched by it as were those in the marginal middle class. The United States had the largest underclass of any first-world country during the global era. Its expanding underclass drew disproportionately from black, Hispanic, and Native Americans, though increasingly from white Anglos as well. Black men began withdrawing from the labor market already in 1965, a time of booming economic expansion and abundant opportunity.[262] The underclass was about 70 percent minority during the mid-1980s, another booming time in which minorities made up only about 17 percent of the population.[263] Notably, the underclass in the United Kingdom was predominantly white. Sam Shepard's plays depict the underclass and near-underclass among inept, unreliable, and miserable white Americans, while Dalrymple's books examine their British counterparts – broken people carrying enormous loads of confusion and disturbance.[264] Such films as *Streetwise*, *Bombay Beach*, and *Christiane F.* poignantly depicted the lives of adults, youths, and children trapped in such patterns in the United States and abroad.[265] Unwilling to get along in the economy or in orderly social life, the members of the underclass tend to be as battered and wretched as they are disruptive for others.

None of the main groups at the bottom of society had been as separated from the middle class during the national era as the underclass became during the global era. The urban, lower-lower class, the national-era pre-cursor of the underclass, was small, and its difference was less pronounced, its fecklessness less thoroughgoing, its segregation less complete, and its alienation less extreme than became the case with the underclass from the mid-1960s. Some northern black ghettos were beginning to approach full, large-scale underclass disorganization between 1945 and 1960,[266] but they were not there yet. More of the bottom decile during the nation-al era had been composed of the good but naïve and helpless traditional poor, over-represented in such places as the Mississippi Delta and Appa-lachia, who struggled to comprehend and cope in a modern world that was impinging upon them. More of it had also been occupied by earnest unskilled workers who tried hard to get by under difficult circumstances. By contrast, those of the global-era underclass lost their caring and fell outside the bounds of morality.

If the underclass is essentially made up of those who lack a superego, the working class is made up of those whose superego is weak and have mixed success in restraining the ego and id. The working class became an unstable battleground terrain with some presence of a superego but not enough to consistently apply discipline. The middle class made up the fourth through the eighth deciles from the bottom, between the broad upper-middle and the working class. Those in the working class were of-ten either high-school dropouts or graduates, while those in the under-class were typically dropouts. Like the former peasants of the early-liberal era, the workers of the global era tended to divide into those able and those unable to get a grip, and the latter were slipping toward the under-class. On the other hand, many who labored with their hands, who by traditional rather than character-based criteria would have been consid-ered working class, were becoming disciplined and orderly and are better viewed as middle class.

Yet, as the underclass was recruiting from the working class, the latter was recruiting from the middle class. Both had been less distant from the middle class during the national era when the recruiting was predomi-nantly upward.

In order to grasp the coming apart that occurred in the United States during the global era, it is necessary to look at the full range of major class divergences and convergences taking place. First, as the gamers arose, they displaced the small, exclusive upper class of the national era. Second, the underclass began absorbing the relatively constrained urban lower-lower class, unskilled working-class poor, and naïve rural poor of the national era. In becoming underclass, those at the bottom escaped from middle-class constraint and influence. What essentially happened was that this country went from being a relatively harmonious three-class society in which the top and bottom classes for the most part paid respect to and deferred to the middle class, to being a querulous, three-class society in which both the top and bottom were antagonistic toward the middle class and it toward them. This transformation brought an immense reduction in societal integration and major decline in societal performance. The nature and implications of these class changes emerge more fully later in this chapter and in the following one.

Community in Europe and Japan. Informal social life remained relatively strong in large parts of Europe between 1965 and 2016, although it receded overall there too. Europeans were more alert to the value of community than Americans and less willing to relinquish it for careerism and consumerism. Club membership remained comparatively vibrant in the United Kingdom. All over Europe, cafes, pubs, trattorias, espresso bars, and public parks drew large numbers of people out to socialize. Especially on weekend evenings in many Italian cities people of all ages dressed up to promenade for hours near and around piazzas and other central locations, greeting each other, chatting, and milling about with friends and acquaintances. Most Europeans were glad to participate in the multi-leveled communities around them, although many Muslims dissented from those communities and turned exclusively to their own. The flowers ubiquitous in Europe (as in Canada) exuded a spirit of communal celebration. Less developed traditional forms of community little known today in the United States such as clientelism also survived, albeit in decline, in Italy's Mezzogiorno, Spain's Andalusia, and other Mediterranean regions.

Yet Europe's generally persisting strength of community was not reflected in greater strength of traditional family than in the United States. Marriage rates fell markedly in Europe, from 8 per thousand in 1970 to 4.5 per thousand in 2010 as opposed to 6.8 per thousand in the United States in 2009. During the same 40-year period, divorce rates doubled from 1 to 2 per thousand in Europe while they reached 3.4 per thousand in the United States. During the twenty years from 1990 to 2010, non-marital births in Europe more than doubled from 17.4 to 37.4 percent of all births.[267] Rates of divorce generally remained lower in Europe than in the United States, but rates of never marrying and of childlessness were higher across the Atlantic.

Where the United States had more whose family formation was haphazard and underclass-like, Europe had more who consciously chose to live in nontraditional arrangements. Many Europeans cohabited in stable, monogamous pairs in which a surprisingly good climate for raising children was maintained. Although nonmarital births increased sharply, many more fathers of nonmarital children in Europe remained in close contact with and supportive of their offspring than in the United States. Overall, cohabiting European parents showed distinctly greater commitment to each other and their children than did their American counterparts.

Many European governments provided extensive state support for families with children, as they did for community generally. European fathers were routinely given and routinely took paternity leave, for example.

On the other hand, at far below replacement, Europe's fertility rates were the lowest in the world, along with Japan's. This "birth dearth" introduced disequilibrium into the age structure and created massive drag on economies and societies. France, where most non-immigrant children became nonmarital, launched family legislation that included the extension of generous parental subsidies and rights that applied irrespective of marital status or citizenship. As a result, that country was able to restore fertility rates to replacement levels, if only with the help of immigrants' heavy utilization of the policies. Viewed narrowly, immigration was a source of communal and familial strength for Europe in some respects, for immigrant community remained stronger than native community in all but a few European countries. But, viewed broadly, it introduced a destructive communal clash between Westerners and Muslims. Neither continuing sources of communal strength nor influxes of it offset the overall weakening of European community.

The dominant pattern of premarital relations in Europe over the global era was starkly different from that in the United States. European young people tended to have series of more exclusive relationships. The early ones usually did not lead to long-term partnership or marriage, but they tended to be relatively caring and meaningful, and they entailed a certain commitment. Europe, in keeping with its more intact community overall, encountered relatively little of the American commodification of sex followed by hardly wanting to say hello the next day, or of the general edge of shallow and raw unfeeling about which many of the young and not so young in the United States were unhappy.

Like the United States, Europe experienced a growing underclass, but it remained small there. The exceptions included the United Kingdom, whose underclass reached 5 percent or more of the population; and some portions of the former Soviet empire, such as Romania, Moldova, and the Baltic enclave of Kaliningrad.

Japan's community remained much stronger than that of the West, even though it too was both receding and changing in form, especially in the younger generations. Nevertheless, rates of divorce more than doubled in Japan.[268] That country retained a prominent shame mechanism that upheld standards of conduct rooted in strong community, although with each postwar generation it too was receding. Hyper-concern with people's regard for others, known as *face*, correspondingly decreased in importance. Japan's longstanding protection of rice farmers from competition was one example of its extensive preservation of traditional community.

Community in the Liberalizing Third World. Liberalizing third-world countries also increasingly developed social marketplaces, and wholesale disruption of the village, tribe, clan, and extended family was taking place. The movement from subsistence communal farming and crafts to a money economy had long been complete in the most developed countries, but it continued in the third world. Many third-world cooperatives formed during the national era, such as Mexico's *ejidos* (with communal/cooperative ownership of land), were driven under or sold off and transformed into profit-making enterprises. As the subsistence economy was receding, and the vibrant community of traditional life was collapsing, former peasants were migrating in vast numbers from villages into cities all over the third world. The uprooting of traditional community left people in more exposed circumstances although the nuclear family generally remained at least moderately strong in the third world, aside from some cities.

Caste, the distinctive overarching structure of India's communal relations, remained strong there, if less so in the South, but it was weakening as a prescribed source of occupation.[269] Intermarriage between castes was also increasing, especially in the cities. Yet 74 percent of Indians still expressed disapproval of inter-caste marriages in 2006 and 72 percent supported allowing parents the final say in their children's marriage partners, although with marked urban-rural differences.[270] Voting with one's caste was pronounced in India. "Sanscritization," in which the lower castes imitated the lifestyles and ritual requirements of the higher castes, was also occurring even as the higher castes sometimes moved on to less traditional concerns.

Community in China and the Muslim World. Community remained surprisingly strong in China despite the massive disruptions brought by Mao's Great Leap Forward of the late 1950s and Cultural Revolution of the late 1960s and early 1970s. It also did so despite the booming economy that drew vast numbers into protracted hours of employment or into migration within the country for jobs, and despite the politically sponsored construction projects that dislocated families, neighborhoods, and sometimes towns or cities without regard to people's livelihoods, often without recompense. Family ties remained particularly strong in China even though the one-child policy, in effect from 1980 until partly rescinded under Xi Jinping in 2013, was traumatic for them.

The social markets were stifled in most Muslim countries during the global era in favor of coercively protecting and supporting robust traditional community. Their hierarchical regimes imposed isolation from the rest of the world and directed severe legal discrimination against those who were different. The traditional suppression and sequestration of women were perceived as integral to the continuing strength of community under the Islamic Resurgence. The widespread support for suicidal murder to advance the faith in the Islamic world was a telltale indicator, reminiscent of imperial Japan, of intense strength of community and weakness of social markets.

WHY THE SOCIAL MARKETS AND COMMUNAL DEVASTATION?

How Did Diversity Undermine Community? The United States and other liberal societies developed social marketplaces in part because, thanks to global capitalism and the accompanying economic growth and technologies of transportation and communication, the scope of the world to which people gained regular access became vast and varied. New technologies enabled diverse people and communities to come into close contact. Bitter experience at home and abroad of the dangers of coercive hierarchy also led people to support the social markets and encourage those of different races, ethnicities, and lifestyles to live and work side by side.

Yet, in keeping with the creation and destruction that all kinds of markets entail, if much was gained, much was also lost in accommodating this enormous human variation. More than a century ago, Simmel wrote perceptively about the ways in which life changes as large numbers of people of varied cultures and lifestyles are brought together in urbanization: They become blasé, reserved cosmopolites, somewhat alienated from

161

others and indifferent to the stimulation, while tending to feel lost and lonely.[271] Urban agglomerations continued to grow, multiplying these effects even as their diversity was increasingly joined by that of virtual cities as well, for the electronic media and especially the web greatly intensified the chaotic-exotic effect of urbanism.

The global era's remarkable encounter with social markets, difference, and diversity brought astonishing freedom and tolerance; but also left many estranged from others in their countries, cities, neighborhoods, and even families. When people agree about a great deal, it is easy for them to identify and feel a sense of community with each other; when they agree about little, affiliation becomes difficult. Community was severely disrupted around great sociocultural markets where vast diversity arose in huge cauldrons of mixing. Often no longer able to feel understood by and comfortable with many who were around them, people pulled back in their attachments, weakening community. As Émile Durkheim compellingly establishes, deep differences within communities and families tend to afflict people with profound feelings of separateness and loneliness.[272] An aching sense of social isolation accompanied global-liberal societies' extensive unbridged differences.

Community was also devastated by the shattered moral consensus that left it unprotected. The many who were well disposed could no longer count on civility in public spaces, or even sometimes their safety, from those ill-disposed. Diminished informal social control in the name of tolerance explained a good deal of why people often became jumpy and kept more to themselves and others like them when in public. Most of those changes were generational, associated with people who came of age after 1965, as they succeeded earlier generations.[273]

The bohemian moral uprising under way during the 1950s was closely associated with rebellion against and withdrawal from traditions of broad communal participation. The beatniks withdrew from the mundane public sphere, hanging wry or long faces amid the good cheer of the time. The 1960s generation greatly expanded that withdrawal. Estranged socially and morally from the middle class, lifestyle revolutionaries wanted little to do with the larger community whose ways and values they regarded with contempt. As is more fully explored in the next chapter, many moral standards that once reinforced community and the family no longer did.

Most of the impoverishing effects of global capitalism on community came indirectly, through changes it worked upon character. Exposed to more instrumental relations than ever before, people became more oriented to self-interest and less to intrinsic appeal.

They more often met for power lunches, less often for simpatico. Because economic markets so strained the genuine, a degree of hardness came to characterize many on the job, in the labor markets, and in their personal lives, that would have shocked and saddened their mid-century predecessors. The hyper-rationality of the gamers threw off community much more than had the modest rationality of the shopkeepers, independent craftsmen, and small farmers of the early-liberal period, or that of the protected white-collar employees of the national-liberal period. Weber and Theodor Adorno's references to the nullity of emotion engendered by modern business were far more apt during the global era than they were during the national.[274] Gary Becker's economistic assumptions about rational calculation in human action were not only no longer extreme but often patently germane.[275] Camaraderie, friendship, family, and civic involvement all suffered under the extreme salience of the economic.

In addition to picking up instrumentalism at work, people absorbed it via shopping and advertising. Imperious capitalist marketing's capture of wants dramatically intensified economic motivation. Ever-present, glamor-soaked media images of a life made more desirable by appealing goods and services became irresistible, drawing people away from almost everything else to dedicate their lives alternately to working and shopping. The experience of having been chronically misled and gypped by cynical marketing ploys hardened consumers and made them tough minded and critical. Lifetime recipients of every high-handed merchandising, advertising, and financial manipulation frequently ceased treating each other with gentleness and trust. Such harshness in everyday life further undercut community.

Increased individualism and decreased collectivism also weakened community, for individualism is complementary to and supportive of markets as collectivism is to hierarchy. Where protected national capitalism fostered the moderate collectivism and regard for the commonweal of the national era, wide-open global capitalism produced much of the global era's greater individualism. Immersion in non-economic markets and isolating media also promoted individualism. As global-capitalist economic growth occurred, society was unable to keep up with the changes; and damaging social lag occurred in this country and the world. Where the economic markets had had their longest and most rapid runs, the communal disruption was most acute.

That contemporary conditions were so difficult for community, often leaving it with insufficient resources to initiate or maintain itself, was why

163

the task of sponsoring community, whether face-to-face or mediated, increasingly fell upon economic entities fostering it for their own purposes. Thus, the dating services, newcomers' organizations, and planned company social activities that were proliferating. Confined as it was in time, setting, and aspect of life, no wonder friendship often became shallower and shorter lived.

Why Did Mediated Sociality Become So Prevalent? Mediated community became so extensive primarily because capitalist technological advance brought unforeseen possibilities. Potential demand for the new forms of community had long been there, and as supply caught up with some of that demand, consumers leapt to make use of it. People could still be sociable in overwhelmingly unmediated ways during the national era because technologies were not yet sufficiently developed to easily and inexpensively allow them to travel or communicate when apart.[276] The question of why mediated community increased largely reduces to an economic one that has already been answered, namely why the new technologies of transportation and communication arose. As people interact more through electronic devices and less through face-to-face engagement, their abilities, skill sets, and ways of perceiving, thinking, feeling, and acting also change.

Why Was the Family Devastated? Diversity strained the family as it strained community generally. Broad social peace is more easily achieved in liberal societies amid diversity than are the happy relationships between spouses or among other family members that constitute foundations of thriving community. Maintaining marriages became more difficult in part because starkly different character profiles, yet negligibly reconciled, were often coming together. It is challenging for combinations of gamer and middle class, democratic and authoritarian, idealist and realist, moral and amoral, and other personality types to adjust to each other in close relationships. Becoming more independent also led women to strongly form their own political views, widening the gender gap and aggravating disagreement between spouses and partners, as among friends. The global era's increasingly mixed marriages, by character, political persuasion, and ethnic and religious background made it more difficult for couples to achieve and maintain close harmony.

Even where difference diminished, the conditions of global-liberal societies could throw relationships off balance. In earlier times women had tended to be more emotional and men more instrumental and rational, but after millennia of reconciliation, this opposition in gender relations had been substantially overcome in the traditional, complementary though hierarchical manner that was no longer appropriate. Their profiles may have converged in this respect as women approached men in instrumentalism due to their intensified economic experience, but adaptation to that global-era metamorphosis of character was not easy from either side.

Coming to terms with a changing power balance between men and women was even more difficult. Women fought for and obtained, in many areas, equal rights and equal opportunity. They came to exceed men in educational attainment and to equal or exceed them in economic potential, self-confidence, and social power. Most men became more democratic figures at home, less authoritarian and more approachable by their partners and children, but many men were also slow to adjust to this new reality and had difficulty abandoning their traditional patriarchal status and lingering sexism. Many women were no longer willing to accept this, resulting in a good deal of relational conflict and increased divorce. Only among the well-educated was the opposition between men and women largely overcome, with men's expectations realigned and decision-making relatively democratic within relationships. This success occurred in part because college graduates were more likely to be adept at working through conflict and in part because they were more exposed to and imbued with liberal culture and informal norms supporting gender equality.

More materialistic values also played a role in weakening the family. Among other things, the entry of homemakers into the labor force, advanced everywhere in the first and second worlds during the global era and well under way in the third, was a ringing endorsement of economic goals and forsaking of communal ones. From the 1960s a woman was widely regarded as more successful in life than her mother or grandmother when she had dispensed nurturant services impersonally, for a salary, and on a large scale that her forebears had conferred voluntarily upon their family and community. She was more esteemed still if she coolly dispensed financial, legal, or consulting services.

Yet moral decline contributed most to the global era's disruption of the family. Many more people than during the preceding era simply no longer cared or only minimally cared about others. Among those who still cared, many adopted relatively untested and often hazardous new "moralities" that invite further damage to community, often with good intentions. When established morality was no longer accepted or was only accepted selectively or when convenient, it became difficult to count on others, with the result that community suffered, and especially the family. In an increasingly amoral society, people became bruisers and the bruised, making them less likely to give of themselves or to trust. Having been taken advantage of by the carnivores, even those with good hearts became tougher and more self-protective. An appalling but revealing joke I overheard one Hollywood screenwriter telling another in Los Angeles in 1994 went, "Do you know how they say 'F--- you!' in LA? ... 'Trust me!'"

The familism paradigm prevalent in the United States during the national-liberal era dissolved through the 1960s, 1970s, and the following decades, greatly stressing families and marriages in all communities. The nuclear family of the 1950s had strong moral support, and considerable resources and time were channeled into it – "togetherness" was all the rage. The youth culture that was already beginning during the late 1940s and 1950s and came into its own during the late 1960s greatly undermined traditional family norms.[277] Self-indulgence or "expressive individualism," as many term it, reacted against and substantially replaced familism. Efforts to support the nuclear family under the social conservative banner of "family values" were ambivalent, retro, contested, and little able to replace the departed familism – *retro* because stylized, defensive, nostalgic attempts to wish thriving traditional families back into existence without the secure, centered middle class or intact, supportive consensus that were the keys to the national-era social nexus.

The moral slippage that began steeply accelerating during the late 1960s as rebellion set in against traditional normative authority, centrally concerned sexual activity. As David Popenoe puts it, "left culturally unregulated, men's sexual behavior can be promiscuous, their paternity casual, their commitment to families weak."[278] Men's vulnerability to disruptive sexual yearnings and their insensitivity to the needs of society and community in the absence of effective consensus led them to seek more sexual partners, postpone and avoid marriage, divorce more frequently, have fewer children, and neglect the ones they had. A consensus no longer supported the family by socializing and enforcing strong personal morals in young people or by buttressing male allegiance to the family. Without such outside moral support, frictions and trials between spouses became much more difficult to surmount. The irresponsibility released by disordered mores brought a series of reverberating effects that importantly included women's reactions to the new conditions.

As men and women pursued their desires with diminished account-ability, women frequently fell victim to circumstances and bore the brunt of the direct, painful consequences of unwanted pregnancies, abortion, and single parenthood. Moral decline and especially the growing unreli-ability of men fundamentally altered the situation of women and prompt-ed much, though not all, of their exodus from full-time homemaking into the world of work.[279] Global-era American feminism grew out of these experiences. Many of the changes that led to the empowerment of women from the mid-1960s were consequences of hard knocks received in the economic and social markets. Single and divorced mothers frequently had no recourse but to enter the labor market off balance while raising children alone. In order to hedge against this vulnerability, young women and their parents quickly realized that they had to be as prepared as men for the labor force. What followed was also realization that along with in-dependence a career could bring unexpected satisfaction. Women, like men, were now prepared to go it alone if necessary. The wholesale aban-donment of homemaking as a career was for the most part forced upon women by the actions of men. Overemphasizing other, secondary sources of this change put a happy face on what was a moral *fait accompli*.

Moral disorder had consequences for the socialization of children as well. Amid moral discreditation, divorced and single parents were often less able to maintain authority over their children or to use well the at-tention and resources they had. Mothers might fill in for missing fathers in many ways, but they tended to have particular difficulty doing so when it came to disciplining teenagers and especially teenage sons in circum-stances of moral complexity.

Divorced parents often spent too little time with their children and then felt guilty about the fact and overcompensated by spoiling them, further un-dermining their self-control. Being fearful of losing contact with their children also often put such parents in an ambiguous position. Widowed mothers or fathers, who gain sympathy rather than bear taint, present the one catego-ry of single parents that had no exceptional moral difficulty raising children successfully (although they certainly endured human difficulty). Steady, en-gaged, thoughtful, loving, uncompromised socialization of children became less common. Sociocultural reproduction occurred, but it was too often car-ried out, not by parents or dedicated surrogates, but by peer groups and the media, which is to say, by sociocultural markets – and in these, children on their own had disappointing outcomes. Global-era American society in many ways became deeply inhospitable and troubling to children.

But the global era's irresponsibility, which was not the exclusive property of any gender or lifestyle, also manifested itself in other ways than sexual impropriety that undermined the family; including refusal to limit spending, inability to avoid substance abuse, failure to do household chores, unwillingness to restrain inconsiderateness, or stubborn insistence on narrow leanings that could only bring anguish to the other. Spouses no longer felt as committed as they once had to the partners who had given them trust and the children who had been placed in their care. Of greater concern to many spouses than their obligations to the family was the thrill of another sexual encounter or escape from a relationship burdened by difference.

Americans' high-marriage, high-divorce pattern is partly explained by Andrew Cherlin as arising from a combination of their culture's extolling of both marriage and strong individualism,[280] but this explanation needs further development. For the high-marriage, high-divorce pattern is primarily middle rather than upper-middle class. Despite their high divorce rates, middle-class Americans keep marrying at a high rate in part because theirs is a bourgeois outlook entailing comparatively intact religiosity and traditionalism. Amid the tattered community around them, middle-class Americans, deprived of sociality and buffeted on many sides, turned more quickly and sometimes desperately to marriage, in part for company and in part as an island of stability. Yet because the many-sided markets were strong in the United States, Americans were more individualist and less protected by consensus, and therefore divorced frequently. In their individualism they were private, kept their own counsel, and tended not to deeply interchange with others. This marital pattern evokes the "gladhanding" that David Riesman lampooned in *The Lonely Crowd* in 1950.[281] The high-marriage, high-divorce profile goes with the bourgeois superficiality that, then as later, manifested itself in relatively shallow friendship. In their market-forged optimism, global-era Americans were venturesome in relationships as they were in business.

What Played Havoc with Meaningful Nonmarital Relationships? The hooking-up pattern between young men and women on college campuses and beyond was largely a joint function of three conditions: First, when society and character become extremely instrumental and rational, informal sociality tends to mean less to people – thus the cold manipulation of this thin form of communal interaction. Second, hooking up was a function of the enormous social power conferred on young men by unbalanced sex ratios, which reached 3:2 overall, women to men, among undergraduates. These circumstances placed young men in a monopolistic position – women could deal with them or do without male companionship. The asymmetry of male-female relations was intensified by the fact that men's biological clocks were ticking at a slower pace than women's; they thought of marrying and having children several years later than women.[282] In the resulting "battle of the sexes," young men and women tugged and negotiated in the social and moral markets over whose needs were to be met and whose not.[283] A good deal of this shortage of men came from greater male dysfunctionality. Third, hooking up also arose from the fact that some of the more immediate and dire negative consequences of combining promiscuity and excessive alcohol intake were reduced in the socially selective and safer, summer-camp-like settings of residential college campuses. Thus also, part of the reversion to dating prevalent after college. That marriage occurred later in life explained much about why there would be more premarital sex than in the previous era but little about why hooking up became the dominant form of sexual encounter between young people.

Many serious, young college graduates wanted to find worthy spouses and therefore moved into dating relationships for that reason as well. The greater mixing of ages in the work world conferred some initial respite for women from the college sex-ratio imbalance, giving them access to older and more mature men. Yet male dysfunctionality in time also created sex-ratio imbalance in the post-college population. Much of boys' educational lagging went back to the more damaging effects of family instability on the rearing of boys than of girls, since that instability mainly took the form of absent fathers. The effects were cumulative generationally and led to further deficits of responsible parenting and supervision, especially on the part of men. The proportionately greater slippage of men in the non-college-graduate adult population had even stronger effects in the same direction.

A major source of this sex imbalance was also that boys were being chewed up and needlessly discouraged in a female-centered educational system more out of sync with boys' than with girls' Piagetian timetables. Primary-grade pacing and curricula were weighted toward the needs of girls by educational institutions overwhelmingly dominated by women. Boys have plenty of natural ability, but most boys mature more slowly. The Finns prioritize social-emotional adjustment, respect boys' timetables, extend low-key preschool play years, and then seriously accelerate performance expectations later. In no small part as a result, they had among the best educational outcomes in the world. Boys aged 5, 6, and 7 needed to be running in schoolyards and playing much more than they were, and not shackled to inappropriate academic expectations and left needlessly discouraged when young.[284] Everyone would be better engaged and society's interests better served by more balanced pacing and curricula, boys especially.[285] However well intentioned, the incessant, nervous pushing of young children by gamers of both genders aggravated this condition. Alienating boys from education harmed their development and weakened their economic and sociocultural resources as adults – no conspiracy here, just the usual, banal obliviousness to the other.

It is seldom noted that the bulk of the sex-ratio imbalance in college attendance by gender came not from the upper-middle and middle classes but from the working class, or that disproportionately much of this imbalance came from minority males.[286] Working-class and especially minority boys encountered greater family disorganization than middle-class white-Anglo ones and were therefore less well positioned to recoup from discouragement in school. Multiculturalist blame worsened the disadvantage by wreaking havoc upon working-class minority machismo. Such undesirable economic, social, and moral consequences as men's diminished labor-force participation, family formation, college attendance, and suitability as partners for accomplished young women flowed from educational discouragement early in life.

Why Did the Gamers Pull Away? The gamers and to a degree the upper-middle class pulled away from the middle class partly in order to celebrate life with similar others and avoid the abrasion and alienation of unresolved difference. The classes were not yet so different in character and lifestyle during the 1950s and early 1960s. Once respect for and consideration of the middle class dissolved amid broken consensus and difference too great for easy, comfortable interaction, the gamers began withdrawing into narrow lifestyle communities, migrating to regions, cities, and neighborhoods with concentrations of like-minded others in order that they could more easily and happily form communal relations and find economic and cultural opportunities. Bringing their increasingly distinct worlds with them, the gamers pulled away in search of their own unity and coherence, even while loudly extolling difference. Local homogeneity gave them more fertile ground for developing communal relations and shared culture.

As to the timing of the separation, Murray says, "Two conditions have to be met before a subculture can spring up within a mainstream culture.

First, a sufficient number of people have to possess a distinctive set of tastes and preferences. Second, they have to be able to get together and form a critical mass large enough to shape the local scene ... in 1963 there was still no critical mass of the people who would later be called symbolic analysts, the educated class, the creative class, or the cognitive elite."[287] The sociocultural division of the late 1960s prepared the way for the separation of the gamers, as is more fully explained in the next chapter. Ten to fifteen years later, global capitalism began coming into its own, producing the character in numbers sufficiently large to break away. The critical mass of gamers jelled during the 1980s.[288]

Why the large, national-era middle class came apart into these two classes is ultimately because society went through another epochal development as radical as that presented by the unfolding of the superego during the late Middle Ages and its consolidation during the Reformation. In the 13th, 14th, and 15th centuries, those with middle-class discipline found it increasingly difficult to accept the institutional arrangements of posturing aristocrats and simple, id-dominant peasants. The middle class had much higher expectations than either of those classes regarding an orderly life, and its members did not feel comfortable with the leanings of those classes. Nor did members of the other classes feel comfortable with the leanings of the bourgeois. Nearly a hundred years of religious wars came out of that profound difference before an exhausted Europe began to settle into partial coexistence after 1648. Wrenching conflict between the classes and the character types and structures associated with them, although diminishing, continued in various forms through the defeat of the Axis powers in World War II.

The global-era tension between the gamers and the middle class rested upon similarly profound differences of experience and character. The gamers' perception of their fundamental difference was neither gratuitous nor spurious. Their distinct character and the conditions out of which it arose were the foundation of this new class divergence. In liberal societies, people who are as fundamentally different from each other as the gamers and the middle class do not easily get along in marriages, friendships, or neighborhoods. A bumper sticker I saw on numerous cars in Berkeley leading up to the 2008 presidential election read, "Friends Don't Have Friends Who Are Republican." America's upper class of gamers was having increasing difficulty recognizing or acknowledging the humanity of the middle class.

Education was increasingly important to how people fared in the social markets primarily because education is largely about learning how to negotiate one's way through the sociocultural markets. It consists of absorbing facts, interpretations, theories, philosophies, aesthetics, and skills regarding the sociocultural and natural worlds, of learning to be critical and creative in coping with them. Society was no longer coherent in any simple, straightforward manner. If people were to discern even moderate coherence in it and become able to move through it fluently, they had to possess considerable critical facility and knowledge. If they did not, they had little hope other than blind faith in a worthy religion, and even then, there were confusing currents to sort out and choices to be made.

Aside from levels of education, the more extensive a community's historical experience with diversity, the better its members were prepared to cope with the social marketplace. Jews, owing in part to their exceptionally cosmopolitan experience, were particularly well equipped to deal with difference. By contrast, communities that were sheltered from difference were particularly vulnerable to disruption. Those of provincial backgrounds often took serious drubbings in the sociocultural markets when they slipped away from their moorings.

How Did the Underclass Get Away? Much of the global-era expansion of the underclass and its growing separation from the rest of society arose as a consequence of the sociocultural markets. As these markets intensified and spread, traditional peasants' idyllic worlds and groupbound moralities collapsed in all but the most backward corners of the world, for the id dominant are utterly needful of tight traditional community and the accompanying sense of shame to enforce social order and moral ways. Peasants and their offspring had been protected for millennia in traditional hierarchical societies and still to some degree in middle-class ones, but refuge for them vanished all over the world under the gamers.

Workers were affected similarly. As the sociocultural markets strengthened, the vibrant nuclear and extended families, neighborhoods, church communities, and substantially groupbound moralities also largely collapsed. Those institutions, often ethnic, had played an important role in stabilizing them through the national era. Without reliable self-control, workers had tended toward some disorderliness in earlier American history, but solid community supplemented by social support and pressures, had generally kept them and their families intact and their children adequately socialized.[289]

The sociocultural markets and tolerance of the global era scrambled working-class community and family, leaving workers badly exposed.

Simple character that had sufficed under the conditions of previous eras became woefully disadvantageous in the global era, contributing greatly to the expansion of the underclass.

Disproportionately much of the underclass phenomenon was associated with minorities possessing limited sociocultural resources such as education and family networks. First- and third-world underclasses included many migrants and their offspring from traditional societies or corners of society who were unable to consolidate rational self-control in the sociocultural markets, and whose lives were upended into chaos. In the United States, blacks from the rural South, Mexicans from the central highlands, and whites from the Appalachians and Ozarks were exposed to the stresses of cosmopolitan diversity in comparable ways. In his memoir *Black Boy*, Richard Wright referred to his father as a peasant who had not made it in the city.[290] Such migrants either achieved self-control, or they slipped into the underclass.

The underclass phenomenon frequently came not from the first-generation migrants of modest sociocultural resources, who had been armored by self-selected venturesomeness and their inheritance of coherent traditional ways but, surprisingly, from their children, who were born in chaotic new settings and had neither sufficient traditional nor sufficient modern resources. Although often themselves protected, the first generation of humble migrants seeking opportunity was unable to assure that its children acquired the discipline and education they needed to succeed in a wide-open society. Upper-middle- and solid middle-class migrants and their children, who possess greater sociocultural resources, had few such problems. The unusually strong community of Asian immigrants better protected its offspring than most, although the less developed Laotian Hmong among them did not fully escaped these problems in the United States.

Nor were those who remained behind in rural areas any longer spared similar trials. For example, in 1965 many in northern New Mexico's remote Rio Arriba County with its Spanish colonial roots still possessed traditional, peasant-like earnestness and simplicity; but by the end of the era comparatively few did. Much of the earlier id dominance was overcome by movement into the middle class, but much of it also turned into underclass fecklessness, indolence, scheming, and attitude. Many Native Americans and Canadian First Nation peoples were in comparable condition. Dynamic and turbulent societies like the global-era United States, Mexico, and Brazil were merciless in the sociocultural challenges they posed to the less able; whose richly textured routines, villages, neighborhoods and extended families no longer existed. The more wide-open the sociocultural markets and more extreme their ethnic and lifestyle mixing, the more these markets worked their disorder.

A great deal of how the sociocultural markets contributed to an expanding underclass was through family disorganization via its impact upon morality. The hard edge of underclass disorganization was rarely found where stable two-parent families were present. Much of the national era U.S. lower-lower class was transformed into the underclass beginning in the 1960s as their families became fractured and unreliable. The middle and working classes were eroding as well. Elizabeth Marquardt *et al.* find that the "disappearance of marriage in Middle America [was] tracking with the disappearance of the middle class in the same communities ...."[291] The dramatic increase in the number of unattached, adult males out of the labor force in the United States was intimately related to the devastation of the family, both as cause and as effect. As the family disintegrated, the underclass recruited, especially among men with only high-school education or less.[292]

Family disorganization was extreme in the black community, but its situation was not unique. Most of its problems were but advanced forms of those increasingly present in other groups as well.[293] Black-American family structure fell apart earlier and more completely than that of other groups in part because blacks became sharply more vulnerable to the sociocultural markets as they migrated into cities during the early and mid-20th century.[294] William Wilson's well-known explanation of the black female-headed family as resulting from male joblessness conveys part of the story.[295] More at fault was that single parents were seldom able to work at a career and raise children well. When children are raised poorly, they have fewer resources to bring to school, employment, parenting, and families of their own, initiating a downward spiral. As in other communities, moral decline and male irresponsibility led to undependability as husbands and fathers, and a generation later to higher rates of dysfunctionality and joblessness. As enabling partners and mothers, women played large roles in these problems too. Accelerated disintegration of the black family from the 1960s was a far larger cause of comparatively low black achievement than lingering prejudice or discrimination. Where blacks form stable families, their incomes approach those of whites. The median personal incomes of blacks who were married and living together during the two decades from 1992 through 2011 were 91 percent those of whites who were married,[296] not bad considering the differences in education. When family structure is controlled for, the enormous differences in crime rates between blacks and whites also disappear.[297]

The robust family and community of Asian Americans and to a lesser degree Hispanics brought them corresponding advantages. From the 19th-century beginnings of their immigration into the United States, Asians utilized strong community as an asset with which to steer group members toward opportunities in business, employment, and education.[298] Their well-earned achievement, attested to by almost 25 percent higher household incomes than non-Hispanic whites,[299] was grounded in the strength and stability of family and community. The weakness and instability of family and community among black Americans, in addition to manifesting itself in family disintegration, did so in a damaging paucity of the social networks through which jobs could be obtained.

The underclass was able to greatly expand and evade middle-class order in large part because of multiculturalism's pervasive negativism that made it difficult for minorities in the United States to find their way. When people busy themselves denying, justifying, or blaming others for their predominantly home-grown chaos, low school performance, low labor-force participation, low income, and high crime, they are not taking responsibility for and resolving to improve themselves. Squarely facing inadequacies, accepting responsibility, and resolving to do better are what everyone must do in life. Bad-faith, defensive denial of the poor performance of disproportionately many blacks with respect to family responsibility was a bedrock distortion of black culture under multiculturalism. Black Americans did better during the global era where their numbers were small, and particularly well in Wyoming where they were exceptionally small,[300] because they were insulated there from the root cause of their problems, the self-fulfilling, black culture of negativism and blame. The analogous negativism that destabilized marginal whites in Britain was the anti-class rhetoric that was already building after the war and reached a crescendo during the 1960s and 1970s.

A related reason for the growth of the underclass during the era was the great expansion of counterproductive welfare programs, also driven in no small part by multiculturalist blame. Life on the dole in its scores of proliferating forms encouraged dependency, fostered helplessness, and underwrote irresponsibility. The excesses of the welfare state worsened the condition of most of its putative beneficiaries and increased the scale of the underclass by removing or diminishing the lessons of the real world. In slack, chaotic settings, the size of the underclass is regulated to a considerable extent by the number of welfare slots made available. The welfare reforms of the 1990s pushed many in the underclass into the world of work, moving them toward discipline and order. President Obama's executive abrogation of those reforms in 2012 reversed this course and accelerated downward slippage into the underclass. Meliorism without tough-minded controls and accountability is a formula for decline.

The condition of the underclass is often referred to as one of poverty, but that interpretation is at once superficial and co-dependent. Essential about those in the underclass is that they lack self-control, a deficiency that bars their route to the middle class, which is one of diligent application at work and in family life. What all too often lies behind their lack of self-control is that those in the underclass have been persuaded to blame society for their troubles. That tragic negativism renders them unwilling to try to do better. American society is hardly to be judged responsible for the lack of will brought on by a multiculturalist framework that became ascendant precisely as equal rights were substantially achieved, or for the inability or unwillingness to form families. All that the vulnerable often needed to nudge them into a downward spiral around powerful and confusing sociocultural currents was exposure to spurious blame, eligibility for the dole, or access to drugs.

Psychiatrist Theodore Dalrymple refers to Britain's worst poverty, as Americans should to theirs, as "poverty of the soul."[301] The income and opportunities of those labeled poor were ample for developing themselves and building a secure future, but those were options they all too often declined. The material want of those in the underclass, such as it was, was overwhelmingly the product of their indiscipline and attitude. The problem of the underclass was within, not without.

The underclass also expanded and got away because the tattered consensus since 1965 allowed it to. Increasing residential and social segregation by class and lifestyle removed role models and agents of middle-class moral enforcement from those most vulnerable. The Wilson thesis presents an instance of this: As the black middle class fled the ghettos, the more concentrated lower class left behind, without the needed models and consensus enforcers, slid downward.[302] The same principle holds in other groups. Yet much of that exodus was motivated precisely by the need to escape endemic nuisances and immorality brought about by the prior removal of sociocultural and legal support for consensus. When combined with the underclass's conflictualist rudeness and high crime, the gamers' radical relativism and extreme civil liberties have made life around the underclass intolerable to the middle classes of all groups.[303] Largely under the banner of social justice, American society came apart during the global era from a big, almost universal middle class into a trifurcated society in which both ends were pulling away from a weakened middle, harassing it as they went.

Why Did Community Remain Stronger in Europe than in the United States? Europe was better able than the United States to preserve community in part because it curbed the economic markets to a greater degree. Largely for that reason, Europeans were more collectivist and less individualist than Americans, to the benefit of community. Among Europeans the British, Netherlanders, and Swiss were supportive of the economic markets and tended toward greater individualism. Nevertheless, the growing force of the economic markets in Europe considerably eroded community and increased individualism during the global era. European societies' historical insularity and comparative harmonization also contributed to their retention of relatively homogeneous and strong community. Community was more off balance in this country because it had undergone great geographical mobility and the chaotic mixing of diverse peoples.

Europe's shielded exposure to capitalism was responsible for its greater stability of families and relationships in particular; its generally more extensive state intervention in support of the family, parenting, and community was part and parcel of its extensive retained economic hierarchy. These conditions, together with the decline of Christianity and mildness of middle-class repression, enabled Europeans to experiment with new communal forms without such destructive outcomes as in the United States. The European pattern of sustained relationships as opposed to the American of greater flux, stemmed from less exposure to the economic markets, more collectivist personalities, and deeper and more profound engagement with close others. European men's and especially working-class men's better integration into society and adjustment to family life than in the United States also arose from the region's greater sociocultural harmony and lesser alienation and conflictualism. Long having been less religious, even as they maintained generally more intact community and consensus, Europeans were able to support less unhealthy alternative lifestyles.

The small size of Europe's underclass owed in part to its stronger community and consensus as well as to its notably restricted immigration until the late 1980s and early 1990s. Its underclass expanded after that as less developed immigrant populations grew in response to liberalized immigration laws, relatively lax welfare policies, and the onset of multiculturalism, in a context of social permissiveness. Stronger European community also posed barriers to the acceptance and integration of the newly arrived that were not as present in the United States. This country's more disrupted community and consensus helped allow it to better take in and assimilate the large immigration it experienced. On the other hand, Europe, until recently, did a better job of integrating black immigrants because its black population was small, diverse, and included a large proportion of well-educated international students. Japan's policy of nearly closed borders played a major role in keeping its community exceptionally strong and homogeneous.

Why Was Community Strong but Vulnerable in the Liberalizing Third World? The liberal culture accompanying global capitalism had a tiered impact on the third world, much as it did in the first world, and this differential impact depended upon the cultural power of the various traditions. Societies that encountered the treacherous sociocultural markets from the 1960s with at least the resources of mature traditional hierarchical societies, including well-established high cultures and world religions, had greater potential for adapting in an orderly way than societies which did not, facilitating their retention of coherent community. Most of Asia was on relatively firm ground while processing the sharply different Western cultures to which it was exposed,[304] but societies that never reached the mature traditional hierarchical stage and thus lacked important sociocultural resources were often unable to digest and manage an orderly encounter with the sociocultural markets, or, for that matter, to effectively resist them. Unable to find their balance, they tended to lapse into chaos following sustained impact. Where many did not have the indigenous resources with which to digest what they encountered, as in sub-Saharan Africa, the sociocultural disintegration was far reaching, and underclasses formed to the extent permitted by economic slack.

India's persistent, though diminishing, strength of caste and community was in keeping with its impressive sociocultural heritage and the continuing relative strength of community in the third world. For strength of community is inversely proportional to the intensity of the economic and sociocultural markets and the duration they have been encountered. That is part of why caste is weaker in urban than rural areas. Caste underwent more erosion in the more developed South because India's openness to the economic markets, though late, was more advanced in that region.

Even mature traditional hierarchical societies with world religions were unbalanced by, and fairly helpless against Western society and culture until the global era. Only when their will and discipline were newly fortified by exposure to the global markets, were most from the stronger traditions able to adapt socio-culturally. Where the economic and socio-cultural markets had been seriously curtailed or had only recently begun to open up, more respite existed for coherent community and the less developed people who depended upon it.

Why the Strong Communal Patterns in Authoritarian Societies? China's community remained considerably stronger than that in the West during the global era because of the country's long hierarchic tradition, the recency of its controlled tolerance of the markets, and its relative sociocultural homogeneity. Nevertheless, economic growth and the Deng regime's highhandedness regarding the effects of its policies wreaked considerable havoc with community in China. Vast internal migration broke and upended community. The one-child policy also disrupted community, conferring significant power on the only children within and weakening authority in families. Yet China was pointed toward communal devastation comparable to that in the worst Soviet and Rumanian areas, where the problem was nihilist totalitarianism's stripping of traditions, and demoralization. Though diminishing traditional poverty continued under the Deng regime, a formidable tradition, economic realities, regime policy, and strong consensus blocked nearly all underclass formation.

Community remained far stronger in Muslim societies during the global era than in most others owing in part to restricted capitalism and economic development. The political authoritarianism and weakness of the rule of law and civil liberties in most Muslim countries also permitted stern consensuses to violently enforce tradition, drastically curtailing sociocultural mixing. All of this was grounded in the Islamic Resurgence's profound authoritarianism and barring of openness and tolerance.

The closed, strictly patriarchal, sociocultural matrix of most Muslim societies, which included the prevalence of highly authoritarian personalities, at the same time fostered ceaseless factionalism and conflict – vis-à-vis those of other religions, other Muslim traditions, other states, other tribes, other warlords, and other clans, as well as against Israel and the West. Outsiders, whoever they might be, were scapegoated as shifting groups of insiders were brought together amid the rejection of reconciliation. Pakistan's bitter ethnic, sectarian, and regional rivalries exemplified this endemic strife. Under the Islamic Resurgence, it was forever "us against them" in an ongoing culture of violence. Among many other consequences, this conflict further strengthened community, in its fractured way. Even the most developed Muslim societies did not escape the seething discord.

Regarding the Era's Changing Community

The global era's new forms of community rooted in emerging technologies held much appeal and even more promise. They were extremely convenient and hugely engaging while allowing effortless, instantaneous reach all over the world. The intensity with which people kept up with hundreds of friends on social websites was remarkable. Yet such mediated community took time away from more meaningful, direct, person-to-person contact with family and friends, and those immersed in it also lost a good deal of the give and take and ability to reconcile that come with face-to-face relations. The sociality that the new technologies supported had little of the vibrant palpability of face-to-face communication and none of the serene contemplativeness of letter writing. Some heart may be taken, however, from the fact that technological change has been swiftly moving toward higher-capacity communication able to support fuller, less intrusively mediated new forms of sociality.

Stressed community was the inevitable concomitant of global-liberal societies' extraordinary economic and sociocultural development, but the ensuing effects on community needed to be watched and managed based on the model of how some of the most developed societies were mitigating environmental impacts. As Switzerland's environmentally friendly tunnels and bridges protect mountains and forests, preserving hillsides that would often have been bulldozed in the United States or China, social policies needed to be as careful as possible with the community they affect. Community is at once fragile and resilient. When damaged, it returns, but like an alpine meadow, it does so slowly. That the economic imperative succeeded brilliantly during most of the global era was most beneficial, but community needed to be encouraged and nurtured as well, especially the family. Let us now take up the morality of the era, keeping in mind among other things its implications for community.

CHAPTER 7

Embattled Morality

The Coming – and the Consequences – of the Wide-Open Moral Markets

*T*he Moral Revolution and Moral Markets. Global-liberal societies witnessed sweeping revolutions against their reigning moral consensuses during the late 1960s and early 1970s.

The sociocultural uprisings of their first decade shattered large portions of the existing moral hierarchy and replaced them with far greater competition in the moral markets, indeed with moral *laissez faire*, in which many different moralities competed openly for acceptance. This wrenching upheaval brought great moral diversity to the United States. (By morality in this chapter, I most often mean in the sense of particular ethical forms, the concrete norms, virtues, or ways reigning or not reigning in people's daily lives; but I sometimes mean the degree to which actions or patterns contribute to the long-term well-being of society as a whole, which is to say, absolute morality.[305])

Much of the 1960s generation abruptly underwent wholesale lifestyle change, adopting the wide-open, anything-goes "new morality" of the time. If people did not care for a norm or virtue, they were frequently able to find another more to their liking or drop it altogether.

Large portions of the established moral order were overthrown, leaving what remained of right and wrong and virtuous and vicious, weak and confused. Many whose character and conduct had been held exemplary under the previous order ceased finding them considered such. As uncertainty arose regarding what rules to follow and whom to emulate, many of the traditional moral ways came to seem arbitrary and confining and were cast aside. By the mid-1970s, large portions of advanced global-liberal populations had gone over to various countercultures. A good deal of the moral variation everywhere apparent had been there all along and had simply come out by then, but much of it was also new. Americans gained enormous freedom to conduct their lives as they saw fit and won respect for their lifestyle choices so long as these did not infringe upon the rights of others.

There were numerous harbingers of the moral revolution of the late 1960s and early 1970s. The illicit drug use of the early 20th-century jazz music scene in large American cities adumbrated and approached it. James Dean's visceral resistance in *Rebel Without a Cause* and provocative slouch in *Giant* also anticipated the moral uprising, as did Lenny Bruce's uproariously foul and biting comedy routines and one-man guerrilla war against censorship and puritanical moral order. *The Man in the Grey Flannel Suit* ridiculed the white-collar conformists of the 1950s, and *MAD* magazine spewed out universal irreverence to its young readers. Above all, the intensifying bohemian tradition, the American branch of which was concentrated in New York, San Francisco, and a few other large cities, reached new levels of public awareness during the beatnik movement of the 1950s. Jack Kerouac, one of its most influential voices, sang comprehensive moral rebellion and abandonment to the senses in his novel *On the Road*. The movement's charismatic literature, music, and lifestyle flourished, reaching further into the populations of liberal societies than had any previous alternative expression, before subsiding. The strands of rebellion wove in and out of each other.

Many university students participated in civil-rights protests in the South during the summers of 1963 and 1964. When they returned to campus, those from Berkeley organized demonstrations and sit-ins protesting discriminatory practices at various Bay Area businesses. The Free Speech Movement was sparked during the fall of 1964 when the University of California administration attempted to block the organizing of illegal protest activities from the campus. Many of the same young radicals then directed the methods of nonviolent protest they had learned in the South against the university administration. The U.S. student movement which spread from that beginning played a key role in the moral revolution. The movement soon began demanding greater personal freedom as well. University administrations dropped most *in loco parentis* regulation of students' lives within a few years.

After a short interlude during the early 1960s following the waning of the beatnik movement, a buzz of excitement began to stir around Ken Kesey and his circle in Palo Alto and nearby La Honda, California. There, many of the anarchic new cultural patterns of the hippie movement, including experimentation with psychedelic drugs, spontaneous art forms, and alternative lifestyles, were being created to little notice from 1963 to mid-1965. In late 1965, this vibrant new expression of long-simmering moral rebellion went public and began swelling into a mass phenomenon. The scene moved up the peninsula to San Francisco where human be-ins and new sorts of music concerts began taking place. Talented rock musicians, including Big Brother and the Holding Company, the Jefferson Airplane, and the Grateful Dead, created the new forms and became key disseminators of the hippie package of sex, drugs, and music. During January 1966 the nascent movement and era reached an initial crescendo as television networks gave it feverish attention, and news magazines blew it up into cover stories. That winter, a full-blown counterculture came into being.

From across the country, youth began flocking to San Francisco to experience the new rage. By that summer, Haight-Ashbury and the nearby panhandle were filled with colorfully dressed, grinning, anarchic, drugged-out hippies. The movement expanded dramatically as the mostly middle-class pilgrims began scattering back home, forming colonies as they returned. From its peak in San Francisco during the "summer of love" in 1967, the movement diffused to receptive cities, university campuses, and rural pockets all over the country, but most densely on the two coasts.

Long-haired and often barefooted, the hippies were naïve sociocultural revolutionaries who opted out of school and work, openly flouted traditional norms and virtues, and advocated peace and love. Yet there were so many of them, and their music and lifestyle were so charismatic that large numbers of young people all over the United States and beyond came under their spell. They had little of the beatniks' intellectuality, but precisely that helped them achieve the wider appeal that had eluded their predecessors. With large portions of a whole generation in bohemian moral uprising, there was little the flabbergasted custodians of the old order could do in a liberal society but grudgingly tolerate them.

Thus began the revolution to dismantle the traditional, Protestant, middle-class morality and replace it with a marketplace in which many different personal moralities were offered for the choosing or rejecting, and little was mandatory. Since the late 1960s, within broad limits, individuals have largely been free in the United States and other developed liberal societies to set and follow their own personal morals or none at all. As Fred Siegel puts it, the sociocultural changes of the 1960s amounted to "moral deregulation,"[306] or in Daniel Patrick Moynihan's famous phrase, they amounted to "defining deviancy down."[307] Already by the 1960s, liberals were defending a wide range of traditional vices against moral authority. Within the minimal new limits, no way of life was deemed too outrageous to be practiced or even put forth as a model. By the end of the 1990s, acceptability moved all the way to consenting sadomasochism, and "spanking" became something that could be talked about on national television in an approving, albeit gingerly, way. Society witnessed a libertarian avalanche extending tolerance and rights to nonmarital sexuality, homosexuality, pornography, abortion, gambling and, increasingly, marijuana use. Even witchcraft and Satanism became practices that people had every right to pursue. Moral permissiveness became sufficiently extreme that discovering how little was left against which to rebel sometimes made those bitten by the impulse to negate quite desperate for new targets. The unrestricted free access to moralities prevailing in the West and increasingly elsewhere exceeded even the unusual moral diversity and tolerance of the Roman Empire. The moral hierarchy of the national era both limited and protected people – they have been on their own since.

Impelled by the earlier example of racial protest, several prominent categories of moral dissidents withdrew from and ceaselessly contested the old moral consensus from the 1960s, becoming aggressively uncooperative with it. Many illicit drug users justified their indulgence by maintaining that they were responsible or moderate users or that what they did was no worse than consuming alcohol or tobacco. Numerous moral entrepreneurs and their supporters pushed beyond demanding toleration toward demanding full acceptance or even toward essentially declaring the once deviant as ideal and the once moral as unacceptable. A striking early example occurred when organized homosexuals hijacked the word "gay" in all its youthful radiance to adorn themselves. Single parenthood not only became accepted by many but was sometimes extolled by celebrities and often by bottom-half teenagers. Refusing opprobrium, the moral dissidents demanded the moral and legal rights to conduct their lives as they would, and they won them.

The countercultural revolution against the established consensual regime was often conducted as moral guerrilla warfare affronting the middle-class moral sensibility. Its tactics, frequently ingenious, outrageous, and effective, ran the gamut from hair length and grooming patterns to foul language, leering innuendo, and flagrant, mocking violation of traditional norms and virtues. The word "queer" was first banned as offensive to gays, and then adopted by them to flaunt their difference and highlight the injustice of their past and continuing mistreatment. The moral revolution was palpable in such phenomena as the exaggeratedly effeminate action of some gay men, parralleling the exaggeratedly ethnic action of some minorities. The bourgeois were harassed by radical transgressions of censorship under the cover of art,[308] as they were by humorous transgressions like streaking and "mooning." Much of the moral war was fought obliquely, as through appeals by the young to peers behind the backs of adults. Negating the traditional consensus and pushing toward a minimalist new one, the unabashedly different employed radical anarchist stunts to counterattack rather than quietly allow their actions to be derogated and their choices limited. The underclass contributed more than its share to the moral uprising through sullen resentment, disrespect, and refusal to work or lead stable family life.

The rhetoric of moral uprising featured the combative use of skepticism and debunking, often on behalf of moral laissez faire and often on behalf of that labeled wrong or vicious. The status quo ante was attacked as priggish, narrow, middle-class, authoritarian, discriminatory, and hypocritical. Heavy irony was a staple trope. Wielding radical relativism, the multiculturalists redefined moral judgments as "'judgmental' and 'moralistic,' [while] to engage in moral discourse became to 'preach' and 'moralize', and to pronounce upon moral affairs became to wage 'moral crusade' or, worse, 'religious crusade.'"[309] After decades of onslaught, Himmelfarb found American "moral language denoting outrage debased and disparaged."[310] Along with in-your-face parading of difference by those once labeled immoral, conflictualist stonewalling was a prominent feature of the contest. The putatively and/or truly immoral no longer acknowledged being such any more than did tyrannical political regimes – they fought back ferociously and dangerously. Foucault combatted those who would look askance at him as did the Kim regime of North Korea. Here, as elsewhere, multiculturalism brought a negational, conflictualist *modus operandi*.

In the process, personal moral issues came to be conceptualized largely in terms of justice toward particular lifestyle groups, of their implications for interested social groups rather than for society as a whole. Some even took the reappraisal of much that had been labeled deviant in the past circularly as evidence for dismissing ethical judgment altogether. Judgment on matters of substantive private morality was often viewed from the mid-1960s as itself vicious and morally offensive, quite a feat for skepticism. Such extremes of relativism were reached that parents sometimes were not even allowed to feel comfortable raising their children under one creed or morality, out of holy deference to the radical-individualist and radical-relativist notion that all sides ought to be heard and the person to make up her own mind. Some may have dropped out of the economy, but many were dropping out of the community and consensus. In the manner of philosophical skeptics, the radical relativists usually had moral views but were elusive and sketchy about them.

Global liberalism brought vindication and legalization of much that had previously been forbidden, albeit in varying ways and to varying degrees. From the 1960s laws regarding private personal conduct were substantially revoked or their enforcement suspended.

Gambling was increasingly legalized and accepted. State lotteries began spreading widely in the 1960s following New Hampshire's lead. Casino gambling spread to Atlantic City in 1976, Biloxi in 1980, and the Mississippi River from 1983.[311] From the 1980s, states allowed Native Americans to build casinos on tribal lands, and these enterprises prospered overall and rapidly proliferated. Illicit drugs in general remained illegal, but there was substantial erosion of disapproval and decriminalization of cannabis use. Pornography in all but a handful of extremely repugnant forms such as child pornography became legal and readily available over the Internet and elsewhere.

Not surprisingly, the incidence of norm violation and vice by traditional standards increased markedly from 1965. Deviance as socially constructed during the national era had not been unusual, but in most categories it was relatively tame and discreet, while in certain others it had been off-limits, at least to all but those in restricted circles. Now by the traditional labels it became widespread and blatant. For example, during the 1930s, illicit drug use was largely the possession of a few bohemians and isolated enclaves in the lower class, aside, that is, from the medically addicted. Drug use increased rapidly during the 1960s and early 1970s, reached peaks in the mid-to-late 1970s, and later returned to approximately the level of 1970, which, with comparatively minor ups and downs, held afterward until the major upticks late in the era associated with legalization.[312] Personal lives chaotic to the degree depicted in Hemingway's *The Sun Also Rises* or Kerouac's *On the Road* now became common. Edmund Burke's worst fears concerning moral chaos are not the half of what became everyday reality more than five centuries into modernity.[313]

As the simultaneous backdrop and metaphor of society's fractured moral consensus, asylums were closed in the late 1960s and early 1970s and the mentally ill abruptly discharged into group homes and/or turned loose on the streets. Ambulatory schizophrenics raw from dumpster-diving now jabbered and barked at pedestrians while panhandling for the illicit drugs and alcohol with which to alternately engage and flee the demons of their cracked poetics. Rendered politically feasible by advances in pharmacology, the new policy issued from an unlikely coalition of civil libertarians and fiscal conservatives. Never mind that the psychotic frequently sold or declined to take medications, or that their prescriptions were often askew. Civil libertarians were also instrumental in dismantling or ignoring previously existing laws governing public nuisances such as vagrancy, loitering, begging, and disorderly conduct; not to mention littering, public urination, and the theft of supermarket carts. The combination of shuttered mental hospitals, liberalized interpretations of disability, and tolerated disruptive conduct installed endowed choruses of madness and disorder in U.S. urban centers and to a lesser extent those of other global-liberal societies. Inhabiting bedlam, the global era's urbanites needed greater income for purchasing insulation from the underclass.

With consensus largely gone, decisions were more often made and enforced by means of politics and power and less often on the basis of consensus and respect.[314] Relationships between parents and children are an arena in which consensus weakened and politics strengthened, for children were frequently paid or otherwise rewarded from the late 1960s to do chores they once would have been persuaded to do with moral force. Relationships between teachers and students became more instrumental in a similar way as behavior modification rather than moral authority became the default means of maintaining classroom discipline, and medication increasingly supplemented it. The weakening of consensus was such that people often found it less uncomfortable to walk out of relationships and friendships than to work through difference or to finesse and tolerate it.

The United States and other liberal societies increasingly relied more upon legislatures, courts, and police through which collective decisions were mechanically produced and enforced, and less upon earnest conversation toward agreement. Larger-scale consensus had been forged spontaneously in the past. When achieved at all during the later decades of the era, it was more often engineered by large economic and political interests and contrived by PR firms operating much as advertising agencies would to mold household product demand. Decisions tended to be reached via negotiations between those directing blocs of controlled opinion.[315] As citizen political involvement declined, "the number of political organizations, partisan and nonpartisan, with regular paid staff ... exploded...." Impersonal "letterhead" organizations, such as AARP, having "more in common with mail-order commercial organizations than with old-fashioned face-to-face associations," were examples.[316] In an era of weak consensus and power politics, the operative rules tended to be legal and the prevailing norms and virtues fewer and thinner.

The Norm of No Norms and the Consensus Remaining. Consensus has not disappeared in the area of personal morality, but what is left of it has been transformed into a much thinner, more restricted, and more abstract one than was in force during the 1950s and early 1960s. The new moral consensus, such as it is, above all emphasizes the need for the inclusion and tolerance of difference, in lifestyle along with race and ethnicity. What largely prevails today is Isaiah Berlin's weak rather than strong consensus, in other words, that in which the moral markets rather than moral hierarchy are respected.[317] In its radical relativism, this new consensus endorses a code of "no norms" whose sole commandment is that there be no explicit moral evaluation other than the minimum transparently required to sustain a liberal society. Thus, the libertarian moral rule that action not be judged unless it objectively interferes with other persons or their property. Denizens of global-liberal American society tended to abstain from judgment in the area of personal morality. Nearly everyone agreed upon being much less hemmed in by moral standards – which is to say, they substantially accepted the moral markets. Personal morality has not simply weakened and thinned in the moral marketplace but has frequently been supplanted by the indignant rejection of any authority whatsoever. Tolerance of difference was the extolled virtue and intolerance the loathed vice during the global era. The law followed suit, largely withdrawing from the area of private morals.

Yet the acts of everyday kindness among families, friends, neighbors, and co-workers – if fewer than 60 years ago – provided evidence not of blanket amorality or immorality but of embattled morality withdrawn to restricted zones of safety and caring, in what has become for many a divided and troubling world. As they have often no longer thought of themselves as part of a larger society so much as members of ethnic, lifestyle, or other groups, most people's zones of caring have receded. Their moral concern has diminished along with their joining.

Moreover, if the ethics of personal conduct has become a wide-open moral marketplace, that specifically pertaining to physical or psychological injury and property damage to others has in many areas witnessed strengthened consensus since 1965. For example, it has become even more strictly forbidden than it was in the past for one to lift a finger against a spouse or partner in anger. Sexual assault and rape have become more broadly defined and steadfastly opposed by informal norms as well as by the law. Elaborate new norms, conventions, and laws have arisen to regulate on-the-job conduct between the sexes. Using corporal punishment

against children in school or even at home has become socially unacceptable in many cases and frequently illegal as well. Considerable attention
has been aimed toward halting bullying in schools. Much increased pressure has been directed against smoking in general and doing so around
others in particular.

Global-liberal societies also reached consensus that racial or ethnic
prejudice is morally unacceptable and discrimination in any form a serious offense. A new consensus, if uneven and less full, was also reached that
sexism is unacceptable. The kind of sexual harassment that was winked at
sixty years ago, an inappropriate pat on the rear or comment about a woman's body, is now disapproved and less common. Comparable consensus
also arose around the need to respect difference in sexual preference. Although contested peripherally, consensus arose as well regarding political
correctness: Which topics may be brought up and attributions of fact and
causation communicated having even quite indirect negative implications
for equality of racial, ethnic, gender, and lifestyle groups. This extensive,
sensitive code supplemented the respect paid to once-disparaged groups.

The Upheaval in Moral Tone. The wide-open, contentious moral markets of the global era were accompanied by a complete upheaval of style.
Cachet was to a considerable extent lifted from the traditionally reputa-
ble and conferred upon the traditionally disreputable, who frequently
became the solicited, respected, admired, and imitated ones. During the
1960s, the upright became "uptight," and everyone was told to "loosen
up" or "lighten up." For many of the young the "grand tour" was no longer
travel abroad but sexual experimentation, drugs, and cross-town low life
in the form of "slumming" that mixed entertainment, illicit substances,
bohemia, and identification with social outcasts.[318] "Bad" became good,
"outrageous" hilarious, and "wicked" virtuoso or alluring. In the era's veritable "emporium of styles,"[319] few were edifying and many not.

For the first time in history the dominant moral style of an entire
society and era rose from the bottom, from bohemians, ne'er-do-wells,
criminals, and the underclass. The dominant style of the national era had
been one version or another of upbeat, middle-class order and neatness.
A mild, secure regime that relatively easily tolerated challenge, it had coexisted from the 1920s on with the detached and ironic counter-style of
cool.[320] *Cool* was for the most part only gently subversive and anti-bourgeois, although for some jazz musicians and big-city sorts it was more
than that. Only incipiently subversive, it pushed the limits of propriety

but tended to do so moderately and playfully. During the global era, cool became radicalized into *hip*, which unambiguously rejects the moral order and inverted its values. The icons of hip from William Burroughs to the Velvet Underground captured abandonment to anarchic sexual freedom, drug use, and negativism. The style of the outs, as in the baggy pants of prison chic, was prominent, while virtue was in short supply. The character of hip was anti-character.

Sinking and Swimming in the Moral Markets. The wide-open sociocultural agoras tossed and churned everyone, leaving the worlds of many fractured and incoherent.[321] Morality and immorality had been clearly defined during the national era, but they no longer were during the global era. The multiculturalists extended respect by transforming those labeled deviant under the old order into victims and directing sympathy toward them. Gays, in all but a few locations, lived in mortal terror of their fellow citizens and the law as late as the 1960s and early 1970s, and still have to be careful in many provincial conservative areas. The sexually libertine or gay or those who divorced, gambled, or engaged in other action traditionally labeled deviant encountered greatly more acceptance and freedom than they had during the 1950s, but many in the middle and working classes who had once felt at home in their societies now perceived chaos and felt anguish.[322]

Nowhere were the moral revolution and moral markets met with greater glee than among the underclass. It was as if tax evaders had been issued rebates. Released from middle-class moral restrictions, drug use soared spectacularly among the disorderly, and the haze of intoxication became their prime state of being. Others who indulged lowered themselves to the same level as they did so. Without either coherent socialization or supportive pressure from family and community, those in the underclass stumbled into every vicious trap posed by the moral markets.

Striking about what happened to morality in the United States was that most young people were seduced into significant wrongdoing or vice during their formative years. This personal experience compromised them, fed the desire in many to justify what they had done, and helped lead them to assume the negational stance of the outsider against their society.

Jaded, many found siding with disorder less onerous than defending or leading an orderly life. Drugs in particular were the perfect experiential wedge between generations and lifestyles. As the baby-boom generation grew older and increasingly attained positions of authority, enforcing moral norms and virtues was particularly fraught for it because of its own past and often continuing deviance.

Middle-class young people's engagement in forbidden sex and drugs during the late 1960s and early 1970s filtered down in no time into the working class, where it wrought immediate communal and moral destruction. As fewer and fewer workers were ensconced in stable families and communities, their accustomed moral adaptation disintegrated. They no longer found the support and guidance upon which they had depended for orderly lives. One thinks of the substance abuse and absenteeism common among blue-collar workers. Drug use, like family disorder, became a much greater problem in the working class than in any other class except for the underclass. Those in the working class found sanctuary scarce.

Understandably apprehensive about the newly pervasive moral tumult, many in the middle class clung to their families, neighborhoods, and religious communities for protection. They too received far less sociocultural support than they had earlier. The moral disintegration and downward mobility among many middle-class young people were particularly shocking.

Initially, conservatives managed little more than a dazed reaction to the sociocultural upheaval of the late 1960s and early 1970s. They were thrown off balance by its suddenness, radicalism, and charisma. Merle Haggard's country and western hit song "I'm an Okie from Muskogee" was a product of the time. For a decade the tide of sociocultural revolution ran effectively unopposed and swept much tradition away, while those resisting the transformation were for the most part confused and quiescent. By the late 1970s, a conservative reaction was at last coalescing, and by the 1980s it was almost able to hold its own, slowing further liberal advance but only for a time. The middle class struggled to hold on to traditional principles and virtues with their now disorientingly uneven moral reception. Insofar as the traditionalists found themselves, they did so for the most part by willfully asserting their morals against the reigning skepticism and chaos. Some rates of disorganization, such as crime and teen pregnancy, receded after the Reagan years, but American society in many ways became radically libertarian. Conflictualists that they are, liberal gamers – including those in, close to, or sympathetic to the media and culture – did not take kindly to the conservative reaction, which was thrown back in the area of morals.

Gay lifestyles were difficult for most from traditional, fundamentalist, provincial, or poorly educated backgrounds to accept, but they increasingly accepted them as the new consensus strengthened. Their substantial recognition of and extension of rights to gay people in everyday life through the early 21st century consolidated this major expansion of the moral markets and represented important reconciliation.

Yet the conservative lifestyle of the global era was not natural and breezy like that of the national era; nor did its middle class muster the dignity of demeanor or aura of the celebratory of its predecessors. For the bourgeois no longer dwelled in a secure moral world – they were embattled. The gamers who occupied the top rungs were of an altogether different temper from the generally sympathetic and discreet members of the upper and upper-middle classes of the early and mid-20th century. Now all too visible were the arrogance, brashness, hipness, and contempt of anti-bourgeois gamers. As the era's middle class struggled to resist the seductive, threatening, and critical presence of the masterly gamers, they were no longer chipper but harried. Shifts from one class morality to another have taken place before in liberal societies, but widespread, significant moral disorder was unprecedented in them.

Moral Decline. The United States underwent serious moral decline from 1965. What I mean is that the actions of large numbers of Americans no longer contributed effectively to the long-term wellbeing of their society as they had during the national era.[323] As Popenoe said, "People no longer treat others as they once did; they no longer feel the same sense of commitment and obligation to others."[324] The concern all too often became exclusively with the self, ignoring or placing far back the needs of spouses, children, friends, neighbors, and fellow citizens. Rates of drug use, welfare fraud, tax evasion, shoplifting, marital faithlessness, and cheating on examinations all increased. Rates of violent crime were down from their highs in the early 1990s due to smarter and more vigorous policing, prison building, and target hardening, not to moral betterment; and those rates were again on the rise by the end of the era. Moral progress continued with respect to a few multiculturalist concerns but little else.

Moral sentiments of social empathy remained, but action based upon them tended to be ad hoc and ineffectual, if not counterproductive. Charitable giving remained comparatively high in the United States primarily because subsidized by the tax code; volunteering, though down, remained as frequent as it did because budding gamers needed to pad their college applications or resumés and the elderly needed to fend off loneliness. The traditional norms and virtues largely fell into desuetude, and few seemed to give any thought to the country as a whole, other than how it might affect their narrow interests or group agendas. After the moral demolition was advanced, a few indeterminate, New-Age platitudes floated to the surface, and moral bits and pieces emanated here and there from fortified islands of middle-class religion and morality, but morality was in shambles. Even as the individual and collective moral casualties continue to climb, it was much of the way back to ethical nothingness. A great deal slipped away in the moral avalanche from 1965.

Moral Consensus in Europe and Japan. Europe's moral consensus also changed, but it remained stronger in most respects than that in the United States. Considerable moral virtue continued to be modeled in Europe, particularly in northern continental Europe. Illicit drug use was less widespread in Europe. Europe remained morally expansive overall, while significant portions of American society tipped into moral reaction.[325] The most notable exception was Europe's Muslim minority, a large portion of which insistently followed its own conservative morality. Yet where Europeans embraced moral reaction, considerable friction arose with the dominant liberals as it did in the United States. Rocco Battagliani was acrimoniously rejected as President of the EU in 2004 over his traditional social-moral values, for example. If less contentious and conflictual generally than their American counterparts, the European upper and upper-middle classes also showed disdain for traditional morality. Europe's relatively few social conservatives were for the most part browbeaten into mildness without much fanfare.

The Japanese consensus, albeit weakened from what it had been during the first two postwar decades, remained exceptionally strong by international standards. Japanese management and politics are able to rely upon consensus to a degree impossible in the West. With relatively little diversity, consensus in Japan was strong enough to significantly limit the moral markets. Japan was distinctive not only for its continuing strength of community and consensus but for the degree to which these were hierarchical.

The Liberalizing Third World. The moral markets were less open in most third-world societies than in the first world. Nevertheless, from starting points of greatly more settled hierarchy, their consensuses underwent extraordinary tumult and were much weakened during the global era. As the moral markets spread in third-world societies, moral disorder radiated out from urban centers. Ethnically diverse societies like Brazil and much of sub-Saharan Africa underwent major disruption of consensus, but the disruption was also advanced in Southeast Asia and throughout Latin America. An especially poisonous demoralization afflicted such countries as Colombia, Mexico, and portions of Thailand in which illicit drug production and trafficking were rampant. Involvement in the drug trade was so corrupting that several Latin American countries became narco-states. By contrast, India's traditional moral consensus remained surprisingly strong, undergoing only moderate disruption during the last 25 years of the era. Nevertheless, incivility of a sort seldom seen earlier began being encountered in that country during the 1980s.

China and the Islamic World. Morally repressive under the Red Guard and Cultural Revolution, China turned somewhat morally expansive under the Deng regime, with its cities in particular experiencing greater play of the moral markets. Informal social control loosened considerably, and the moral markets gained more room.[326] Divorce laws were liberalized, and the stigma against marital dissolution lessened.[327] Although still comparatively low, China's divorce rate increased significantly. Block leaders largely disappeared, going the way of the United States' neighborhood busybodies and France's intrusive concierges. Neighborhood authorities who once held moral sway over family matters and could force couples to remain together against their will, weakened and tended to avoid involvement.

Yet both extended and nuclear family ties remained robust in China, limiting the effects of the moral markets. Chinese families extensively assisted their members but also still controlled them. China became only a little more tolerant of gay lifestyles, for example. A lesbian woman would seldom dare to openly act upon her preference and live her lifestyle in China; for if she did, her family would ostracize her and cut her off from the many benefits it provided. A gay man would not face as much pressure and would have more options, but he, too, would face difficulties. Since connections still determined opportunities and careers in China, if a family or person fell into disrepute, they lost massively.[328] External rather than internal forces kept people from openly challenging the consensus. From long experience living in that country, Fallows observed, "China seems like a bunch of individuals who behave themselves only when they think they might get caught."[329] If Chinese consensus remains relatively strong with regard to the family, it weakened considerably in politics.

Where other societies have mostly accommodated the moral markets and accepted varying degrees of freedom, nowhere was the reaction against the moral markets stronger than in Muslim societies. The Islamic world's moral consensus strengthened and became more authoritarian, suppressing individual choice. The Islamic Resurgence was so intense and the rule of law and civil liberties so weak that violators of traditional ways, norms, and virtues were often summarily dealt violence by the consensus around them. Among the world's large traditions, only in the Muslim world were accused adulterers stoned to death and independent-minded teenage girls regularly murdered or disfigured. Seven-eighths of Egyptians favored the murder of apostates and adulterers.[330] A similar fraction of Pakistanis did.

Islamic societies' traditional consensuses had been rigid enough that Muslims had been spared most other countries' discomfort with proximate moral markets. Their moral regime was associated with extreme personal authoritarianism and intolerance. Fundamentalist Muslims were nearly as violent toward their co-religionists of divergent sectarian persuasion as they were toward non-Muslims. Under Iran's coercive regime, for example, the intolerant rural moral police (the *besaaj*) of humble origins terrorized cosmopolitan, venturesome, middle-class urbanites.[331] The Islamic profile of coerced consensus in the micro arena and severe dissension in the macro was the polar opposite of that in global-liberal societies, while also quite different from that in China.

WHY THE COMING AND CONSEQUENCES OF THE MORAL MARKETS?

The Moral Revolution and Moral Markets. How did the United States, a relatively prudish and parochial national liberal society in its morals, become overnight the most tumultuous, anarchic, and cosmopolitan of global-liberal societies; a stupendous sociocultural bazaar in which everyone had to find their own path among myriads of proffered norms, virtues, and ways? The advent of global capitalism was in numerous ways a factor behind the rise of the moral markets and weakening of consensus. Capitalist economic growth and technologies of transportation and communication made migration and exchange relatively affordable all over the globe, leading to massive sociocultural diversity. Capitalist geographical mobility between and within countries disrupted community, consensus, and morality. The capitalist media delivered floods of content to, from, and about immensely varied societies and cultures all over the world. The much-increased education and personal development made possible by market-driven economic growth also enabled today's kaleidoscopic moral variety.

Since the experience of economic markets leaves more rational-instrumentalism and less emotionality, politics and negotiation now came more naturally than consensus with its appeal to common norms and virtues. That is part of why exhortation was increasingly directed to interests rather than obligations. If appeal to shared commitments is no longer able to bring people to cease and desist from activities that interfered with others, they had to invoke politics and the law, move elsewhere, or continue to suffer. Experience of the economic markets also undermined consensus by increasing individualism and decreasing collectivism. Politics was displacing consensus for reasons analogous to those behind economy displacing community, beginning with increased rationality and individualism from experience with economic markets.

As people withdraw from community under pressure from the global markets, they withdraw from the consensus it bears. By becoming one-sidedly concerned with the economic and working long hours, they sequestered the social influence their less driven and less harried forebears exercised. They had fewer informal social connections to activate and less time available with which to teach, model, monitor, and enforce morality.

Another condition lying behind liberal societies' weakening and changing consensus was the way in which technology and the media displaced the direct human contact that sustains vibrant consensus, interposing themselves between adults and children, friends and acquaintances, and the elderly and everyone else, while frequently bypassing neighbors altogether. As attention turned from face-to-face social interaction to television sets, computer monitors, game consoles, and hand-held devices, chains of direct personal influence withered. Nowhere was this displacement more strongly felt than in socialization, where the sundering of generations and explosion of youth culture revolved around shared experience in generationally segregated media. Cut out of the loop, parents and members of the community were no longer as able to wield informal social power to inculcate or enforce norms and virtues. Mediated human relationships at the same time brought out further individualism, making consensus more difficult to achieve.

A crucial explanation for the American moral transformation lay in the discreditation of established moral authority during the 1960s and early 1970s. The main indictments of the country and its incompletely universalistic white upper, upper-middle-, and middle-classes of the national era were for injustice toward racial and ethnic minorities. Charges of racist beliefs and practices were followed by those of sexism, homophobia, and the suppression and exploitation of third-world peoples such as Hondurans, Iranians, and Vietnamese. As national-liberal societies and particularly their dominant classes were blamed for injustice, much what was associated with them was rejected, making room for a new respect for moral difference.

The racial and ethnic uprisings prompted by that guilty verdict paved the way toward toppling the established moral order. The subsequent extension of sympathy and respect to unjustly treated lifestyle groups opened the doors to the moral markets and their striking diversity of unfamiliar norms, virtues, and ways. Respect for lifestyle diversity rendered the moral markets overpowering.

Understandably annoyed with narrow aspects of the traditional Christian moral consensus, American Jews played an important role in toppling the Protestant middle-class moral order remaining hegemonic through the early 1960s. As perennial wanderers, Jews have long borne and developed the perspective of the outsider. Traumatized by centuries of anti-Semitism, pogroms, and finally the Holocaust, their experience has understandably tended toward acute sensitivity and even jumpiness regarding sociocultural rights. Many Jews have been highly uncomfortable with paternalistic moral concessions made to Christians of modest sociocultural means. They have felt apprehensive about lower-middle- and working-class Christian intolerance in all its forms. Echoing the dismissive, traditional Yiddish "Goyim kaput" (gentiles are all messed up), numerous Coen brothers films humorously express an at once bemused, contemptuous, aggressive, and fearful sentiment of many Jews toward naïve gentiles. Their tendency has been toward distancing and protecting themselves and, more recently, toward supporting other vulnerable groups similarly situated. American Jewish intellectuals, writers, artists, and members of the culture indistry were the leading participants in the diffuse 1950s and 1960s cultural assault on conformity, which constituted one of the major currents flowing into the contemporary moral upheaval. Most American Jews strongly support the moral markets.[332]

Consensus is set back by new encounters and broadened horizons; however desirable these may be for other reasons. Even much of the Maslovian moral growth enabled by the reign of extreme tolerance stressed society by posing additional moral diversity and uncertainty. What Hayek says of political consensus holds for consensus in general: "As the range of persons extends among whom some agreement is necessary to prevent conflict, there will necessarily be less and less agreement on the particular ends to be achieved: agreement will increasingly be possible only on certain abstract aspects of the kind of society in which they wish to live."[333] Reaching consensus anew takes time, conversation, and mulling over.

The epochal but disorienting rise of the gamers lay behind much of the upending of moral consensus and rise of the moral markets. The gamers' irresponsible action and negative example spread to much of the rest of the country, propelling its moral decline. Their radical relativism was a central source of the repudiation of traditional morality and arrival of moral chaos. Lacking a sense of the whole, the gamers declare moral judgment to be arbitrary. In their cynical critique interestedness, politics, and power lie behind every step of the process of moral regulation, from the initial imputation of immorality to its sanction. The higher reflexivity and social constructionism of the gamers outshone the traditional middle-class ethics, greatly undermining moral authority. Of the gamers, cultural gamers in the media, academia, the arts, and popular culture caused much of the grief.[334] Economic gamers did not usually have the same personal stake in potentially disruptive sociocultural patterns. They also more often had to work closely with the middle class, giving them empathy for the latter. Yet most economic gamers fell under the influence of their cultural peers.

Among cultural gamers, intellectuals were a major force opposing the traditional consensus and supporting the moral markets. Their publications and media exposure disseminated rebellious moral ideas through the population. Long experience of sociocultural independence led them to recoil from sociocultural authority. They were autonomous creators in their realm and accustomed to their distinct sort of freedom. Most such creators, for opinions related to their work, had experienced heated attacks from traditionalists seeking to invoke the established consensus, via the media if not personally. Cultural gamers chafed at restrictions on civil liberties, in part out of resentment arising from such attacks, which threatened their beings and livelihoods. The overrepresentation of intellectuals in the media gave them strategic positioning from which to criticize or ridicule the old order and defend the moral markets and counterculture.[335]

Skeptical scholars in the human sciences also undercut the existing consensus and its enforcement by giving powerful support to the opinions of other intellectuals. The sociology of deviance played a leading role in inverting the moral order and declaring the traditional norm-violators victims. Its message tapped deeply into the era's tolerance of and sympathy for the marginal, along with its hesitancy to enforce traditional morality. Sociology dramatically turned its identification from society as a whole to those labeled deviant, in such notable works as Erving Goffman's *Asylums*, Howard Becker's *Outsiders*, and David Matza's *Becoming Deviant*.

Edwin Schurr argued forcefully in *Crimes without Victims* that, when it came to such "victimless" crimes as gambling, prostitution, abortion, and homosexuality, people were harmed not by the illegal activities but by the laws and stigma against them.[336] There was so much truck between many of the sociologists and the purported deviants they studied that their positions often merged with the self-justification of the putative deviants, whom their resources also provided with a sophisticated exculpatory rhetoric.

Modern anthropology's foundational skepticism and radical relativism were also influential in undermining traditional moral authority and opening doors of tolerance. Cultural relativism might have been no more than an analytic tool with which to systematically view varying structural patterns – along with admonition to students of ethnography to be cautious about imposing narrow assumptions and values that might easily be outflanked by reality.

Instead, under modernist, anti-bourgeois impetus, anthropology's cultural relativism developed into an overarching skeptical precept forbidding moral judgment. Its aspiration had been to present the widest possible array of human practices in morally neutral-to-sympathetic tones, tacitly brushing against its own norm of refraining from moral judgment. Anthropology's moral message was so concentrated upon its construction of cultural relativism and so delightfully illustrated with back-from-the-bush zaniness that this small field was punching above its weight and exerting a surprisingly large impact upon global-era morals.

Psychology's acceptance and relabeling of many formerly proscribed actions as healthy also contributed to establishing the moral markets. Freudian and other antinomian schools of psychology undermined the superego and middle-class morality. Thomas Szasz's *Myth of Mental Illness* and other writings were influential. The therapy movement exposed large portions of the population to culture embracing the once forbidden. Its heavy emphasis on feelings undercut moral discipline. The popularization of therapy took its influence far beyond the tiny analyzed group of the national era. Leaguing itself with the id, a great deal of therapy was in evasive, self-indulgent denial of the immorality that brought on many of the problems it treats.

The medicalization of deviance contributed further demoralization. Arguing that medicalization of illegal drug use offered a more effective and humane approach than stigmatization, many physicians and natural scientists came out for the decriminalization of illicit drugs. Conveniently wielding science to dissolve guilt, many of the dissolute ceded blame for their condition to biology, abjuring personal responsibility.

Large numbers of artists and writers also continued the rebellion they have been mounting since the early 19th century, whose chief target was the traditional moral order. Taking the necessary disorder of their own creative progress as the ideal norm for all, they sought to impose anarchy generally. As they became liberated from censorship formal and informal, they too posed grave difficulties for middle-class propriety.[337] Many artists and writers viewed conformity with traditional norms and virtues as anathema and felt compelled to push the limits of moral revolution. Approaching the global era, which was postmodernist in the arts and culture, J. D. Salinger's *Catcher in the Rye* decried the phoniness everywhere present in the bourgeois order; Arthur Miller's *The Crucible* flailed away at Christian moral tradition for witch trials that occurred under isolated, provincial circumstances centuries earlier; and Kesey's *One Flew over the Cuckoo's Nest* declared the ill sane and society a cruel, fascist asylum. Jean Genet and Norman Mailer attributed superiority to the underclass and deviant. Artists and writers' heroes became anti-heroes who broke rules and held out against the moral consensus. Stanley Kubrick's Alex in *A Clockwork Orange*[338] took this rebellion to an extreme, unflinchingly directing random violence amid absurdist hilarity against a society of less than zero moral value. Greater wealth and more auctions and galleries also meant that larger numbers of artists could be supported in alienated bohemian lifestyles. As they had been during the national era, artists and writers were leading moral revolutionaries from the 1960s.

When norms and laws governing personal life began more rapidly liberalizing during the 1960s, those governing the media and higher education also began dramatically loosening.

Where modernist literature had been able to bring a few million quiet, mostly disciplined readers into contact with the rebellious culture of intellectuals, artists, and writers during the national era, providing them a certain familiarity with long-simmering anti-bourgeois ways of thought and life that would otherwise not have been known to them; the mass media exposed hundreds of millions in the West to moral dissent from the 1960s, vividly amplifying bohemian lifestyles. Large portions of a whole generation were won over to alternative lifestyles during the years of the hippie movement's maximum catchiness. Timothy Leary played the pied piper, popularizing psychedelics as the panacea. *Easy Rider*[339] peddled alienation, drugs, and hip lethargy. Media entertainment posed alluring countercultural models for lives of dissoluteness. Marijuana began spreading to middle-class youth from around 1960, but its use only became widespread a few years later as the media began presenting it as hip, essentially advertising it and other illicit drugs. Under the new openness, moral rebellion and the moral markets were supported and disseminated in the media as never before, further weakening consensus. Artists and bohemians had charisma during the national period, but they had been few in number and relatively isolated. Even as true bohemianism was disappearing, artists and intellectuals' way of life was disseminated via the media and accepted by large portions of the public.

Mass higher education, too, exposed large numbers to anti-bourgeois thinking and sensibility, greatly spreading the critical stance that few had possessed earlier, although it did so under circumstances that better facilitated coming to terms with the dissonant sociocultural content everywhere evident than was likely to be attained by those dropped into the media and life less prepared. Intellectuals and artists' cultural influence considerably increased with the great expansion of universities during the 1950s and 1960s.[340]

Capitalist cultural entrepreneurs, who were at once cultural and economic gamers, have had strong economic interests in fanning the flames. The private media rarely hesitated to film or broadcast whatever made money that they could get away with – sex, drugs, violence, baseness, or foul language. Propriety not having sold well, the media presented bourgeois morality as tired, mean-spirited frump. The outrageous captured attention in such television programs as MTV's *Beavis and Butthead*, films as *The Last Temptation of Christ*,[341] and music as gangsta rap. Advertising brought its own interested wedge of demoralization, stirring desire for goods and services by association with abandon, sex, profligacy, or whatever else was profitable. Although every bit as deadly, the ill effects of these cultural products were sometimes no more deliberate than those of the toxic effluent their economic brethren pumped into rivers and the air from manufacturing plants.

The crude manipulation permeating television soap operas and hyperbolic amorality suffusing Hollywood movies, though, often reflected more than that they sold; they also reflected how the industry viewed the world. Those who would make their living fawning to a vulnerable public to its detriment for maximum profit – whether there, elsewhere in the economy, or in politics – tended by initial selection and again by experience to be cynical, those to whom civilization was an oyster to be pried open, cut at the root, and ingested alive. Like the wallpaper in *Barton Fink*,[342] their special moral contribution oozed corruption into all with whom it had contact. The global era's moral disorder was heavily conditioned by the entertainment industry.

How Did Radical Relativism (with Some Exceptions) Become the New Consensus? Relativism became more radical and gained momentum during the civil-rights movement and then sharply more so with the ghetto riots and black power movement as they and their supporters increasingly utilized radical relativism to attack racism. Drawing upon cultural relativism, they appropriately asked who the bigots were, given the immense human variation found all over the world, to think that their narrow construals of reality were any more valid than those of the people whom they demeaned and mistreated. Feminists employed similar arguments against male chauvinism.

A larger source of the era's radical relativism came as the supporters of the traditional categories of deviance began widely and forcefully using analogous arguments against the wielders of moral authority. Their comprehensive moral skepticism left moral authority befuddled and speechless. Brandishing radical relativism, the sociocultural revolutionaries, the gamers, the broad upper-middle class, and their allies trounced the middle-class opposition on all of these issues and left them reeling. As traditionalists were successfully skewered by their talented opponents, skepticism became integral to the global-liberal paradigm. Never mind that radical relativism was inherently negative and devoid of moral substance – it worked for the overriding concerns of multiculturalism's constituent groups. In their socially constructed alienations, the moral revolutionaries, cultural gamers, and allies were in no mood to consider the needs of their middle-class opponents, of children, or of anyone else and temper their skepticism. From their outsider points of view, all that was needed was overthrowing the old establishment and redistributing the social and symbolic benefits. Negativism and conflictualism having been in the air, most of the best educated and credentialed became alienated from and unconcerned with the whole, arrayed against their society rather than with it.

Radical relativism has in large part been about release from moral responsibility. Consciously or unconsciously lying behind much effort to stave off enforcement of the traditional moral consensus was that many no longer wanted to be moral. Since acknowledging this fact was more than most were able to bear or bare, a great deal of blatant sophistry and nonsense filled the air. Saying no to objects of immoral desire is difficult for many, and fewer had the resolve with which to do so. Moral skepticism in large part represented refusal of this reality. If some used the moral markets and moral diversity to move up the needs hierarchy, many more found in them a convenient if transparent justification for abandoning themselves. Since the gamers cared little about what others did or felt, radical relativism both expressed and abetted their alienation and unconcern. In their moral indifference, many found radical relativism convenient. Withdrawal from morality paralleled withdrawal from community.

Why the Upheaval in Moral Tone? A natural home of the dominant hip lifestyle of the global era was the postmodernist nether realms of the underclass and those traditionally labeled deviant, including bohemians, rebellious youth, and dissenting minorities. Particularly vicious versions of the lifestyle were associated with the criminal class.[343] The hip lifestyle emanated from such groups because it expressed the resentful or contemptuous sentiments of those with assorted moral chips on their shoulders. Its supporters bore grudges against middle-class morality – they had attitude.

Hip gained a great deal of cultural power because many of those in whom it was based became a spurious leisure class generating charisma, for leisure nurtures flair. During the global period, this pseudo-elite emanated from those on one form of dole or another, freed from the burden of employment. Having far too much time on their hands, they were able to devote themselves and their underreported, not inconsiderable resources to popular culture and vicious pursuits. In so doing they were able to acquire the catchy styles of speech, manner, dress, and grooming with which to raise themselves to positions of sociocultural influence, facilitating the explosive diffusion of countercultural style. The slack welfare system of the 1960s and 1970s was an infamous source of leisure for large numbers of the disorderly, and many more later wiled away their days on one government pass or another, enabling them to cultivate their manner and charisma. Inmates had nothing but subsidized time on their hands, as did under-challenged, under-supervised, under-socialized, and underachieving youth. During the national era well-socialized middle-class homemakers had the leisure and cultural power, but now the alienated did. Amplified by entire industries, cultural rebellion became a mass phenomenon in which the vicious, as in the lifestyles of Santa Monica teenage runaways or New York heroin users, developed charisma and recruited to their lifestyles.[344] Meanwhile, responsible, hard-working adults were busily advancing their careers and supporting families, leaving them unable to develop flair. In its sturdy diligence the middle class had a difficult time competing.

The media were another home of the hip lifestyle, facilitating its development in part by creating a large class of entertainers whose success required an acute sense of style. By selection and by professional experience, singers, announcers, screenwriters, actors, directors, comedians, models, advertising executives, and the many associated with them also tended to develop flair, and the most successful dwelled predominantly in the world of style.[345] Given their emotional gifts and lifestyles, entertainers, actors, artists, and musicians easily acquired a sense of superiority to and rejected the middle class and its moral order. Notoriously libertine, their leanings contributed disproportionately to the radical expansion of the morally permissible.

The aesthetic sense had long been promoted as well by urbanization, which provided exposure to great variation in personal style, stimulating perceptual acuity and giving access to many traditions, but increasingly much of this exposure took place via the media. Cinema and television communicated lifestyles far more widely than direct observation and more vividly than print or radio. Exposure to the hip often contributed to the descent of the vulnerable.

Why the Abrogation of Informal Social Control? Those who were different and their sympathizers amassed a great deal of power in the moral markets, with which they contested enforcement of the traditional consensus through the era. Their newly organized pressure groups were a large source of this power. Earlier in the period, such amateurish efforts as the Sexual Freedom League and COYOTE (Call Off Your Old Tired Ethics), the whimsical organization of prostitutes in San Francisco, fought uphill battles against moral opposition. Organized PR campaigns soon become decisive political forces shaping opinion and policy. The National Organization for Reform of Marijuana Laws (NORML) labored ingeniously from the early 1970s to win acceptance for cannabis.346 During the first decade of the 21st century, the deft, tactical, and well-financed use of medicalization as an entry toward full legalization of marijuana brought that goal considerably nearer to realization. Rapidly picking up momentum, the movement then mounted successful campaigns for legalization in liberal states and cities. Wielding multiculturalism's language of group difference and justice, the broadening gay rights movement powerfully asserted the rights of the LGBT community and won judicial victories. The gambling lobby became powerful and successful. Changing power constellations amid contentiousness and dwindling concern for societal consequences delivered much of the moral transformation.

Government policies, especially constitutional ones, also helped overturn enforcement of the consensus. During the 1950s, national policy in the United States supported what was a humane and wise normative order in many sectors, albeit with imperfections. Legal support for consensus substantially collapsed during the 1960s and early 1970s, making it difficult to sanction immorality. American society had a "homelessness" problem primarily because mental hospitals were shut down, drug offenses ignored, vagrancy euphemized, and nuisance laws unenforced. Nor have many difficult young people any longer been controllable by the great majority of teachers and administrators who were not exceedingly adept at wielding behavior modification or moral suasion now that the administration of corporal punishment in schools and often homes was deemed barbaric and/or made illegal. Bureaucracy, regulations, diversity, and radical relativism so bogged down public schools that they had great difficulty instilling or enforcing morality.

The judiciary and academia were long the two strongest bastions of multiculturalism because institutionally fortified. Distant from the economic and many of the social markets, both were sufficiently aloof from the trials of the struggling members of the middle and working classes to ignore their widely felt moral anguish from the advancing sociocultural chaos. This phenomenon strikingly echoes the lag of the American judiciary far into the 19th century as the lone citadel of elitist Federalism dug in against the advancing Jacksonian populism and spreading middle-class morality of the early 19th century. Secure in their insularity, these quintessentially multiculturalist institutions were insensitive and unfeeling toward the havoc of spreading moral disorder.

Homemakers' disappearance as full-time consensus enforcers left a moral vacuum no one else could fill, contributing a great deal to the sharply increased threat to the social order from the 1960s and 1970s. That teenage drug use and pregnancy were associated with after-school hours was a direct consequence of their lack of supervision. That rates of nonmarital pregnancy in offspring were as low in single parent-grandparent households as in those in which parents were married also gives testimony to the importance of adult supervision.[347] As Durkheim says, the more elders are present, the better consensus is enforced.[348]

Why the Variable Outcomes in the Moral Markets? What is at stake in the moral markets is the ability to prosper or even to survive in life. The greater the education and cultural resources, the greater the ability to navigate the moral markets. A university education is among other things a boot camp in finding one's way amid moral diversity. At the other end of the spectrum, the underclass was largely made up of those unable to cope with moral hazards. In U.S. enclaves like small-town northern New Mexico and southeastern Missouri, many lacked the sociocultural resources with which to handle the destructive influences now far more numerous than they had been in 1965. Such areas desperately lacked the coherent, strong community and consensus with which those who were morally shaky might be nudged or pressured into conforming despite their confusion.

Of all the effects of the American moral revolution, none was more startling than encountering limits with respect to how much disruption of consensus was possible while society was still able to pass on rational self-control and moral responsibility from generation to generation. One of the great benefits of the rulebound, superego-dominant character is that, once well-socialized, it is capable of making sound moral choices throughout a lifetime without much support from the informal social pressure whose presence was required throughout life to shelter peasants and workers' traditional, groupbound moralities of social approval and disapproval. But a condition of the superego's durable strength and the middle class's with it is sufficient moral solidarity through childhood on the part of the consensus carrying out socialization – the family, school, church, neighborhood, youth program, and especially a combination of them working together. During the critical period of its minority, the rulebound character has at least as much need of moral solidarity as does the groupbound. Under the conditions of the moral marketplace, many fewer were raised than before with the reliable self-control prerequisite to an orderly middle-class life. There have always been problems with properly socializing some in large cities, but during the global era the inability to provide the moral coherence required for middle-class socialization became widespread. In the many jumbled and rebellious areas, adults found it extremely difficult to pass on discipline and moral direction to their children. A central cause of the decline of the middle class was the sociocultural disruption flowing from this inability to reliably pass on its character and morality to younger generations.

A fuller grasp of the plight of the contemporary working class requires understanding that most of its woes have occurred because traditional community and consensus collapsed. The working class had been acutely dependent upon and held in suspension by the community and consensus around it. When these supports dissolved, workers either had to develop new inner resources, or they sank toward the underclass. The struggles of the American working class have never been primarily an economic phenomenon. The underclass was largely the roadkill of the wide-open moral markets and the wholesale attacks on moral authority that delivered those markets.

Brazenly skeptical gamers having risen to dominate American institutions, those in the middle and working classes, with limited resources for finding their way amid sociocultural disorder, were acutely threatened by the ensuing moral chaos. Many of those who were so threatened in the moral markets responded to their disintegrating worlds by turning to moral reaction and the reaffirmation of tradition. Many among them had the good sense, humility, and faith to seek additional religious grounding. Many had to rally themselves to hold on, not unlike the way in which dangerously drowsy late-night drivers caught between cities open the windows, bounce around behind the wheel, blare the radio, and talk to themselves to stay awake.

Sensible Americans of various backgrounds and persuasions were deeply concerned for their society. If the middle class was losing far too many members to disorder, and the working class was in free-fall, it was not unreasonable to be alarmed. Such apprehension was often particularly strong among those with families. If all moral authority were suspect, what standing did parents have vis-à-vis their children? When a great many self-identified as deviant, how were young people to be brought up? The vehement opposition of many gamers, especially cultural gamers, to the middle-class way of life and of being, inflicted most of the peculiar discomfort of the global-era middle class by comparison with its national-era predecessor.

Why Did Morality Decline? Morality declined in the United States and most other advanced liberal societies during the global era, first, because the loss of the consensus and arrival of the moral markets sowed confusion and doubt. A great deal of traditional morality that was regarded as optional and cast aside remained valid, and those who discarded it did so at their own and at society's peril. The acceptance of great moral diversity and suffering of high moral casualties are two sides of the same coin.

Morality declined to the extent to that it did because of the waning of Christianity. The religious markets and assaults on belief increasingly threw the West into moral crisis and dysfunction from the 1960s. As Peter Berger says, "Traditional religious definitions of reality" suffered "widespread collapse," leaving uncertainty in their wake.[349] It was perturbing for large numbers of those who could no longer take direction or draw solace from religion and had to find sustenance as best they could from a mélange of arid secular beliefs and ethics.[350] The waning of Christianity through the era was part of a larger, interrelated matrix including changes of identification, character, law, community, and morality.

Class conflict was at the heart of global-era moral decline: The wide-open moral markets left some in joyful freedom with self-fashioned, creative lives; some in cautious apprehension huddled in resisting enclaves; and others in baleful despair stripped of all coherence. In the immense human diversity now encountered daily, what seemed bracing to the sophisticated was often disturbing to the traditional, and what felt comforting to the latter often felt stifling to the sophisticated. The era's questions of civil liberties entailed deciding how many of the socioculturally independent were going to have the full panorama of the world unveiled exhilaratingly before them, and how many of the dependent were going to wake up with nightmares.

The moral politics of the global era was forged of the tension between secular moral independents and religious moral dependents. Where the gamers were morally expansive and confident about human nature, many in the middle and working classes were distressed and fearful.[351] The gamers' ebullition was the middle class's anguish. The gamers tended to be liberal on social issues and on good terms with multiculturalism, the middle class to be conservative on social issues and resistant to it. The gamers and broad upper-middle class possessed the sociocultural market experience and development with which to feel relatively comfortable with stark moral difference, whether wisely or not was another matter; those with fewer such resources did not. Extending tolerance to activities traditionally condemned as immoral made it more of a challenge for people to know the difference between right and wrong or virtue and vice or how to lead their lives. Abortion was a central battlefield upon which social and moral conservatives and liberals fought pitched battles from the 1960s on primarily because it was enabling for the era's liberated sex, which was emblematic for moral liberals and anathematic to conservatives.

Social liberals were ranting, miffed at the well-intentioned if sometimes narrow middle class whose sturdy morals built this great country. Lacking insight into and empathy with those traumatized by the moral markets, they brooked nothing short of moral laissez faire. With supremely hollow cant and cruel hardness, they denounced those who were genuinely moral in a rulebound manner and sought respite for themselves, their families, and their society from the moral markets. Much as entrepreneurs are averse to economic hierarchy, those with broad sociocultural experience are averse to sociocultural hierarchy. They cannot stand sociocultural dependence for the same reason those in business cannot stand economic dependence. Gamer intellectuals, writers, and artists were boldly and haughtily libertarian in the sociocultural markets where they were the well-prepared and experienced entrepreneurs, but when it came to the economic markets, they morphed into timid hierarchists whimpering for protection. Bonding dogmatically to the morally expansive and open for all times and places, radical relativists were oblivious to human nature and destructively inconsiderate of the needs of the middle and working classes and of society.

This one-sided imposition of the sociocultural world of the gamers again evokes Hegel's dictum that those new to a higher form of self-consciousness tend first to negate difference and only later to begin reconciling it. The gamers' higher reflexivity was in the initial phase of new awareness in which those who attained it were enthralled with themselves and imperious toward others. The central moral problem of global-liberal societies was the gamers' severely limited sense of sociocultural responsibility.

On the other hand, while modest middle-class norms and virtues may have enabled the United States to become what it was through the early 1960s and even to a degree into the early 1990s, that morality also required adherence to its norms and virtues by a consensus – at least with regard to how young people were to be socialized – otherwise it failed to reproduce and faltered. That requirement of closedness restricted and inconvenienced growing numbers of others who either did not need rulebound morality; or did, but lacked the good sense or discipline to adopt it. Bourgeois morality has always had difficulty enforcing itself on the classes below it, but that morality became positively fragile when large numbers also outgrew it. As the middle class had outgrown and chafed at peasant morality centuries earlier, the gamers had now outgrown and were and chafing at middle-class morality.

None of this is to say that some successful moral accommodation to multiculturalist and bohemian disorder did not also occur in the middle class. In their way and to a degree, some members of the middle class became market-savvy in today's free moral surroundings. This tier of the global-era middle class moderately and thoughtfully drew upon pragmatism and good sense informed by moral rules and virtues. This quiet, relatively solid center was neither as sophisticated as the cultural gamers nor as morally threatened as most in the middle and working classes but presented a hesitant, partial analog to the independent, universalistic, often mainline Protestant middle class of national-liberal societies. However, under the difficult circumstances of the moral markets, this middle-class center was unable to reliably pass on its moderation and equilibration to its children.

Demoralization also proceeded as far as it did because, thanks to the social ethic and interested lobbies, welfare benefits were widely and abundantly made available, irrespective of desert, such that many of the natural consequences of unwise personal decisions were lifted. Most learn from their own and others' mistakes if they have to face their consequences. Distinctly fewer learn if people are shielded from them by government intervention and subsidy. Just as today's Americans in large numbers indulge themselves, they indulge others. To the extent to which human nature is co-dependently enabled, it ignores and pulls away from the healthy fear of moral disorder over time. Such fear, flowing from hard lessons, would have helped a great many.

In the broadest horizon, global-liberal demoralization may be said to have been cyclically due. After the period of the Reformation was morally repressive, that of the Enlightenment during the late 17th-18th centuries was morally expansive in liberal societies like Great Britain and the Netherlands, until 1793, and a generation later in the United States. The 19th century was predominantly repressive until about 1885, and the 20th overwhelmingly expansive again until the late 1960s. Given human nature, whatever the challenges and events of the later 20th century had been, it is unlikely that the excesses of one sort of ebullient moral blowout or another could have long been avoided.

The odds were stacked against it by much-increased prosperity and urbanization alone. The growing permissiveness of the national era – held partially in check by the hardships of the 31-year crisis – long invited moral excess and therefore eventually a repressive response.

Expansion of the welfare and regulatory states did the same. Once the conditions got out of hand – as they did with a vengeance during the late 1960s and early 1970s when the large, unruly U.S. postwar generation came of age – acute moral disorder arose. Understandably but inauspiciously, the boomers' parents had wanted to make things easier for them. Peace, prosperity, slackness, and indulgence brought selfishness and the willful ignoring of consequences – for young people themselves, for others, for society, and for the long term. This self-indulgence was strongly related to that from the larger macro co-dependency associated with the excessive tender mindedness and sentimentalism of the social ethic and government expansion.

The last general repressive movement in liberal societies began in the late 18th and early 19th centuries[352] in reaction to the enormous excesses of the French Revolution and of out-of-control rural migrants entering the burgeoning industrial cities. Time itself prepared the way for the 1960s and 1970s by blurring the memories and distancing the relevance of the horrors of the Jacobins and of terminal exasperation with irresponsible, rural and newly urban labor, occasions for the 19th century moral distress. Time also dated the language of bourgeois morality and rendered the circumstances unpropitious for it.

The expansive phase of the global era was in a league of its own, much more radical and much more strongly defended than those of the Enlightenment or national era. No moderate repressive response to moral decline was able to gain majority support, much less a consensus during the period. The gamers dug in, contested it, and successfully defended the open moral conditions they found congenial against middle-class moral reform. The lopsided balance of power enabled moral decline to gather momentum and pose more serious moral threats than any faced in the West since the fall of Rome.

Indeed the moral disorder of the global era presented nothing less than the return of the grand moral cycle that was the nemesis of all the great traditional hierarchical societies – the bane of civilization for millennia – largely for which reason Rome fell, the Chinese dynasties collapsed, and a decaying Ottoman Empire blew away in the winds of World War I. Moral decline badly damaged the United States on countless fronts, particularly the political corruption and family disintegration from which disorder was spiraling on all sides. The future of the United States and the world depends upon reversing this moral cycle. Welcome back to the history and human condition many thought to be left behind! This moral decline presented decadence like that Gaetano Mosca and Vilfredo Pareto wrote about more than a century ago and Ibn Khaldun, Augustine, and Polybius did far longer ago than that.[353]

Consideration of the intensified moral cycle from 1965 and liberal societies' unfortunate new position in it brought into relief the astounding secret that early-liberal societies inadvertently discovered – about which the skeptical, anti-free-market, anti-bourgeois scholarship of the global era was in denial and oblivious – that the economic markets confer moral discipline as a most important side effect, discipline that overcomes the grand moral cycle of traditional hierarchical societies.[354] Market-induced discipline is what tamed the grand moral cycle into the mild one of modern liberal societies from 1500 to 1965. A key condition of the reappearance of the grand moral cycle since 1965 has been the displacement and hobbling of economic markets by the welfare and regulatory states. The scores of new welfare programs and hundreds of thousands of new regulations arising since – nearly all of them delivered to interested parties by cynical gamers amid PR deceit of the well intentioned but naïve – have brought about a great deal of the current moral disorder. Big government has dried up business investment, shrunk labor force participation, and restricted exposure to the economic markets.

A second key condition of its reappearance has been the accession to power of a blinkered gamer elite that would allow society to collapse before relinquishing its predation and imposition. Hierarchical societies have known such unscrupulous ruling classes over the millennia, which exploit all other classes and foil reform until the bitter end, but this was the first time major liberal societies had known them.

Why Did Moral Consensus, though Weakened, Remain Relatively Intact in Europe and Japan? Moral consensus remained stronger in most European societies than in the United States during the global era primarily because of Europe's continuing though diminishing sociocultural homogeneity and delayed multiculturalism. Among other things, these conditions somewhat better enabled European agents of socialization to teach morality.

Greater sociocultural coherence, stronger community, and more collectivism combined with more extensive urban life and a richer aesthetic tradition to bring more wholesome character and modeling of lifestyle. Europe's comparative harmony, in particular its lesser and milder experience of the gamers and underclass and larger and healthier middle classes, were important results. Substance abuse was considerably less serious in most of Europe than in the United States because the former underwent less demoralization overall. Without the Hunter Thompsons and Howard Sterns they had less need of the Dr. Lauras. On the other hand, increasing numbers of gamers, influence of the media, and sociocultural mixing were pulling Europe in the direction of the United States. Insofar as its economic and political woes permitted, Europe's comparatively intact moral consensus and more secure middle class underlay an ongoing spirit of celebration, although one that was hushing under attack by its Muslim minorities.

The moralities of some of the liberalizing former Soviet peoples on the other hand were ravaged by tyranny and radical modernism, breaking down religion, family, and self-respect, leaving portions of their populations in profound despair. Yet through force of national, communal, familial, and religious tradition, some of the former dependencies were better able to protect themselves morally or more quickly rebuild than others – although their heavy doses of secular ideology largely inoculated them from the morally repressive. For better and worse, the West was relatively well prepared for the moral markets of the last half century by long experience with markets of many kinds.

The continuing strength of Japan's consensus and its hierarchical cast had everything to do with the country's longstanding and thoroughgoing sociocultural homogeneity and tightly restricted immigration. These conditions preserved strong tradition and enabled policymakers to actively intervene in support of community and consensus, as by protecting small farmers. Japan presents a contrasting approach to that of the West to community, consensus, and morality, one from which the West could learn things of great value.

Why the Patterns in the Liberalizing Third World? Rapid economic growth and urbanization along with massive exposure to the international sociocultural markets of the global era brought great development but also wrenching moral dislocation to the liberalizing third world. Consensuses remained stronger in third-world societies than in most first-world countries due to the recency and unevenness of their opening to the world; but the newness of their liberalism interacted with the localism and tribalism still strong in many such countries to aggravate those sources of difference and dissention. Together, these factors resulted in the common third-world pattern of relatively strong consensus at the local or tribal level but weak consensus at the national level.

Nevertheless, some third-world societies took the moral markets in stride. India, for one, with its rapid economic growth, educational advances, and comparative openness, was moving overall in the direction of the consensual profile of more developed countries even though relatively strong consensus and lingering provincialism restricted acceptance of the sociocultural markets in many parts of the country. India was among those better prepared for sociocultural liberalization thanks to its highly developed universalism, long familiarity with diversity, and well-rooted democratic traditions. When encountering the moral markets, societies, social classes, and ethnic groups largely fared in accordance with the resources of their traditions, education levels, and economic experience.

Why the Patterns in China and the Islamic World? China's moral consensus loosened significantly in part because the dynamism and upheaval of the economic markets undermined it, particularly by hampering its enforcement. Some of the effect occurred through increased urbanization and education levels that weakened informal social control. Divorce, for example, was on the rise in China in part because of diminished consensual and legal sanction along with diminished disapproval. Married couples once domiciled in extended family compounds became dispersed in apartments of their own, freeing them from considerable family and neighborhood interference. Chinese women's improved employment opportunities and greater economic independence gave them more options as well. The Deng regime has not sought to coerce compliance with traditional norms and virtues because its political acceptance has not depended upon religious approval in the way that of Muslim rulers has. On the other hand, China's moral consensus did not liberalize more than it did because of the continuing force of long hierarchical tradition. China possessed considerable universalism but much less familiarity with sociocultural markets than the West, while India was no better than moderately well prepared for them. Yet its totalitarian regime remained able and willing to intercede to curb them as needed.

To some extent the Islamic Resurgence, like the far milder and more limited contemporary efflorescence of popular evangelical Protestantism in the United States, has been a reactionary response to the presence of moral markets and their disorienting difference. The sociocultural and historical sources of this reaction have already been discussed, but no small part in the Islamic world's increased moral repression has also been played by the West's increasing decadence, which has presented an opening for contempt by Muslims, as opposed to the well-earned but grudging respect more common during the national era. Islam no longer faces a West with cultural power emanating from abundant moral strength; it now faces an aimless and effete West manifesting a dearth of leadership, courage, and consequence. The Islamic Resurgence has been fueled in part by an understandable collective pride in the strengthening of moral seriousness among Muslims. On the other hand, their severely authoritarian tradition and limited resources for digesting sociocultural disorder have worked against consensus within Muslim societies, as has been evident throughout the Islamic world, in post-Gaddafi Libya, post-Mubarak Egypt, Syria, Iraq, and Pakistan for example.

Islamic civilization has been the least well prepared of the large civilizations of the world for the moral markets because of the stark moral authoritarianism, intolerance, and insularity of Muslim tradition, all the more so as hardened by the Islamic Resurgence.

Rejection of the earnest sociocultural working of difference goes back to the foundations of Islam. Islamic societies' tight moral consensuses ill prepare their members for respecting the rights of others in an interdependent world, beginning with those of women and those of different Muslim faiths. In all but a few unusually progressive and balanced places, Muslims who develop morally do so in resistance to the hierarchalism around them. Islamic men are indulged in their indiscipline by veiling and sequestering women, which does not encourage the independence and development of either. As a charmed Ayatolla Khomeini effectively admitted in his famously ingenuous 1979 interview with Oriana Fallaci, the shari'a (as his regime narrowly interprets it) would collapse in moral markets unprotected by coerced consensus.[355] Although its contemporary forms may be overwhelmingly backward, there is nothing inherently wrong with the shari'a; it just needs a great deal of the free criticism and updating that morality has long undergone in other major traditions.

THE IMPLICATIONS

The Central Problem. Global-liberal societies' acceptance of much of the moral diversity they inherited and more that arose during that era was appropriate and just. Liberalization of gambling, pornography, and sexuality was predominantly a matter of shedding paternalism and paying respect to others. For, as John Stuart Mill says, "different persons ... require different conditions for their spiritual development; and can no more exist healthily in the same moral than all the variety of plants can in the same physical, atmosphere and climate...."[356] The inclusion of new moral forms better fulfilling the needs of thoughtful human beings constituted important moral development.

This is true despite the fact that in the moral markets it is caveat emptor – participation in the contest is guaranteed but not the choice or following of wise precepts or wholesome models. The moral markets permitted a great deal of Nietzschean ethical experimentation, much of it accompanied by good sense but also much of it not.[357] Wide-open moral markets inevitably sustain numerous human casualties. A much more vulnerable middle class, a working class in disarray, fewer and more troubled children, and a growing underclass were key portions of the balance sheet on the moral markets. As traditional restrictions were removed out of respect for freedom and the different, people were at once granted rights and made more likely to lose their bearings. As in all markets, creation and destruction are found together in the moral markets.

The opening up of the moral world was not as problematic as the failure of the better-prepared gamers to recognize the stalwart worthiness of the middle class whom they mercilessly attacked and needled, or as their failure to acknowledge the moral devastation.

When the middle-class is endlessly lampooned in movies, television, and music lyrics, what are the struggling members of the middle and working classes of all ages who consume this content to make of it? Through savage disparagement, middle-class order, life, and accomplishment may be depicted as hardly worth the effort. Where the bourgeois once sought to jostle peasants into demanding but uplifting middle-class morality, the gamers now seek to prod the bourgeois into unsuitable moral minimalism. The gamers' intolerant, negativist thrusting forth of their own particularistic ways, when these could not possibly become general models, amounted to terrible class centrism. That the gamers had difficulty recognizing the moral anguish of so many good people and were not taking their well-being and that of their families, communities, and society into consideration is entirely in keeping with the harshness of the gamers' rudimentary higher reflexivity and awareness. The obligations that come with membership in society do not decrease but increase as one moves up in it.

Moral conservatives also often displayed excesses of intolerance and shrillness. Their efforts to roll up the moral markets and put forth morality too rigid for most to accept were examples. Taking cues from their antagonists, they sometimes pushed their program as conflictually as liberal gamers did theirs, but moral conservatives had genuine apprehensions that required urgent attention. They raised the alert about the serious moral disorder that arose in the United States and other advanced global-liberal societies. They posed the question of how such societies were to overcome the modern world's first large-scale moral decline – much of it, as we have seen, joined at the hip to what was also significant moral advance. The antagonism between the worldviews of the classes must be overcome, as must moral decline.

What Is to Be Done? If Americans do not want more and more of our population to be underclass and our country and the world in ruins, we need to do several things simultaneously with respect to morality: First and foremost, we need to let reality teach its stern moral lessons directly and indirectly to a greater degree, allowing the economic markets to selectively punish persons, families, and communities for their moral slackness, foolishness, mistakes, and sometimes evil. A society that does not allow those who choose the path of nullity to suffer the consequences individually or in groups – one that maintains an indiscriminate welfare state cushioning those who have been harmed, if at all, by their own wrongdoing and vice – postpones, multiplies, and collectivizes the moral destruction. For more than half a century, advanced global-liberal societies have been undergoing moral decline that will not be halted until people are sufficiently chastened to come to their senses. Progressives have absolved irresponsible parents, gamblers, substance abusers, workers, fraudulent benefit claimants, and even violent criminals of responsibility for their actions, ascribing victimhood to *them* rather than to society. Tenderhearted solicitousness toward the troubled, irrespective of moral desert, allowed that category to expand in all directions, not least among the circles of its deluded admirers. The economic markets, insofar as we permit them to operate, are society's moral ally and benefactor, helping keep disorder at bay. If the seriously irresponsible are not required to take the natural consequences of their actions – and they do deserve them – then everyone does.

Second, we need to teach moral lessons symbolically. Children may be the primary concern, but adults floundering in the moral markets and remiss in their obligations should also be subjected to middle-class moralism on behalf of propriety and order. People have been so browbeaten with radical relativism that they have a difficult time teaching moral principles and virtues. No matter what the devastation, Hamlet-like gamers cannot bring themselves to judge others' personal morality and chastise it when it is out of line. What previous liberal societies have taught by moral authority was reinforced through personal experience and observation. The moral content so gained may not have been as coherent, but the discipline, prudence, and independence have been there, acquired more in adulthood than in childhood by many. What could be more fitting in a time of turbulent moral markets?! Working together, a free society and bourgeois morality brought about the enormous expansion of the middle class during the 18th and 19th centuries and on through the early 1960s. They have been doing the same in many liberalizing third-world countries and ought to be allowed again to do so in the United States.

Third, we need to teach moral lessons homeopathically. Just as it doesn't matter much what major language young people are brought up in, only

217

that they learn it well, so there needs to be a language of morality rather than a mishmash: Thoughtful parents of various secular and religious persuasions bring up children well while living aware and centered lives in wide-open societies like the United States, United Kingdom, or Brazil by forming loose, partially protected moral-cultural enclaves around coherent traditions while providing resources for criticizing and transcending what is corrosive in the broader society and culture. Such parents establish good family settings and find neighborhoods and schools that stand opposed to what is most harmful in society. They teach children by steps to navigate through much that is amiss. They expose them to homeopathic doses while insulating them from full ones, steadily increasing their freedom as children develop critical facility until strong enough to fend for themselves in the sociocultural markets. Large numbers of thoughtful conservative and liberal parents follow kindred routes with their children while themselves negotiating the full range of available society and culture, naturally shunning what is base in it. The two camps may lean in different directions on where the limits for children and adults should be, but their approaches and personal lives have much in common.

Fourth, we have to upgrade education at all levels, for as knowledge and sophistication increase, greater familiarity with and understanding of sociocultural difference are acquired, and people become more astute consumers of the rich human variety presented to them, transforming threats into opportunities. There is no excuse for the United States to be four years behind Finland and South Korea in achievement scores by the end of high school.

Academic standards at all levels were deliberately dropped, caving-in to pressure from organized interests, particularly including cynical administrators and unions, often along with, of all people, minorities who acutely need better education. That dropping of standards was frequently carried out, under the false banner of social justice, to spare students and their parents from hard work or miffed feelings. In order for this educational deficit to be turned into excellence, people need boldness, courage, resolve, and confidence in the power of education and freedom. Moving U.S. student achievement scores up to the world's best could be accomplished within a decade if its citizens were willing to take back their country.

President Eisenhower initiated the last fine, though modest and mainly mathematics-, science-, and engineering-oriented, effort in this direction during his second term. Simultaneously, educational institutions need to be pruned, made more efficient, and their administrative costs sharply cut.

Fifth, the United States and other liberal societies need to pursue consensus-friendly social policy. We need to accept sensible restraints on egregious public conduct and on the sociocultural content to which children are exposed. Nuisance laws such as those against loitering and vagrancy need to be revived and tailored to contemporary conditions. A range of consensus-empowering measures, including the extension of legal authority to landlords, tenants' organizations, neighborhood associations, school administrations, and communities to enforce standards of public conduct is also needed. Strengthening consensus may include policies like the United Kingdom's civility laws that empower citizens against public nuisances through the use of anti-social behavior or dispersal orders, among other remedies.

The care and maturity in many European countries' responses to the moral markets have reduced their devastation. People earn the right to highly liberal societies by fashioning pragmatic solutions to the problems arising from them. To the extent to which society were successful with intelligent consensus-building/supporting policies, many of the criticisms of social conservatives would be mooted; to the extent to which it were not, more weight would need to be placed upon their moral prescriptions. As liberals are able to overcome their radical relativism and cease denying morality, and as conservatives are able to overcome their know-nothingism and cease trying to impose narrow views beyond their limits, society can get on with the work of renewal.

The moral conflict of the global era arose from different characters in different positions vis-à-vis the sociocultural markets. Smooth gamers have their moral needs, steady bourgeois have theirs, and they are not the same. A fundamental question of injustice arises when a society allows itself to become so extremely libertarian that people need a strong university education to survive in the moral markets. The newly educated can be as crass in their way as the newly rich. The gamer chiefs on both liberal and conservative sides need to understand that the different characters and moral stances can be reconciled, with each given due recognition. They need to extend the practice of the tolerance, diversity, and inclusion that they all support with respect to racial and ethnic difference to these important moral differences of class and politics.

American society was coming apart in every major way except economically between 1965 and 2016: In its national security, identity, class structure, politics, family, and morality. Even its economy was becoming more unequal from the late 1970s, and growth slowed in the early 21st century, hit hard by the Great Recession, only to then experience its worst recovery since the 1930s during the closing years of the global period. The United States entered the global era the greatest nation on earth and one of the greatest in the history of the world but left the era riven by conflict and disintegrating. An astute English observer of the United States said of this country already in the early 1970s that he had never seen a nation pass so quickly from youth to senescence. Perhaps the most dangerous element of how the country was faring by the end of the era was the precarious, partially suspended Pax Americana of its last four years. The country's national security was being dangerously challenged on multiple sides, most ominously by China. I know of no better succinct assessment of the circumstances at the end of the global era than Henry Kissinger's of two summers after it ended, that they were "very, very grave." The conditions responsible for the precariousness of the Pax Americana were no less grave.

The United States was coming apart and in grave circumstances by the end of the era, most fundamentally, because of the global-liberal paradigm that had dominated it for 51 years, and in particular the multiculturalism that we have examined, with its subtle but profound change in cast of mind. Rejecting the traditional classical and Christian universalism that had reigned in the West from antiquity, though with lacunae and lapses, multiculturalism had broken society into factious, alienated groups. Nearly all of the sundry domestic wars of the global-era United States were ultimately about whether this society and civilization were to be reorganized on the basis of resentful splintering. Accepting multiculturalism represented a fundamental coming apart that contribute mightily to all of the other comings apart, a progressive national disintegration, that was passed on to Europe after a 25-year lag.

Part III
The Return of Paradigm Conflict Since 2016 Amid the Crisis of Democracy

CHAPTER 8

Trump's American Restoration Meets Asymmetric Top-Gamer Resistance

Global-Era Problems Posed by Gamers and Multiculturalists as the Setting

2016 was another of those extraordinary years like 1648 and 1789 in continental Europe or 1885 and 1965 in the United States when the ground gave way beneath us. Donald Trump's successful campaign for the presidency overthrew central tenets of the global liberalism that had reigned as the tacit consensus in the United States since 1965. Trump alone among the more than twenty presidential candidates critiqued the established paradigm, sketched a new one addressing neglected national needs, and vowed to implement it as chief executive. The United States again entered paradigm crisis in which its basic assumptions were in question. The elite of top gamers and upper class of gamers have been relentless in their attacks upon President Trump and his movement, trying at all costs to reverse their gains. American society has been in tension since the 1960s and increasingly so since the 1990s, but it substantially fractured in 2016 as the contest degenerated into a melee in which elite officials and journalists were the chief brawlers. Social ties have been torn apart over politics as only rarely before in the nation's history. More than four years into the new era, we are again in circumstances resembling those of 1968, early in a paradigm crisis in which nearly everyone is apprehensive.

Analyzing the current paradigm conflict must begin with the fundamental problems of global liberalism against which Trump and his movement rose up, those posed by gamers and multiculturalists. The foundations of American society were turned upside down during the late 1960s and early 1970s as the multiculturalist disunity of the global era overthrew the relative domestic unity of the national era that had reigned since the late 19th century. The country lurched from embracing reconciliation to embracing conflict, from an overriding sense of national pride to one of national blame, and from power being predominantly Christian to its being predominantly anti-Christian.

The first fundamental problem of the global era was the character of its upper class of gamers, the talented and disciplined but amoral strivers who gamed their way into and through prestigious educations and into impressive executive and professional positions which they then used without restraint to increase their power and wealth. The central problem the gamers posed and continue to pose for American society has been that they feel next to no responsibility toward the larger society and are unconcerned with the effects of their actions upon it. Massive problems were building and festering in all institutions because they disparage their country and eschew leadership. An important manifestation of the gamers' estrangement is the way in which they badly treat the middle class. In their smug disdain, the gamers, although highly disciplined, cannot bring themselves to respect middle-class lives of simple but sturdy discipline. Their class-centric unwillingness to recognize themselves in the other has led to more than half a century of deprecating the main ladder on which the vulnerable might rise into or secure themselves in the middle class. The gamers rose to power, stormed the bridge, and furloughed the old crew in the global era; but virtually none of them took the helm, navigated, watched the radar, or monitored the ship. In their self-centeredness, shortsightedness, indifference, and hubris, the gamers divided the country, jeopardized national security, undermined democracy, battered the family, and shattered morality. The challenge of how to promote leadership and restraint in a talented upper class without a sense of responsibility is as old as civilization.

The second fundamental problem of the era was the multiculturalism which shaped the revolution of the late 1960s and early 1970s, the ideology of identity politics, the radical doctrine that people ought to think of their societies as collections of racial, ethnic, gender, lifestyle, and similar groups rather than as national units; and value the aggrieved groups among them rather than their larger societies, indeed value purported social justice for the groups above all other concerns. Multiculturalism holds that the descendants of the subordinate groups of the past ought to blame the descendants of the dominant groups for alleged collective injustice, associate contemporary American society with that injustice, and blame it as well. That fundamental persuasion opposes nation-states but supports supra-national entities like the UN and EU that weaken or displace the nation-state, hence much of their globalism. Multiculturalism values the parts and denounces meaningful societal wholes, as if Americans had nothing in common but membership in antagonistic groups.

The gamers' character and multiculturalists' doctrine that posed fundamental problems of global liberalism form an interrelated gamer-multiculturalist nexus. The gamers developed multiculturalism and were its strongest proponents, their support for it was one of their strongest claims to legitimacy, and that support was pivotal to the alienated groups' alliance with them. Multiculturalist disparagement of American society was at the same time the key source of the gamers' amorality and indifference. With searing rhetoric, gamers fomented multiculturalist division, curried favor with the resulting groups, and then slyly stepped into and exploited the void of engagement and leadership left by the spreading alienation. The global-era American coming apart and senescence were run by and for the gamers.

The natural, easy, unassuming Christian genuineness and kindness of the United States, its heritage, and the great majority of its people, national traits that were necessary for this country to become the leader among nations, are why Americans cared and were willing to do their best for decades to improve group relations. Although taken aback by the destructiveness of many manifestations of multiculturalism, they did not grasp for a long time that they were getting with it something very different from their sincere desire to overcome prejudice and discrimination: They were getting an effort to dismantle their society, politics, character, and civilization and fundamentally restructure them along permanently and dangerously divisive and hierarchical lines.

The dying gasp of the expiring national-liberal paradigm in its passage of the equal rights provisions of the civil-rights acts attained a balance nobler than any achievement of gamer multiculturalism. It is appalling that those who obsess about one issue to the extent of jeopardizing everything for themselves and for their country should get away with blaming the United States and the West for alleged narrowness. Like so much else of the doctrine, that accusation is both false and all projection. Not surprisingly, black Americans experienced less economic progress overall under multiculturalism than they had during the national era.

Who gains power in a society has immense influence upon its members' identifications and attachments. At the birth of the global era, gamers and multiculturalists drew deeply from intellectual, bohemian, Jewish, black, and generational disaffection and blended it into radical rejection of this society's foundational Christian reconciliation and relatively harmonious modern secular-Christian synthesis in the previous era's mainline Protestantism. The global era was instead *post*modern and conflictual. As its multiculturalism took hold, the Watts riot occurred, and the civil-rights movement metamorphosed into one expressing anger and demanding governmental and symbolic benefits. As that doctrine picked up momentum and became more alienated, much of the uprising embraced illicit drugs. Multiculturalism's banishment of meaning played the central role in delivering the boomers' "me" generation. The precious but fragile idealism of Camelot, still a product of liberal modernity, competed through the 1960s to inspire the young of talent, but multiculturalism dissolved its universalism and hope, leaving it spent by the end of the decade. Gaming and multiculturalism have been intertwined not only with each other but also with moral decline, the third fundamental problem of the global era and the one about which Trump and his movement, like most of their fellow Americans, have so far been in denial.

Much of the gamers and multiculturalists' alienation was *from* the United States, the world's leading country, flagship democracy, and largest economy as well as modern history's greatest society. Gamers and multiculturalists have wrongly disparaged this exemplary country and its institutions, citizens, tradition, and history for more than half a century now, and they have badly damaged them. The gamers have rejected moral rules and virtues, expressed contempt for Christianity, and dismissed reconciliation. Amid their all-encompassing upper-class presumption and many-sided alienation, practicing civility toward their fellow Americans has been out of the question. With boundless hubris, they have thought, "What could we smart, privileged members of the 'meritocracy' – la crème de la crème – possibly owe to our forebears, posterity, or the middle and working classes of this country?" The gamers have been consumed by a will-to-power that they have had the temerity to interpret as universal ordination. Americans no longer trust Congress, the administrative state, journalism, or higher education. Gamers repeatedly attempt to present the problem as one of lack of trust, but institutions are unworthy of trust insofar as they are run by gamers and suffused with multiculturalism.

The paradigm crisis in the United States arose from the gamers' use of multiculturalism's societal demolition to maximize their power and wealth, against the settled judgment of most Americans that this country required and deserved reconciliation and working together. As growing excess brought gamer multiculturalism toward an inflection point under the Obama administration, the sense grew among levelheaded Americans that the United States was not going to survive unless it fundamentally changed course. Global liberalism was overthrown in 2016 because the threats gamers and multiculturalists posed to the long-term wellbeing of this country and its citizens had become dire. Yet Americans could only do so because an able and determined leader, Donald Trump, founded a movement dedicated to replacing the earlier paradigm and overcoming the fundamental problems to which it led. The many-sided markets (political, social, moral, and cultural as well as economic), the other core element of the global-liberal paradigm along with multiculturalism, performed well overall, posing no problems of comparable magnitude except where influenced by gamers, skewed by multiculturalism, or compromised by moral decline.

DONALD TRUMP, THE AMERICAN RESTORATION, AND THE REVOLT OF THE MIDDLE AND WORKING CLASSES

Where the gamers elevated the alienated groups and their engineered resentment to become the apparently overriding concern of domestic policy for 51 years, Trump and the Restoration's first principle has been to make America great again, to restore the greatness that the United States had achieved from its origins through the early 1960s and even in part into the early 1990s. They believed that after half a century of neglect, the United States again needed to focus upon what contributes to the general interest, to the common good of the American people, not to what benefits one group or class or another. Unlike a robust majority of citizens, most gamers have lost all comprehension of what this imperative could even mean and, in their insularity, trained obliviousness, and radical relativism, even ridicule it. Average Americans' discernment of that anomalous incomprehension was crucial to why Trump won the 2016 election and has been able to fundamentally contest gamer multiculturalism. Trump and the Restoration again make society the main reference, not the group, the larger whole the reference, not the part. Doing so maximally benefits the American people, including those in aggrieved groups.

Making America great again has been about the return of working together for the long-term wellbeing of this country and its citizens. Trump and the Restoration support those who pursue the best interests of the country as a whole and oppose those who instead elbow and cheat for their individual or group interests. They blame and hold accountable those who disparage, subvert, and exploit America and its middle and working classes.

Trump was able to win the presidency in large part because his message of working together for society as a whole was uplifting, hopeful, and resonant with large numbers of Americans who have continued to believe in

227

their country and oppose its naysayers. He was able to win because under his leadership the middle and working classes rose up against the elite and upper-class dividers, rejecting the meanness and destructiveness of their anti-Americanism. Trump also won because he was able to burst the bubble of spurious collective guilt the gamers had socially constructed to sustain the reign of multiculturalism, in keeping with their class and group leanings and what they saw as their interests. He did so by pointing out its contradictions and modeling how its codes might be transgressed, albeit not always with perfect sensitivity, while withstanding nearly unanimous elite and upper-class accusation and denunciation. The reservoir of collective guilt has run dry in a majority of American citizens if not yet a consensus. Many had been there or almost there for a time, and Trump's leadership took them a decisive additional step in breaking the global-era tacit consensus. Most Americans no longer accept the upside-down history that prejudicially attributes virtue to the groups and vice to the majority. Long patient with the excesses of multiculturalism, the white majority has seen itself for decades as alone in putting aside group attachment and trying to do what is right for the country as a whole. Sixty percent of white voters supported Trump in the 2016 election, which was by no means the potential upper limit of their support.

The Restoration applies the goal of making America great again to the crucial question of immigration by establishing economic, political, social, and cultural compatibility with and assimilability to the United States as the governing criteria for immigration; not proximity to the border, percentage of the world population, having relatives in the country, or drawing random numbers. The Restoration advocates priority to Christian, Jewish, and secular Western backgrounds and to democratic experience and leanings. Its criteria mean no to those who do not accept this country and its basic principles. They mean plusses for English language proficiency, needed entrepreneurialism, education, skills, and economic resources, but no to criminality. They mean yes to compatibility with the labor market but no to most low-skill, low-education immigration that undercuts American workers; which still leaves room for a large, orderly guest-worker program for labor few Americans are willing to do. Its criteria mean citizenship or residency only sparingly extended as a salve to the social conscience and never as a device for building a party's voter rolls. The Restoration supports instilling basic knowledge and values of this country and reinstating American history and government requirements at all levels of education. The melting pot has been operating all along, but where multiculturalism discouraged and slowed it for more than half a century, the Restoration encourages it.

The second principle of the American Restoration, a corollary of the first, posits strengthening and expanding the middle class as essential to making America great again. The sociocultural changes of the global era weighed heavily on the middle class. Under gamer-multiculturalist animus and dysfunction, the middle and working classes of nearly all groups weakened, the underclass expanded, and the great economic progress of two centuries slowed. Trump and the Restoration's policies aimed at increasing economic growth and employment have been strengthening and expanding the middle class, as would thoroughly reforming education and sharply raising standards at all levels. Strengthening and expanding the middle class does not leave out the working class, minorities, or the poor – all the opposite – they are the only genuine solutions to the needs of the vulnerable. Opportunity, aspiration, and hard work toward becoming middle class and securing one's place in it offer those who are struggling the chance to progress and flourish.

The gamers need to be brought front and center into analysis of how the middle class has fared since 1965, for their failures of leadership and responsibility lie behind most of its woes. The gamers' ability and skills can be extremely valuable to society, but their character and orientation have been disastrous. An upper class may have its great rewards, within reason, but in return it must provide leadership and be responsible – that is a law.[358] Ayn Rand makes a lively sophomore argument but passes neither empirical nor moral muster.

A necessary condition of reforming the gamers and righting the upper class's relationship with the country is freeing liberal-arts education of gamer-multiculturalist anti-American, anti-Christian, and anti-Western venom. The academe that ensconced itself early in the global era excoriated and banished the classics of Western Civilization – for their elitism no less, a gem of gamer-multiculturalist wisdom. Complex societies cannot but have upper classes; the issue is whether those upper classes are to be moral and responsible. For if they are to be, we had better immerse the young of talent in the civilizational foundations of morality and responsibility. As the West forgets its classical humanism and abandons the Christianity well integrated with it, it is grounded upon little but sand.

Without the classics, humanities, religion, and more than rare examples of a worthy upper class to inspire and sublimate the super-achievers, in our time gamers, things become a lot like *Lord of the Flies*.[359] When sections of the middle class get on steroids, take hardball competition and striving to vicious extremes, and become amoral upper classes – which has happened repeatedly in history – only upper classes of distinction and morality are capable of overcoming them while protecting that which they neglect and those whom they mistreat. Well-balanced, civilized, caring human beings able to perceive the unity in diversity and act in the interests of the whole are always needed to temper and restrain the ruthless. Even small true upper classes and their milieux take the hard edges off their irresponsible peers and partially sublimate them.

Trump and the Restoration depart dramatically from global liberalism with respect to its multiculturalism and treatment of the middle class but not with respect to its other policies. They have sought to strengthen the Pax Americana by building up the military; dealing effectively with China, North Korea, Russia, and Iran; and persuading unserious, free-riding, sometimes passive-aggressive allies to pull their share of the load. Trump and the Restoration support the many-sided markets, with relatively minor qualifications, as have the previous paradigms of liberal modernity. Global capitalism continues, but mercantilist cheating on the rules of international trade is no longer accepted. Trump and the Restoration's economic policies have brought needed economic reform and growth. All institutional arrangements are in question in the current paradigm crisis as they have been in previous ones. To the extent to which the Restoration is successful, important fundamentals will change markedly after being tested but most will change only by degree. Trump and the Restoration's efforts to overcome multiculturalism, reorient society toward the common good, and strengthen the middle class have been their key reversals of global-liberal policy.

The uprising of the middle and working classes has largely been their reaction to the devastation of 51 years of global liberalism, to the sense that this country was approaching a point of no return. By early 2016 we were headed toward major woes in all institutional areas and toward ruin in some of them. One of many examples was an opioid crisis that was wreaking terrible damage with hardly anyone in the elite or upper class seeming to care.

Movements of restoration analogous to that in the United States are under way in Europe, but only those in Hungary and Poland have yet dethroned multiculturalism although others in the United Kingdom, Denmark, France, Italy, Austria, Slovakia, and Croatia are getting close. As in the United States, the inability of gamers and multiculturalists to consider national needs other than those to funnel resources to and indulge themselves lies behind the uprisings.

Restorations are necessary when great countries have suffered terrible devastation. An example was the restoration of ancient Rome under Diocletian and Constantine during the late 3rd and early 4th centuries in recovering from the disasters between 180 and 284 AD. That restoration won Rome nearly two hundred years of additional vibrancy in the West and 1200 years in the East after its society had been on the rocks. Another example was France's restoration of the Bourbon monarchy from 1815 to 1830, following the devastation of the French Revolution and Napoleonic wars, which returned the country to normalcy and provided the platform upon which Louis Philippe's long and productive reign could build as could that of the Third Republic later.

THE ANATOMY OF RESISTANCE: TOP GAMERS AND THE DPASM

The central opposition to Trump and the Restoration is the left-leaning, top-gamer elite of the United States in lockstep with the consolidating Democratic Party-Administrative State Monopoly complex (DPASM). Considered narrowly, the monopoly complex comprises the crony-capitalist monopolistic and oligopolistic corporate entities hovering about the government; but considered broadly, the DPASM comprises a single, immense monopoly complex. It represents all that is large and monopolistic seeking to control and exploit all that is small and independent; which is to say, it represents government at all levels remote from the people, large corporations and unions in various stages of consolidation, and aligned NGOs of many descriptions. Most large organizations are on board, most billionaires are on board, large tech companies are on board, and the alienated groups are on board. The DPASM is isomorphic with the large special interests that Trump and the Restoration anathematize.

As the gamers were the dominant class of the global era, the top gamers are making a determined bid to become the dominant class of the new era. The elite top 1 percent of gamers, the top gamers who run and staff the DPASM at high levels, are buttressed by large majorities of other gamers and the upper-middle class, even as the top gamers are now increasingly rising above them. Scary smart and having median net worths in the tens of millions, the top gamers are exceedingly cunning, calculating every word and gesture to advance their interests. Around the top gamers, nothing is as it appears: Their actions speak to who they are and what they are about but never what they say, and even their actions do so extremely subtly. The top gamers are now pulling away from other gamers to form their own distinct upper-upper class and becoming aware of themselves as such. They have begun congealing as a distinct class in large part by capitalizing upon ordinary gamers' withdrawal from their society and obsequiousness before the special interests. The top gamers pose a more imminently dangerous problem to the country than have the gamers.

Top gamers manifest most of the traits of the ordinary gamers from whom they have emerged, only more extremely. Where the gamers are single-mindedly ambitious in their drives to power, the top gamers are ambitious to totalistic extremes. Where relatively few gamers stand out as completely unscrupulous, most top gamers regularly manipulate, deceive, and betray. Their careers are littered with figurative and, where the rule of law is weak, real corpses. Unscrupulous top gaming has become pervasive in and around American politics, government, journalism, the media and academia.

An important section of the elite is drawn from cultural gamers the vast majority of whom also line up with the DPASM. They form the church to the DPASM's state, justifying and legitimizing it, running interference for it, and sharing in the spoils. The DPASM rules, as Michael Anton says, with the full support of the *Megaphone*, the "progressive" corporate left media-journalism-academy-arts complex.[360] The top gamers reward the Megaphone's loyal hacks with employment, resources, access, and recognition. The free press was beginning to gingerly transform itself into a central part of the Megaphone during the 1980s and 1990s, selectively doing so during the next decade and a half, and furiously completed the process in 2016 and 2017. The Megaphone abets the DPASM's benumbing of naïve idealists, buying off of low-income voters, and fanning of multiculturalist flames while attacking their critics with oppo research, selective coverage, fake news, trash-talk, libel, character assassination, and radical relativist smokescreen.[361] The Megaphone is the propaganda arm of the DPASM, turning fact into advantageous assertion, statistics into sophistry, critical inquiry into inquisition, universities into madrassas, and history into PR doled out to client groups. It wages culture wars to stifle political and intellectual opposition to itself, the monopoly complex, and their supporters. It wields vast power to define or redefine what it wants, as in the way in which it arbitrarily switched the color designations of progressive and conservative states without meaningful opposition, shedding the well-deserved but symbolically disadvantageous red and appropriating the symbolically desirable blue. One must now read the *New York Times* and *Washington Post* as one read *Izvestia* 50 years ago, by carefully looking for the guileful concession toward the end of a long feature article or critically interpreting the short article buried at the bottom of Page 26. With almost all of its resources commandeered by the top gamers and DPASM, propaganda is flourishing, but journalism is barely hanging on in America.

The stage set by its locked-in resentful groups, the Democratic Party has been drawing a supermajority of top gamers entering or approaching politics since the 1990s, by primarily representing them and winking at and facilitating their plundering. As their power and wealth have grown, the operators have cloaked their predation with unctuous, hypocritical appeals about inequality. "Trust the government to save the poor and victimized," the top gamers say to the naïve and alienated. "Come to my shell game," they whisper among themselves as they further monopolize the economy, increase inequality with surreptitious government assistance, and set up zombie-staffed clones of the Post Office and DMV. The top gamers support "redistribution" to acquire additional levers of power and privilege, big government to advance their monopoly interests, and open borders to import Democratic voters and cheap labor. The top gamers' multiculturalism may have an important aspect of shared religion, but it is to them above all a means to divide and conquer. Under their control, the Democratic Party has become a coalition of fraudsters, the naïve, and the resentful.

Although nominally opposing the developing DPASM and Megaphone, the fewer top gamers of the Republican Party establishment had substantially failed to oppose them until Trump arrived. They had gained electoral advantage from the fact that their ideas sometimes reflected common sense and concern for the country, but diffidently accepting the assumptions of gamer multiculturalism, those junior partners in corruption dithered, hesitated to play hardball, and lost most of the administrative, legislative, and judicial contests if not the electoral ones. Under Trump's leadership, the Republican Party has somewhat come around to stand up against the DPASM but not with much spirit. The younger Republican gamers taking up the banners of Trump and the Restoration may typically bring less sophistication to the table than their Democratic opponents, but many more of them both grasp and care about the country's opportunities and problems. As Trump overcame the Resistance attacks upon him, open support for establishment Republicans and Never Trumpers collapsed, but more than a little sandbagging has continued, as in Mitch McConnell and the Senate Republicans' gratuitous backlog in confirming Trump's administrative appointments and remarkable lack of outrage and action regarding DPASM sedition and corruption. Granted, they have done an excellent job on court appointments.

The administrative state has been another core element of the developing DPASM. Ignoring their oaths of office, federal bureaucrats, especially top ones, have come to feel that it is now theirs to rule, not to faithfully execute the laws of the United States as enacted by Congress and directed by the President. Having increasingly felt superior to their fellow citizens and above the law, they were attempting to transform themselves from civil servants into commissars under Obama's coaching and have been intensely doing so since 2016, if more cautiously. Paid as well as sworn to defend the constitution, intelligence agents have instead been using their spycraft and surveillance for political purposes. Chuck Schumer speaks gleefully of their power, "Let me tell you: You take on the intelligence community – they have six ways from Sunday of getting back at you."[363] Sharing the nihilism and hubris of other top gamers, administrative-state elites have played teamwork with Democratic administrations and sabotaged Republican ones, as have hundreds of thousands of its run-of-the-mill gamers. Rogue political behavior has become widespread and blatant in the federal bureaucracy and that of the larger states, especially blue ones, as the top gamers and DPASM have been attempting to suppress democratic opposition. When the DPASM gathers in all communication, illegally weaponizes leaking, and monopolizes the media, opposing it becomes exceedingly difficult. The enormous size, power, and entrenchment of the administrative state have added greatly to its corruption, as has the estrangement of its gamers from the American people and their institutions and values.

Large corporations are also a core part of the DPASM. They leaned toward the Republican Party for its support of the free markets through most of the global era as they had during the national era, but the larger and more monopolistic of them began throwing in with the Democratic Party later in the global era, a trend that accelerated as Democratic politicians were virtually hanging out neon for-sale signs, and establishment Republican ones were not far behind. The top executives of monopolistic and oligopolistic companies were concluding that a lot more money was to be made in partnering with corrupt officials than from enduring the rigors of free-market competition. Their money bought the support of the officials, who in return gave the companies and their wealthy owners tax breaks and barriers to entry strengthening their monopolistic positions. Big tech played its role on the team also by using its formidable control and censorship to throw huge assistance to the Democratic Party. Top executives wagered that government had become large and corrupt enough and democratic oversight tenuous enough that they could get away with it.

The bit players and extras among the gamers and upper-middle class have also been part of the story if mostly oblivious to the larger drama within which they have been acting. The naïve may have good hearts and feel sincerely democratic, may be concerned for the country and its middle and working classes, and may have apprehensions about the top gamers, but they have failed to notice that the elites, including those owning the media and suppressing the news, have crept over into their party. The naive mostly still believe in much of what they have long believed in, but the Megaphone has too stirred them up to notice that their party has done a 180 and has not for decades been what they thought it was, and has too incited them to notice that they who were once proudly open and tolerant have become personally authoritarian.

Nor have they noticed that theirs has become the party of Big Brother, everywhere displaying parallels with *1984*. Notice how Big Brother is watching with police and computer cameras, listening with transgender aliases like Siri and Alexa, and recording every click, keystroke, and GPS location. Notice the ubiquitous doublethink in the news and commentary, the omnipresence of the Thought Police, and the imputed "thought-crimes" they watchfully punish. Notice the sweeping rewriting of history. Notice the "Big Lies" with which top gamers smirkingly play along. None of them believe that discrimination is a major factor in the tribulations of black Americans. None of them care about the large numbers of black lives lost to violent crime arising from woke attacks restricting the police. None of them believe the Russia collusion story they have pushed. Notice that the top gamers' philosophy remains as Orwell described more than 70 years ago: "Not merely the validity of experience, but the very existence of external reality was tacitly denied by their philosophy. The heresy of heresies was common sense."[363] Big Brother's representative O'Brien tells the protagonist Winston, "The more the Party is powerful, the less it will be tolerant; the weaker the opposition, the tighter the despotism."[364] At the most profound level, all of their nonsense, which is to say, all of their non-technical cultural content and all of postmodernism, is meant to confuse and control you. It is all sparring and gaming intended to separate people into the few controllers and the many controlled.

Truly dangerous is not any single element of the DPASM but that the top-gamer elites who operate all of its elements have come together into a tight, exclusive consensus and have been marching together in close formation for the first time in American history, other than briefly under the extremely different circumstances of World War II. Also truly dangerous is what they are marching for and toward.

The Means and Ends of Resistance: Unrestrained Methods in the Elite Pursuit of Power and Wealth

The Resistance has been about elites' unrestrained pursuit of power and wealth. The real top-gamer/DPASM program – behind the toxic multiculturalist one they dispense as they do junk food, opioid medications, violent video games, and unsound mortgages – is self-seeking but now with a vengeance; which is to say, feverishly and by every means possible, flouting morality, the rule of law, and constitutional limits. The top gamers cloak themselves with inflammatory appeals to multiculturalism, effusive promises of government benefits, and mawkish deception of the naïve as they scheme with fellow operators on behalf of their interests. American national security, free markets, democracy, way of life, culture, education, beliefs, and values are all for sale by the top gamers, who have insinuated themselves as brokers auctioning it all away. Their slash-and-burn MO is as destructive to the country as their looting and pillaging.

The top gamers and DPASM's shrouded new paradigm alternative for the country is full-bore, pedal to the metal on the road toward elite monopolistic control of power and wealth, which is the road toward authoritarianism and totalitarianism, although few of them are looking even that now potentially short distance ahead. Authoritarian by inner and outer experience, the top gamers are hard, hard men and a few hard women long used to commanding themselves and others mercilessly. They are hell-bent upon and have no compunction about dictating to their fellow Americans and suppressing any who get in the way. They have been abandoning democracy not by deliberate choice in the manner for which the French existentialists mournfully pleaded through the mid-20th century but as the unthinking, cumulative consequence of their habitual transgressions of reason and restraint in pursuit of what they take to be their interests. They represent Plato's Thrasymachus again, scoffing in the Republic at the very notion of morality.[365] Their will to power has been of a piece with the Clintons' brazen pay-to-play corruption, their moving entourage-cum-cabal, Obama's devious partial remaking of federal agencies into instruments of political repression, his systematic sabotage of his successor's presidency, intelligence agencies' politicizations, and the mutation of the free press into the Megaphone. Much more devoutly than ordinary gamers, top gamers worship at the altar of Nothing, the Latin nihil.

Essential checks and balances had been dissolving since the early 1970s, but American democracy began nearing crisis as President Obama politicized and weaponized the administrative state and larger DPASM for war to suppress the loyal opposition. A key part of the run-up to the Resistance was the way in which he coopted federal agencies to have his way outside the law for political purposes. He invited Commissioner of the IRS Lois Lerner to the White House an astounding 47 times, systematically politicizing the agency to audit and suppress hundreds if not thousands of conservative organizations all over the country, threatening and often imposing dire tax penalties, killing the Tea Party, and badly disrupting Republican campaign activities. His politicized Small Business Administration harassed and punished Republican donors in a similar manner. Among many examples, the agency arbitrarily confiscated the venerable Gibson Guitar's valuable supply of exotic woods, nearly bankrupting it. Its offense was having been a small business whose owner supported the opposition. Obama may well have won reelection through his widespread use of the administrative state to suppress the Republican Party. One heard virtually none of this from the Megaphone. Silenzio!

The crisis of democracy was fully upon us when Donald Trump dared to stand up to and frontally challenge the top gamers, DPASM, and Megaphone in becoming a serious contender for the presidency in early 2016. The effort by Trump and the Restoration to democratically and lawfully overcome top-gamer predation and machinations, veiled by a multiculturalism that almost unanimous elite and upper-upper class opinion took to be foundational after its 51-year roll, is what "triggered" the Resistance. Under Obama's direction, administrative state top gamers, who had been spoiling for a fight and playing fast and freely with the law, struck against Trump and his campaign, tapping phones and sending in spies. In November of that year, on the verge of de facto hierarchical rule under the Clintons; Trump, the Restoration, and American voters shunted them off the road. Incensed to find themselves defeated, the top gamers quickly marshaled their forces, resolved to destroy Trump and key associates without procedural restraint, and began goose-stepping to achieve that purpose. The largest swarms of elite attacks, with knowing falsehood, first accused him of colluding with Russia. No sooner had those charges been demonstrated to be patently false than the deep state (i.e., the law enforcement and intelligence sections of the administrative state) contrived another set of bogus charges regarding Ukraine while elites attacked any who mentioned the Clintons' crimes or Bidens' corruption. Having long gotten away with increasingly arbitrary action, they disrespected the election and constitution, doubled down, and sought to have their way above the law. Trump's elite opponents have tasted blood in their unrelenting attacks on his candidacy, presidency, family, and very being.

A key part of the picture lies in understanding how such extremely intelligent and rational attorneys as James Comey, Peter Strzok, Andrew McCabe, Lisa Page, and their analogs in the Department of Justice could have deliberately chosen to commit their numerous felony crimes against our democratically elected president and his top associates. The answer is that a whole new elite sociocultural matrix was rapidly jelling in and around the DPASM as the conditions of democracy were slipping away and those of authoritarianism were going into place. They all took for granted in their Washington bubble that Hillary Clinton was a done deal. They all knew that, given the circumstances, the Clintons meant the effective end of American democracy. Ambitious to rise under the new administration and regime, they jumped the gun to further their political stock.

As a backup, they all knew that, with many hundreds of billions in negative advertising and PR from all sources against Trump and the Restoration, their fellow top gamers had created so much agitation in naïve and resentful Democrats, so much division and polarization that progressives could no longer be convicted of any crime against the opposition by a unanimous jury verdict. Even that was only in the unlikely event that elite prosecutors would bring charges against them in the first place and elite judges would allow proceedings to go forward. They all took out professional liability insurance with which to pay legal expenses. Moreover, they were aware that with the Megaphone having a more than 90 percent monopoly on the news, giving unqualified, blanket propaganda support to elites and the DPASM and with tech giants controlling nearly 100 percent of social media, neither the rule of law nor democracy was any longer sustainable without fundamental restoration. Democracy crumbles when unified billionaires control the entire public square within which political discussion and organization occur. Little public space is left within which freedom of speech and freedom of organization are possible.

We Americans have allowed the top gamers and DPASM to become so powerful that anyone who threatens to significantly slow the traffic on their road to authoritarian rule and the serfdom of the American people becomes the object of extreme vituperation, false accusation, spying, and arbitrary legal action with punishing financial consequences. President Trump and the Restoration have opposed elites' tyrannical rule, and they have been ruthlessly attacked for doing so. American politics has become so brutal and treacherous at the hands of the incipient tyrants and henchmen that only an extremely small subset of otherwise highly qualified potential opposition leaders has the toughness and courage to withstand it. The top gamers and DPASM have turned American politics into a commodity exchange defended by blood sport. Who else could have taken what Trump has as president? Any Republican or independent contender for the presidency, other than an establishment cipher whom elites already own, will be taking escalating versions of the broadside fusillades and foul play they have directed at Trump.

Gamers have long been attempting to tighten their political grip by fueling leftist hysteria, evoking the incendiary enragés of the French Revolution. As they were coming into their own in the 1980s and pulling back into upper-class enclaves especially numerous on the two coasts, the hysteria began being directed against Reagan. I first paid attention to it when Ted Kennedy began whipping up the hysteria as it was building during the 1990s. Gamers were beginning to know hardly anyone who was not upper class and to hear hardly anything that was not from the corporate left media. Their increasing insularity and waxing hubris brought fierce intolerance of any diversity that was not politically beholden to them.

The insularity and intolerance have been accentuated in youth who have grown up under helicopter parenting. The worsening myopia of their political correctness is an important manifestation of the constricting circle. They demand conformity with an ever-encroaching multiculturalism while fatuously virtue signaling each other. They impute a microaggression if someone gestures, speaks, writes, or votes in a manner of which they disapprove. Unseen is the macroaggression of their expanding attempts to bully and dictate to their fellow citizens, in the fraudulent names of inclusion, diversity, and tolerance no less.

The hysteria sharply intensified in 2016 as the top gamers, DPASM, and Megaphone began increasingly orchestrating it. Their assaults upon Trump and the Restoration have been calculated, higher-stakes versions of the piranha fests by self-appointed political correctness police upon insufficiently conformist speakers, administrators, professors, and students at Yale, Claremont, Middlebury, Berkeley, Evergreen State, and other universities and colleges. The "moral police," the ANTIFA and BLM brownshirts who often accompany them, and those who permit their riots and hate crimes call themselves progressive, but progress toward what ends could that represent? Most among the long-harassed and increasingly surly middle and working classes pay little or no attention to such attacks, but nor has their elected president been fully able to govern amid the ceaseless libels, conspiracies, and sabotage. The top gamer/DPASM PR barrages and star-chamber legal assaults constitute mobilization for a rebound – resistance, as in the French resistance against the Nazi occupation, they call it in accent-free 1984-speak.

At a receding apex of the congealing DPASM during and just after the campaign lay the Clintons, fresh from almost half a century of sprawling political corruption, culminating in their hugely lucrative fake charity. As the Clinton campaign rigged the Democratic nomination against Bernie Sanders, the otherwise near-certain party nominee, it sought Obama's help in first attempting to derail the Trump campaign and then to nullify the election. The libelous Russia conspiracy subterfuge that greatly disrupted the Trump campaign and presidency was Clinton-sponsored oppo fiction concocted and disseminated by Fusion Research and its MI6 alumnus-for-hire Christopher Steele, with Obama administration, CIA, FBI, NSA, and as it turns out, FRS teamwork.[366]

Obama has been and remains at a central apex of the developing DPASM, first as president and then behind the scenes. He and top associates conspired to determine the election outcome; when that was unsuccessful, to remove the new president from office; and when that failed, to mangle his presidency. Obama utilized the deep state, with CIA Director John Brennan acting as a chief agent, to frame Trump. The Megaphone went into high gear, pulling out all the stops to crank up the fake news hysteria machine with ceaseless false and exaggerated accusations against the president. Immediately after Peter Thiel dared to come out in active support of Trump at the 2016 Republican National Convention, the Obama Labor Department landed hard upon one of his companies. The retribution operated as it had with Gibson Guitar and as it routinely does in Putin's Russia.

In deploying a wide range of dirty trick assets against Trump and the Restoration, Obama, the Clintons, their top associates, the administrative state, and their billionaire monopolist backers ramped Saul Alinsky up to Vladimir Putin. Free institutions were menaced, compromised, and weakened as the Democratic Party transformed itself into a base camp for subverting American democracy, like the German Nazi Party did during the Weimar years and as the Communist parties of France and Italy attempted to do during the postwar decades. The extra-legal assaults against the elected president were begun not in the straightforward manner of Fort Sumter but in the complex, deceptive, asymmetric manner of the top gamers, a domestic and international manner with which Putin has acquainted the world. The top gamers shamelessly brawl, feint, throw tantrums, spout bald-faced lies, and act with lightening quickness in ways surprisingly and deceptively intended to further their interests. The Resistance's Fort Sumter moment was its launching of multiple overlapping illegal conspiracies to first control and then to reverse the outcome of the 2016 presidential election.

CIA and FBI fingerprints were all over Nixon's removal from office. Trump too has squarely take on the administrative state, and again CIA and FBI fingerprints have been all over the serial attempts at his removal. Closely observing comparable travesties in the early 20th century, Hayek warned that the government's coercive control apparatus is its aspect most dangerous to democracy.[367]

Watching multiple FBI chiefs sit in judgment of a newly elected President of the United States and maul his first term in office as part of a larger conspiracy that included the outgoing administration, scores of Department of Justice officials, and multiple intelligence heads while the Megaphone cheered them on was an astonishing spectacle to any supporter of democracy. They spied upon Trump and his campaign, framed them, withheld evidence, destroyed evidence, perjured themselves, and lied to Congress while overseeing the cover-up of the Clintons' high crimes. If the top-gamer impresarios of those and similar outrages had been able to destroy Trump's presidency, they would have raked in the short-term spoils, heedless of the fact that in doing so they would have terminally embittered the white middle and working classes of this country and severely damaged its democracy and national security, with dire and far-reaching consequences for themselves and their fellow Americans.

The conditions of democracy have been receding in the United States because, wielding multiculturalism as a wrecking ball, the top gamers have been able to accumulate and exercise immense power and resources while they and ordinary gamers have been steadily undermining the middle class and rendering it politically, socially, and culturally ineffectual. Their great power, wealth, and ability have in turn fed the top gamers' hubris, emboldened them, and dissolved their tolerance and restraint. Controlling the administrative state, they cover for and fail to enforce the law against each other and sabotage lawful directives from conservative officials. Elites' substantial locks on the media and education, exposure to little but their own propaganda, isolation in homogeneous neighborhoods and metropolitan areas, and formation of overlapping fraternities of character and culture aggravated their tension with the rest of society until paradigm conflict exploded in 2016.

The conditions of democracy have been receding because after half a century of obsessing upon difference under gamer multiculturalism – half a century of gratuitous alienation, blame, and conflictualism – the sense of and concern for their country have largely dissolved at the top of American society. Such are the workings and wages of top-down moral decline, the third fundamental problem carried over from the global era, accompanying and aggravating gaming and multiculturalism.

Who are these cruel, soulless Phi Beta Kappas and Ivy Leaguers without breadth, history, heart, or morality? Not only are American journalists now acting more like their Soviet counterparts of half a century ago than like the American journalists of the past, but American civil servants are acting more like Soviet apparatchiki than like their predecessors, American billionaires are acting more like Russian oligarchs than like the very wealthy of the mid-century, and American intelligence officials are acting more like KGB than like most of their predecessors. How could anyone ever again utter the word "merit" without irony after watching this elite plot, prey, deceive, ransack, and stonewall? Do not forget for a moment that the FRS successor to the KGB now rules Russia.

In addition to the fundamental problems carried over from the global era, the new era has added its own with American elites' push toward hierarchical rule, with grave assaults upon our democracy and its elected officials and citizens in the exercise of their constitutional rights and duties. Several tens of thousands of elite Americans attended by a few million gamers have quietly reached the conclusion on some level that it is right and just that they rule dictatorially over 330 million of their fellow citizens. The top gamers' intransigent doubling down, abandoning of the rule of law, and embracing of Leninist methods have represented the metastasizing and spread of the problems of the global era.

Accordingly, the third basic principle of the Restoration has become that as a high priority we must restore and strengthen the U.S. constitution and democracy against the top gamers' drive toward authoritarianism. If we value our freedom, our property, and our lives, we must make certain that the Resistance is soundly defeated and transformed into the blowout of a bankrupt gamer multiculturalism – sending progressives back to their drawing boards and the once and hopefully future liberal foundations they have forsaken. That is going to be a decades-long struggle without respite, for the top gamers and DPASM are pursuing their authoritarian quest on all fronts, at every opportunity, and with all of their resources engaged. As if all of this were not sufficiently alarming, those resources are just now beginning to be supercharged by the industrial revolution of the new era, at the absolute center of which is AI.

Repudiating the wisdom and courage of the past that have bequeathed to us supple, hard-won democratic mechanisms and traditions enabling difficult oppositions to be peacefully reconciled, Democratic Party insiders' paradigm alternative to Trump's Restoration has in effect become hierarchical rule by the top gamers and DPASM. Its unstated party platform poses a haunting shadow regime for the United States, the first such regime the United States has faced since Appomattox and only the second in its history. The towering domestic issue before us now and for the next few decades is whether this country ought to remain a democracy or ought to adopt authoritarianism. If you do not know that already, you had better come out of your slumber. In sixty years, our elites have sunk from the best and the brightest to the worst and the brightest. The American people know what they must do about their unwanted new predicament: They must stand up for themselves and what they hold dear after having allowed themselves to be bludgeoned and trampled upon by contemptuous elites and gamers for 55 years. They can do so, but first they must wake up, throw off the yoke of the Megaphone in all of its manifestations, and organize.

READING TRUMP

President Trump with his bold insights, outsized charisma, earnest patriotism, and empathy with mainstream America has played the lead role in the paradigm conflict embroiling the United States. His complex character is intertwined with his experience as an entrepreneur and entertainer of genius and his having grown up, come of age, and flourished in New York City, one of the nation's epicenters of gamers and multiculturalists. Like Andrew Jackson, he is an executive force Americans have but rarely witnessed in the White House. Trump honed his formidable social and communication skills as a reality TV host wielding verbal and behavioral kung fu. How else would one attack the smooth, treacherous top gamers with their ratcheting control of the country? He utilizes those skills when he wields the truth in blunt, courageous ways to expose top gamer/DPASM misconduct. Who else among presidential contenders since Reagan has spoken authentically to the middle and working classes? Who else has worked with anywhere near Trump's effectiveness on the country's and their behalf?

While faux-delicate top gamers and tens of millions they influence have respectively worked themselves and allowed themselves to be worked into states in which they find the middle- and working-class vernacular, manners, and morality startling and offensive, Trump is a most unusual top gamer who grew up absorbing the language of those classes in rebellious disgust with his fellow elites, to the subsequent delight of his many supporters but the outrage of gamers. In a similar manner the Federalist elites scorned and conspired against Jackson, the blunt and courageous bearer of an earlier middle-class paradigm.

Trump possesses a comprehensive vision of where the country must go if it is to be saved from depredation, authoritarianism, and ruin. As Marini says, Trump has been attempting to reach out to all citizens over and above the factious groups. He has appealed "to the rule of law and attacked bureaucratic rule as the rule of privilege and patronage...."[368] He may use contention and he must, but he reconciles what gamers and multiculturalists have compulsively divided since the 1960s: He keeps the well-being of the larger society in mind and sees worth in all classes and groups of Americans.

Insofar as Trump and the Restoration are able to win support, they will defeat the elites and reconcile the vast and acrimonious difference that those top gamers have brought about and used to further their interests. Refocusing upon the wellbeing of the whole, reemphasizing commonality, overcoming conflict, and strengthening and expanding the middle class represent extremely important reconciliation that restores and strengthens America. Acting with consequence internationally, obtaining cooperation from allies and trading partners, reducing and redirecting social programs, cutting and redirecting regulations, and reforming taxation, if less dramatic, also do.

If you were *there* fifty-plus years ago but said of Jerry Rubin and Abbie Hoffman that their manners were just dreadful, my goodness; you were sleepwalking through 1960s – you were *out of it!* The same goes for reading Trump today. Many critics regard performance art to be the leading genre of contemporary art. Those who do not actually *get* what Trump is doing had better engage in extensive preparation before visiting the Whitney Museum. The meaning of conservatism and composition of conservative parties have been changing before our eyes because the threats to Western societies, Western Civilization, the world, and freedom have been changing, as have the ways in which those threats might best be overcome, all rapidly since 2016.

The gamers have been unremittingly contentious from the outset toward any who disagree with them, turning democratic conversation into the brutal combat of identity politics. Republican presidents and candidates from the late 1960s on, even Reagan, dared not contest them on ideological basics until 2016.[369] Elites and gamers have finally met in Trump a leader able and willing to do high-stakes battle with them. The relationship between the camps is no longer combative one way and capitulatory the other; it is combative both ways. Once the gamers were fundamentally challenged, once they for the first time met head-on opposition and were defeated by it in battle, they hyperventilated for a moment and then went apoplectic – Trump's unthinkable effrontery in failing to honor their entitlement, returning fire against their continuing barrages, and labeling their multiculturalist and other poisons what they are! Most middle- and working-class Americans grasp what legions of naïve idealists do not, that an extremely valuable leader may have a different style and manner, that in the largest view the foibles of an Admiral Nelson or a Jackson, Patton, Kennedy, or Trump pale toward insignificance when weighed against the extraordinary importance of their public service – and that today's smart, polished, credentialed, and superficially correct elites are routinely void of concern for their fellow citizens and coldly act in ways that, if not overcome, will destroy their societies.

Middle- and working-class Americans have not only retained their tolerance but greatly augmented it since 1965. Not so our elites and gamers. They fought their way kicking and screaming into the global era, and Trump and the Restoration have been doing their level best to drag them kicking and screaming out of it. Why would we expect that upper class to be an iota more decent, cautious, wiser, less obnoxious, or less dangerous in its exit than it was in its entry?! Simultaneously in paradigm and regime crises, this society has to pull itself together again, but as 160 years ago under Abraham Lincoln, it has to do so in the right manner.

TO RECONCILE OR NOT TO RECONCILE? THAT IS THE QUESTION

As the Restoration sees the circumstances of the United States in the new era unfolding, societies come apart for a time, and they must be brought together again through mutual adjustment and understanding. The immense difference that arose during the global era must be worked into a constructive and coherent relationship with the larger society; it must be made more understandable through conversation and learning, not seen as something alien and strange but as familiar variation along well-understood dimensions. We must learn to perceive the unity in seeming difference and make our country the dominant reference again. Reasons of overriding importance required that the work of multifaceted inclusion be undertaken; reasons of no less importance now compel harmonization between groups and classes. Most Americans have better learned since the 1960s to appreciate those of different racial and ethnic backgrounds, and, while relearning what is exceptional and exemplary about our country and its history, we must now emphasize doing the same with those of different classes. The wise path forward neither goes back to the omissions of the earnest and exemplary but imperfect universalisms of the early- and national-liberal paradigms and eras nor simply rejects multiculturalism; it rises above and overcomes the opposition between the earlier leadership and unifying devotion to the country amid lapses in accepting difference, and the global era's selective sensitivity to difference amid multiple worse lapses.

Yet, more than four years into the new era, we find no trace of the top gamers' willingness to peacefully reconcile with their fellow citizens; we find only their solipsistic, "woke" ultimatums and conspiracies of escalating aggressiveness. Where the Restoration embraces reconciliation in a spirit of good will, the intensifying anti-universalism of the last 55 years arrogantly rejects it. Our elites' negativism and conflictualism are no coincidence, for where the previous paradigms of liberal modernity were grounded in the Greco-Roman-Christian syntheses of late antiquity, the Middle Ages, the Renaissance, Reformation, and Enlightenment, the global-liberal paradigm pointedly was not. Gamers and multiculturalists have waged war on the universalism that made the United States and the West great, and they have brought disintegration and decline in their wake. The top gamers of the DPASM have intransigently doubled down on gamer multiculturalists' unreason in the new era. So long as we retain our democracy, the choice is ours. The United States does not have to keep coming apart, and it does not have to continue in its senescence.

The most difficult of all oppositions to reconcile are those between universalists and conflictualists, those who think in terms of, lean toward, and routinely justify conflict.[370] Hard-core conflictualists, whether they be hardened criminals or most of our top gamers, are impervious to good will and the desire and ability to reconcile. Amid bad hombres with settled dispositions to foul play, good and fair-minded people's only recourse is to sufficiently empower themselves that such people are either deterred from their wonted ill behavior or defeated in political or military conflict. The same thing goes with respect to the elites of the Chinese Communist Party.

However important our country's grave domestic challenges, the implications of the emerging paradigm alternatives for the Pax Americana, our national security, that of our friends and allies, and particularly for what is by far our largest national security threat, that posed by China, are even more important. We face a massive, determined, comprehensive, long-term Chinese juggernaut aimed systematically at world domination. They no longer even try to hide the fact. The global domination the Chinese Communist Party elite envisions for itself has a name as of Xi Jinping's recent constitutional proclamations, the "community of common destiny."[371] Xi's Belt and Road Initiative, investment in and movement toward domination of numerous strategic industries, extension of influence around the world, and consolidation of crushing totalitarianism at home are deeply rooted in the Dung regime's paradigm of more than four-decades duration. The overarching global ambition of the Communist Party in control of the resources of China's 1.4 billion people is more dangerous than were those of the USSR forty years ago or Germany and Japan together eighty years ago. They are allocating huge resources to developing military technologies that could enable them to destroy the United States in a decisive first strike. This threat from China will be the crucible of the new era for the United States, Europe, Japan, India, South Korea, our other friends and allies, our several civilizations, and freedom and liberty everywhere.

The prerequisite to achieving all other goals is that we overcome the many-sided security challenge China poses and do so by comprehensively defending ourselves and our allies to deter that adversary and others militarily if at all possible or by defeating them in war if we must. If the United States and its friends and allies are able to reconcile their domestic oppositions and revive the sense of the whole that they have allowed nihilist gamer multiculturalists to persuade them to abandon, we will in all likelihood be able to successfully meet this supreme challenge without even firing a bullet, and go on to work with all nations toward a world of peaceful accommodation. If we are not, we will yield to China's cunning, expanding coercive grip, and the future will not be kind to this country, the West, or the world. Our elites' frenzied irresponsibility has higher stakes than any of them realize.

Only rising above our differences, marshaling our national resolve, building defenses, nurturing diplomatic relationships, and enacting international policies that leverage the advantages of freedom and humane constraints will enable us to secure the future. The sooner and more seriously we rise to this world-historical challenge, the better positioned we will be to address other crucial emerging challenges, particularly including the imminent domestic threats now present to our democracy. As we enter the new era, we may hope that it will be one of national Restoration whose most important domestic task is to reconcile difference, enabling us to work together as a strong, effective, humane, and free society.

Much of the global era looks familiar and reassuring in the fading, slow-motion, rear-view cinematography: Its Pax Americana, global capitalism, democracy, and even aspects of its ascending gamers were natural developments of liberal modernity going back to 1500 and earlier, to liberalizing trends well established during the Middle Ages. Even the era's family disintegration and moral disorder were familiar, if anything but reassuring, but the gamers' apotheosis of a multiculturalism that is profoundly anti-American, anti-Western, and utterly toxic to everything good, decent, liberal, democratic, or middle class is deeply disturbing.

The contradictions, caroms, hubris, and pathos of gamer multiculturalism are right out of Euripides. It wrought devastating consequences wielding gratuitous guilt, for minorities, the United States, the West, and the world during its 51-year reign and continues to work them in its irascible dotage. If the angry groups and the top gamers fomenting and auctioning that anger were to continue on their course, they would come to tragedy. Like Medea and Pentheus, they would lose all as we who are bound to them would lose all. If that tragedy is to be averted, we have only a few years within which to be well under way with national restorations capable of guiding the United States and the West wisely through this time of massive upheaval and mortal trial, on the basis of reawakened seriousness and rediscovered national, civilizational, and global interests.

EPILOGUE

THE HISTORICAL CONTEXT
THAT IS NEVER PROVIDED

The multiculturalism that began assuming a foundational place in the American consciousness already in the mid-1960s has done so on the basis of a badly misleading narrative and false accusations that unjustly blame this exemplary country. In essence, its proponents have accused the United States of being a bad or even evil country for having had slavery during the first 75 years of its independence and for having declined to contest Jim Crow in the South as a national priority during the 85 years between 1880 and 1965. They have also regularly blamed this country for allegedly having continued to allow major and systemic prejudice toward and discrimination against group members to the present. So often as to become a mantra, gamer multiculturalists have asserted that Americans and particularly white, male, gentile Americans are an unworthy, bigoted, and anti-Semitic lot prone to prejudice and discrimination toward those who are different, beginning with blacks and extending to the expanding ranks of other multiculturalist groups.

I would like to close with a critique of the multiculturalists' narrative supporting those accusations against the United States, which were foundational to the global-liberal paradigm and era and have continued to be highly influential since, by placing it in the broader historical context that, sadly, is never provided in the press, the media, textbooks, lectures, or historical scholarship. This broader context reveals the extent to which multiculturalists have falsely accused, distortedly interpreted, and unfairly attacked this outstanding country, wrongly castigating the world's indispensable nation and painting it over from hero to goat.

As to the multiculturalists' first accusation against the United States, pertaining to its having had slavery, I would aver that, to the contrary, this country, along with a few other exceptional liberal countries, is exemplary for having institutionalized liberty and abolished slavery. Indeed, its international leadership has forged the way in making free societies possible at all in our time and by enabling a majority of countries in the world to attain liberty and democracy. Without the United States there would have been no large societies in the world that were not hierarchical and did not institutionalize a great deal of coercive labor.

America's elite accusers never go far enough and broadly enough back in time to note the rarity and precariousness of liberty in world history. Riveted to next month's or next year's depredation, they would rather not acknowledge the fact that essentially all premodern civilized societies were extremely hierarchical, with elites like themselves ruling over subject masses seldom having more than insecure subsistence incomes and minimal control over their lives, that virtually the entire history of civilized humankind from 4000 BC until 1500 AD was hierarchical, and that the vast majority of it remained such until the late 20th century. Elites and most gamers take their own liberty for granted and are unconcerned with anyone else's.

The foundations of modern liberty and modern democracy were laid in part during the Middle Ages as scores of free cities and a few relatively free small regions managed to escape the worst of elite exploitation. The Netherlands, among the freest of these regions, became home to the densest clustering of economic markets in the world by the end of the Middle Ages, supported by independent small farming unfettered by more than minimal feudalism. Its decisive turn into modern liberty and modernity occurred when the Netherlands (which then included today's Belgium) with its commercial center in Antwerp, became the first liberal nation-state as its economy tipped predominantly from hierarchy to markets and its political system from authoritarianism to republicanism around 1500 AD.

The emergence of a political coalition in the Netherlands between a flexible, relatively liberal aristocracy and the middle class during the Late Middle Ages made that beginning possible, as had the West's cultural background of Christian universalism with its emphasis upon reconciliation. The Low Countries were not fully or perfectly liberal, but they developed strong property rights and republican institutions over centuries around successively the counts of Flanders, dukes of Burgundy, and princes of Orange. Switzerland also came together early into a loose, liberal nation-state. The political experience of the Netherlands became a cornerstone of English and American liberty.

England only became predominantly liberal and republican almost two centuries later with the Glorious Revolution of 1688. English citizens of different classes had had enough of the would-be absolutism of the Stuart monarchs who disrespected the country's liberal achievements of the Middle Ages and Reformation. When democratic forces became strong enough to accept and defend self-determination and modernity, an upwelling of support arose for exiling King James II and bringing in the Netherlands' Prince of Orange, widely known as a monarch who respected the economic and political markets, to become King William I of England. National leaders invited him and his Dutch army to depose the detested James – it helped that the prince's wife Mary was the daughter of an earlier English king, Charles I, and became William's co-monarch. Throngs of English citizens welcomed and cheered them as they marched to London. William and his supporters established the modern English democracy in this Glorious Revolution. As subject to the crown, colonial America was part of this great English transition too little remembered in the United States. Not long afterward, Sweden also became liberal. No democratic nation-states existed anywhere in the world in the late 18th century other than a handful of European ones and the nascent United States.

These countries' epochal early-liberal transitions and those of the few other countries like France that joined them in the 19th century developed analogous leading coalitions which represented the partial overcoming of difficult oppositions of class, culture, and institutional structure. They overcame comparable threats to liberty. Their powerful aristocracies controlled a great deal of land and labor, providing those classes with huge resources and leaving them with hierarchical experience and leanings. These liberal countries' middle classes worked in independent businesses, craft shops, and small farms, leaving them with market experience and leanings. The aristocracies permitted capitalism and representative government only to the extent to which doing so coincided with their interests. Those aristocracies entered early-liberal coalitions at all only after long, difficult processes of learning and reconciling where in a few places like Flanders and Alsace, some aristocrats slowly came to understand during the Middle Ages and afterward that instead of commanding and arbitrarily lording it over everyone and everything, they could increase their revenues by only moderately taxing the middle class and business, allowing them to flourish - in what was an early, precocious apperception of the subtle principle behind the Laffer curve. Liberty, modernity, and robust middle-class society hinged upon this delicate process of learning and reconciliation. Aristocrats had so much power and wealth that no one could think for centuries of comprehensively imposing middle-class norms and values upon them, infringing upon their traditional hierarchi-

251

cal rights, including that of coercing labor. There was no other chance for freedom than by long working patiently with relatively liberal aristocrats. Although slavery was peripheral to Western Europe in the Middle Ages, serfdom was widely practiced, and even in early-liberal societies many powerful aristocrats continued to own large estates with partially coerced labor and/or plantations abroad, or at home in the U.S. case.

Moving from traditional hierarchical to modern liberal societies was an extremely long, difficult slog requiring cooperation and compromise with the relatively liberal sections of aristocracies, even when they owned slaves, until, centuries later, the middle class and its free institutions were strong enough to dominate on their own. The middle class did not become dominant in Britain until 1833 after passage of the Great Reform Act, and four years later in 1837 it democratically and peacefully abolished slavery throughout the British Empire, against the will of the resisting aristocracy. The success of that early-liberal coalition demanded the principled realism, steadiness, and patience of middle classes and their dedicated leaders.

Each American colony had its distinct balance between aristocracy and middle class under the sovereignty of early-liberal Great Britain. Soon after the colonies became states within an independent, unified United States, our nation formed its own early-liberal coalition as reflected in the compromises embodied in the U.S. Constitution. That document reflected a power balance between the Northern states with their relatively strong middle classes and the Southern ones with their relatively strong aristocracies. Slavery was comparatively little present in the middle-class North and old Northwest; it was heavily present in the aristocratically dominated South. The Northern and Northwestern middle classes were not yet strong enough to begin manhandling the South over slavery until 1860 with the election of the nation's first Republican president, Abraham Lincoln; and even then, it had to fight and win the Civil War to enforce that new domination. The ante-bellum United States was an early-liberal hybrid society that was partly free and partly authoritarian. The new United States under middle-class dominance was forged when the North and Northwest forcibly imposed modern liberal standards on the South, reconstituting and purging the country of aristocracy and slavery during the Civil War and Reconstruction.

How could the solid, middle-class citizens of the United States, Great Britain, or the Netherlands have developed the strong free societies that eventually overcame aristocratic hierarchy and coercive labor without having worked together with relatively illiberal aristocrats for centuries, slowly and incrementally strengthening themselves and building the foundations of liberty? Had they indignantly fought all or nothing for complete liberty from the beginning, as our fake utopian multiculturalists would foolishly demand of them, they would have been crushed; and the West would have become one more of the world's standard-issue hierarchical regions like China, Russia, and the Middle East. Engaging in utopian and quixotic revolution might have felt virtuous to out-of-touch idealists, but it would have been suicidal to their long-term cause and therefore morally wrong. Middle-class Europeans and Americans worked together with relatively flexible sections of aristocracies over centuries to lead their countries, the West, and then for a time a majority of the world's nation-states to democracy and liberation from coerced labor and coerced conformity to elite dictates. Since all historical development has gone into, and, if fortunate, fought its way out of prolonged stages of authoritarianism, it is supremely ironic that hierarchally oriented gamer multiculturalists should blame, attack, and weaken the world's leading democratic society, the United States, vis-à-vis its authoritarian adversaries international and domestic for having committed the imputed collective "original sin" of having fought its way out of authoritarianism![372]

Putting up with morally repugnant slavery for centuries while slowly restricting and eventually abolishing it was the wise and necessary course under extremely difficult circumstances for those who loved liberty and justice and would one day sacrifice and prevail in building an even greater society. Societies do not progress toward civil liberties and mature, stable democracies with radical French, Russian, Chinese, or Cuban revolutions. Wise, steady, realistic middle-class societies even rightly worked together for a time with a genocidal Stalin when they had no other choice. Neither unscrupulous, hyperrealist top gamers nor their "useful idiots" whom our Leninists devote vast respources to manipulating, have sound historical analysis upon which to stand when they condemn the United States for having had slavery. But let us turn to the second spurious charge against this country and its citizens.

As to elite multiculturalists' second accusation against the United States, that it was immoral or even evil for having left Jim Crow to the states from about 1880 until 1965; this country had focused intensely upon the problem of race from the 1830s through the 1870s as it struggled peacefully to overcome slavery during the prewar decades, waged the Civil War during the early 1860s (by far this country's bloodiest) when it had to, and then followed with Reconstruction to try to give emancipation as much substance in liberty as possible. After those wrenching, exhausting efforts to overcome slavery, circumstances required that our nation turn its focus in the 1880s to emerging priorities and largely put aside the issue of race.

Gamer multiculturalists essentially argue that the American citizens who fought and supported the Civil War and maintained Reconstruction for fifteen years afterward before turning to other priorities, were immoral or even evil for having done so – that after losing some 700,000 dead in the war out of a population of 31 million. This loss represented approximately 2,250 of every 100,000 Americans. The Vietnam War, by comparison, took approximately 26 of every 100,000 Americans. We recall the extreme outrage and intense social protest about the sacrifice of life as the latter war was conducted, the way in which public opinion was so finished with the war by the mid-1970s that it threw away the successful outcome in hand, and the way in which it wanted nothing more to do with any such involvement for long afterward. Our country's loss of life in the Civil War was approximately 87 times greater per capita than was that in the Vietnam War! Gamer multiculturalists nevertheless excoriate the battered, sickened, grieving, exhausted Americans of the 1870s and 1880s who had had the energy to keep the war going and Reconstruction afterward for another 15 years, even while they were enduring the depression of the mid-1870s and the unrest accompanying and following it. Not only had the loss of life in the Civil War been staggering, but this country now had massive new problems to face.

The ferment and agitation intensified in 1885 as the United States went into paradigm crisis for more than eleven years. Labor unrest became acute with the Haymarket bombing and riot in 1886, the Homestead strike and violence in 1892, and the nationwide railroad strike and disruption in 1894. By 1885 this country had grown immensely in territory and population. Its contiguous land area had more than tripled through the century to 3 million square miles, and its population had increased more than ten-fold to 56 million. The frontier had closed, and the now-continental country had no choice but to pull itself together into a governable and defensible nation. It had to do so while coping with the comprehensive, ramifying, unfamiliar effects of the industrial revolution, rise of large business, and urbanization. The late-19th-century United States had to forge tens of millions of diverse, polyglot European immigrants, many of them with little or no experience of self-determination, into an effective democratic society together with their American predecessors. Most challenging, this country also had to take the lead in resolving the 31-year crisis – the larger West's cataclysmic civil war, one might say – which was looming for decades, under way from 1914 to 1945, and followed at once by the Cold War defense against Soviet attempts at global expansion. After the late-19th-century paradigm crisis was resolved with the election of William McKinley as president in 1896, the United States began in earnest to overcome every one of those complex and daunting problems over the next seven decades. The magnitude of what this country took on and accomplished during the national era was stupendous.

Given the colossal new structural and existential challenges the United States faced and the widespread devastation and deep bitterness in the defeated South, the opportunity costs would have been prohibitive for it to have to have continued prioritizing the divisive and refractory issue of race. Of course Jim Crow with its continuing prejudice and discrimination was bad, but where did its injustice rank among all of the harmful conditions this country had to face during the national era? What would the costs and risks have been of continuing to take on race as a focal concern at the national level under the circumstances? Had we prioritized it, what on that crowded national-era agenda of existential challenges could we have dropped? Could we have put aside adaptation to the industrial revolution, large business, or urbanization? Could we have put aside participation in World War I or World War II? Or could we have pursued armistices rather than the complete surrenders of Nazi Germany and Japan in the latter war? Under the circumstances, the wise and moral course for the country was not at all to neglect but to benignly deprioritize racial problems at the national level, to for the most part let the states deal with them as best they could during the era.

After World War II, some relaxation took place in the generations of Americans who had pulled the gigantic load for this country and the world. A decade and a half later, the relaxation was fuller as a moment of respite, release, and hope arrived with President Kennedy, if a bit prematurely until the Cuban missile crisis was over and Khrushchev had stepped down. Thirteen months after that perilous confrontation, tensions with the USSR had subsided, Kennedy was assassinated, Johnson was newly sworn in as president, and the United States could allow itself to address omissions of its aging but venerable national-liberal paradigm and society. Once a level of security had been reached in which the country's most basic and pressing needs had been successfully met for a time, it could again devote sustained attention and energy to problems of collective justice regarding race.

The last finale of the national era then arrived quickly with passage of the equal rights provisions of the landmark civil rights laws of 1964 and 1965, but it was not the grand finale – that had been 1945. Days after passage of the second law, the Watts riot broke out, the country was badly shaken, 1880s- and 1890s-scale turmoil was again upon us, the waning national-liberal paradigm and era expired, and the global-liberal paradigm and era began unfolding. Under completely different circumstances, the no less terrible Detroit riot of 1942 had rightly fallen upon deaf, impatient ears. By 1965, the United States again had circumstances that allowed it to work hard to overcome its remaining problems of collective injustice. That does not mean it would conceptualize equal rights in a way that boded well for the country or choose constructive policies with which to try to bring them about. Christopher Caldwell argues brilliantly in his new book *The Age of Entitlement* that the draconian enforcement provisions of the civil rights laws at once institutionalized multiculturalism and contradicted vital civil liberties granted in the constitution, that they in effect radically changed or even substituted a new American constitution for the old one – all without having formally amended the constitution or convened a constitutional convention.[373] An addled America failed to notice what it was doing. Such monumental sleight of hand required both the distraction that only inflamed racial tensions could provide and execution that only the slipperiest of top gamers in Lyndon Johnson could pull off, as fitting a stroke with which to introduce the troubled new era as was his contrivance of the Tonkin Gulf incident.

Whether our having struggled all out to end slavery earlier than we did would have done more good than harm is vital counterfactual historical analysis that is virtually never engaged in. No one who looks carefully at how precarious the Union effort was in the Civil War, almost throughout, even with the new industrial might of the North and Northwest behind it, is likely to conclude that this country would have been advised to wage that war earlier than it did. Whether it would have been wise to continue with the problem of race to the fore during the national era is another necessary analysis that essentially never took place amid the anger, din, myopia, and excess of the 1960s and early 1970s and never takes place today. Nor were the rapidly improving economic conditions of black Americans through the national era much noticed or discussed during those years of paradigm change. Gamer multiculturalists excise such exonerating historical context from the narrative.

Multiculturalists' additional core accusation against the United States was that it was continuing to permit major and systemic prejudice and discrimination toward minorities during the global era. Multiculturalists subscribe to a foundational myth about race and ethnicity in America that may not always have been a misrepresentation but has long been one. The myth is that white Americans are disproportionate perpetrators of racism and black Americans disproportionate recipients of it, that Anglos are disproportionate perpetrators of injustice toward Hispanics and they disproportionate victims of it, and that gentiles are disproportionate perpetrators of antagonism and Jews disproportionate victims of it. Those charges are untrue! There is as much prejudice and discrimination by blacks against whites in the United States, as much ethnic aggression by Hispanics as by Anglos, as much negative sentiment by Jews as by gentiles (regarding this last, little in either direction by the way). There is patently not a surplus of virtue in U.S. minorities and vice in the majority, and it is prejudicial falsehood to assert otherwise. Consider that 85 percent of violent crime occurring between blacks and whites is committed by blacks,[374] or try having a white child attend an overwhelmingly black-dominated inner-city school. Watch the brutal bullying of Anglo children in many Hispanic-dominated neighborhoods and schools or the harassment of Anglo women in the Southwest. As to gentile-Jewish relations, a few with resentment here and there the one way, a few with contempt here and there the other amid a great deal of intermarriage and excellent relations overall. Human nature is complex enough that one is never going to achieve perfect harmony between racial and ethnic groups. Considering its great diversity and all aspects of needed adjustment, the United States has done as good a job with collective justice as any country in the world. Vis-à-vis these relationships, let's just call it a wash and work to reduce rather than exacerbate the abrasion.

In negating the American, Western, Christian, and classical traditions, multiculturalists have hardly been aware of the neurotic, socially constructed resentment permeating their paradigm. They are allergic to self-abnegation and self-punishment in their personal lives but wantonly sadistic in their practice of collective self-abnegation and self-punishment. They cannot cease their rhythmic, vengeful flailing upon society. Like Sam Shepard's Henry Moss, they breathe and they yell.[375] This modern, democratic United States of America is not to blame for slavery, it is not to blame for Jim Crow, and it is not to blame for ghetto demoralization. Multiculturalism and identity politics lead toward endless division, acrimony, despair, and dysfunction; toward segmentary structures like those of Austro-Hungary, Yugoslavia, Lebanon, Rwanda, and South

Africa; toward failed societies, the ruin of the West, and the end of democracy. While the United States needed to pay increased attention to race relations in 1965, the multiculturalist framework under which this was carried out was radical, negative, one-sided, and destructive to this and every other country that accepted it. When so many come to consider themselves outsiders and bear resentment toward and disparage their society, who is to lead or otherwise contribute to that society, and what happens if no one does?

All of this means nothing to today's elites whose modus operandi we know well by now. They have zero inclination toward either the truth or fair mindedness, they use anything they can as a cudgel against anyone who significantly opposes them. They bring slash and burn political conflict on behalf of their personal and class agendas to what was not long ago a respectful democratic conversation. They use group blame and division as tools, laying waste to our country and countless millions of its citizens' lives. These elites do not grasp that if they continue on their march to dictatorship, they themselves will be its most likely victims. At a certain point they lose control. For Girondins are succeeded by Jacobins and Mensheviks by Bolsheviks. In Rubashov's meditations while awaiting execution, Arthur Koestler's novel *Darkness at Noon* poignantly describes the nightmarishly vacillating razor's edge of conformity demanded of everyone but especially of elites once civil liberties and the rule of law are gone.[376] As Nikolai Bukharin and Alexei Rykov learned in Moscow and Trotsky in Mexico, there is no escape.

Yet perhaps the greatest irony is that our elite aspiring dictators, oligarchs, and commissars use bogus historical blame to discredit this outstanding liberal society as a means toward their own authoritarian and ultimately totalitarian rule, which then inevitably brings its new slaves, new genocides, new ethnic cleansing, new misogyny, and new lifestyle taboos. Except for the all-too-rare heroic leaders of the new era, one should never listen to a thing our elites say except to critically pry apart and combat their ceaseless machinations and deceit.

Edith Hamilton's reflections from nearly a century ago upon the fall of Rome bear pondering: Rome toward the end, she says, was most lacking in "wisdom and disinterestedness…. If the people had held together, realizing their interdependence and working for a common good, their problems, completely strange and enormously difficult though they were, would not, it may well be believed, have proved too much for them. But they were split into sharpest oppositions, extremes that ever grew more extreme and so more irresponsible."[377] Always oppose our elites so long as they remain divisive and destructive; always fight to reduce their power and resources, open their monopolies to competition, lay bare the wreckage they strew, and shine light upon their nefarious schemes – and we might just barely hold on to our freedom and humanity, against the odds, through the extremely rocky decades to come.

BIBLIOGRAPHY

Abrams, Richard M. *America Transformed: Sixty Years of Revolutionary Change, 1941–2001*. Cambridge: Cambridge University Press, 2006.

Adorno, Theodor. *Minima Moralia*. London: Verso, 1975.

Ali, Ayaan Hirsi. *Infidel*. New York: Free Press, 2007.

Anand, Geeta, and Amol Sharma. "For India's Lowest Castes, Path Forward Is 'Backward.'" *Wall Street Journal*, Dec. 9, 2011, A1.

Anton, Michael. "The Empire Strikes Back," *Claremont Review of Books*, Vol. 19, no. 4 (Fall, 2019): 8-14.

Aristotle. *Politics*. Hammondsworth, Middlesex: Penguin, 1962.

Augustine. *City of God.* Hammondsworth, Middlesex: Penguin Books, 1972.

Baltzell, E. Digby. *The Protestant Establishment: Aristocracy and Caste in America*. New York: Random House, 1964.

Banfield, Edward C. *The Unheavenly City Revisited*. Boston: Little, Brown, 1974.

Barbieri, Pierpaolo. "A Lesson in Crony Capitalism." *Wall Street Journal,* Aug. 9, 2012, A11.

Bartlett, Tom, and Karin Fischer. "The China Conundrum." *New York Times*, Nov. 3, 2011, Education Life Sctn., 1–10.

Barton Fink. DVD. Directed by Joel Coen. Beverly Hills, CA: Twentieth Century Fox, 1991.

Baudrillard, Jean. *Consumer Society: Myths and Structures*. Thousand Oaks, CA: Sage, 1998.

-----. *System of Objects*. New York: Verso, 1996.

Baumeister, Roy F. *Identity*. New York: Oxford University Press, 1986.

Becker, Gary S. *A Treatise on the Family*. Cambridge, MA: Harvard University Press, 1991.

Becker, Howard S. *Outsiders: Studies in the Sociology of Deviance*. Glencoe, IL: Free Press, 1963.

Bell, Daniel. *The Cultural Contradictions of Capitalism*. New York: Basic Books, 1966.

Bellah, Robert N., Richard Madsen, William M. Sullivan, Ann Swidler, and Steven M. Tipton. *Habits of the Heart: Individualism and Commitment in American Life*. Berkeley: University of California Press, 1985.

Berger, Peter L. *The Sacred Canopy*. New York: Anchor Books, 1967.

Berlin, Isaiah. "Two Concepts of Liberty." Pp. 118–72 in *Four Essays on Liberty*. New York: Oxford University Press, 1969.

Bhagwati, Jagdish, and Arvind Panagariya. *Why Growth Matters*. New York: Public Affairs, 2013.

Bishop, Bill. *The Big Sort: Why the Clustering of Like-Minded America Is Tearing Us Apart*. Boston: Houghton Mifflin, 2008.

Bogle, Kathleen A. *Hooking Up: Sex, Dating and Relationships on Campus*. New York: New York University Press, 2008.

Bombay Beach. Directed by Alma Har'el. Boaz Yakin Presents, 2011.

Bourdieu, Pierre. *Distinction: A Social Critique of the Judgment of Taste*. Cambridge, MA: Harvard University Press, 1984.

Brooks, David. *Bobos in Paradise: The New Upper Class and How They Got There*. New York: Simon and Schuster, 2000.

Brooks, Geraldine. "Teen-Age Infidels Hanging Out." *New York Times Magazine*, Apr. 30, 1995, 44– 48.

Brown, Claude. *Manchild in the Promised Land*. New York: Macmillan, 1965.

Buchanan, James M. and Gordon Tullock, *The Calculus of Consent: Logical Foundations of Constitutional Democracy*. Ann Arbor, MI: University of Michigan Press, 1962.

Burke, Edmund. *Reflections on the Revolution in France*. Oxford: Oxford University Press, 1993.

Burnham, John C. *Bad Habits: Drinking, Smoking, Taking Drugs, Gambling, Sexual Misbehavior, and Swearing in American History*. New York: New York University Press, 1993.

Caldwell, Christopher. *The Age of Entitlement: America since the Sixties*. New York: Simon & Schuster, 2020

Caro, Robert A. *The Years of Lyndon Johnson*, Vol. 4. *The Passage of Power*. New York: Vintage, 2012.

Carroll, Jim. *The Basketball Diaries*. New York: Penguin Books, 1995.

Chen, Adrian. "The Agency." *New York Times Magazine*, June 2, 2015.

Cherlin, Andrew J. *The Marriage-Go-Round: The State of Marriage and the Family in America Today*. New York: Alfred A. Knopf, 2009.

Chow, Emily, Scott Cleist, and Peyton Craighill. "Exit Polls." *Washington Post*, Nov. 5, 2014.

Christiane F.: Wir Kinder vom Bahnhof Zoo. Directed by Ulrich Edel. West Berlin: New World Pictures, 1981.

Churchill, Winston S. "The Sinews of Peace." Pp. 7285–93 in Robert R. James, ed., *Winston S. Churchill: His Complete Speeches 1897–1963*. Vol. 7, *1943–1949*. New York: Chelsea House Publishers, 1974.

Claassen, Alfred. *An Inquiry into the Philosophical Foundations of the Human Sciences*. New York: Peter Lang, 2007.

Cleveland, Margot. "Schumer: Intelligence Agencies Have Six Ways From Sunday of Getting Back At You." *The Federalist*, September 27, 2019. At https://thefederalist.com/2019/09/27/schumer-intelligence-agencies-have-six-ways-from- sunday-of-getting-back-at-you/

Clockwork Orange, A. Directed by Stanley Kubrick. New York: Polaris Productions, 1971.

Congdon, Tim and Steve H. Hanke. "More Bank Capital Could Kill the Economy," *Wall Street Journal,* March 14, 2017, A17.

Congressman X, *The Confessions of Congressman X.* Minneapolis: Mill City Press, 2016.

Conley, Dalton. *Elsewhere, USA*. New York: Pantheon Books, 2009.

Daft, Richard L. *Organization Theory and Design*, 11th ed. Mason, OH: Southwestern Cengage Learning, 2013.

Dalrymple, Theodore. *Life at the Bottom: The Worldview that Makes the Underclass*. Chicago, Ivan R. Dee, 2001.

DeParle, Jason, and Sabrina Tavernise. "The New Normal: A Child Out of Wedlock." *New York Times,* Feb. 18, 2012, A1 (L).

Deresiewicz, William. "Solitude and Leadership." *American Scholar*, Vol. 79, no. 2 (Spring 2010): 20–31. At http//www.theamericanscholar.org/solitude-and-leadership/.

De Soto, Hernando. *The Mystery of Capital: Why Capitalism Triumphs in the West and Fails Everywhere Else*. New York: Basic Books, 2000.

Diamond, Larry. *The Spirit of Democracy: The Struggle to Build Free Societies throughout the World*. New York: Henry Holt and Company, 2008.

Dicey, A. V. *Lectures on the Relation between Law and Public Opinion in England during the Nineteenth Century*. London: Macmillan, 1962.

Didion, Joan. *Political Fictions*. New York: Vintage, 2001.

Dobson, William J. *The Dictator's Learning Curve: Inside the Global Battle for Democracy*. New York: Doubleday, 2012.

Dunlop, John B. *The Moscow Bombings of September 1999: Examinations of Russian Terrorist Attacks at the Onset of Vladimir Putin's Rule*. Stuttgart: Ibidem, 2012.

Durkheim, Emile. *The Division of Labor in Society*. New York: Free Press, 1984.

----- *Suicide: A Study in Sociology*. New York: Free Press, 1966.

Duverger, Maurice. *Political Parties, Their Organization and Activity in the Modern State*. New York: Wiley, 1962.

Easy Rider. Directed by Dennis Hopper. New York: The Pando Company/Raybert Productions, 1969.

Ehrenreich, Barbara. *The Hearts of Men: American Dreams and the Flight from Commitment*. Garden City, NY: Doubleday, 1983.

Eichengreen, Barry. *Globalizing Capital: A History of the International Monetary System*. 2nd ed. Princeton, NJ: Princeton University Press, 2008.

Fallaci, Oriana. "An Interview with Khomeini." *New York Times Magazine*, Oct. 7, 1979, 29–31.

Fallows, James. *Postcards from Tomorrow Square: Reports from China*. New York: Vintage, 2009.

Fan, Maureen. "Chinese Slough Off Old Barriers to Divorce." *Washington Post*, Apr. 7, 2007, A1.

Ferguson, Niall. *Colossus: The Price of America's Empire*. New York: Penguin, 2004.

Fisk, Catherine and Erwin Chemerinsky. "The Filibuster," 49 *Stanford Law Review*, 181-254, January 1997.

Freedom in the World 2015: Discarding Democracy – Return to the Iron Fist. Washington, DC: Freedom House, 2015. At https://www.freedomhouse.org/report/freedom-world-2015.

Freedom in the World 2016: Anxious Dictators, Wavering Democracies. Washington, DC: Freedom House, 2016. At https://www.freedomhouse.org/report/freedom-world-2016.

Freeman, Kathleen, ed. *Ancilla to the Pre-Socratic Philosophers*. Cambridge, MA: Harvard University Press, 1948.

French, Patrick. *India*. New York: Alfred A. Knopf, 2011.

Friedman, George. "The Crisis of Interdependence," George Friedman," October 3, 2016. At www.realclearworld.com/articles/2016/10/03/2008_interdependence_globalization_nationalism_georgefriedman.html.

Friedman, Milton, and Rose Friedman. *Free to Choose: A Personal Statement*. New York: Harcourt, Brace, Jovanovich, 1980.

Friedman, Milton, and Anna Jacobson Schwartz. *A Monetary History of the United States, 1867–1960*. Princeton, NJ: Princeton University Press, 1963.

Fukuyama, Francis. *The End of History and the Last Man*. New York: Free Press, 1992.

Gaddis, John L. *The Cold War: A New History*. New York: Penguin, 2005.

-----. *Surprise, Security, and the American Experience*. Cambridge, MA: Harvard University Press, 2004.

-----. *The United States and the Origins of the Cold War, 1941–1947*. New York: Columbia University Press, 2000.

Gilbert, Neil. *Capitalism and the Welfare State: Dilemmas of Social Benevolence*. New Haven, CT: Yale University Press, 1983.

Glazer, Nathan and Daniel Patrick Moynihan, *Beyond the Melting Pot*, 2nd ed. Cambridge, MA: MIT Press, 1970.

Goffman, Erving. *Asylums: Essays on the Social Situation of Mental Patients and Other Inmates*. Garden City, NY: Anchor Books, 1961.

Goldberg, Jeffrey. "The Obama Doctrine." *The Atlantic*, Vol. 317, no. 3 (Apr. 2016), 70-90.

Goody, Jack. *The Logic of Writing and the Organization of Society*. Cambridge: Cambridge University Press, 1986.

Gurevitch, Michael. "The Globalization of Electronic Journalism." Pp. 178–93 in James Curran and Michael Gurevitch, eds., *Mass Media and Society*. London: Edward Arnold, 1992.

Gutman, Herbert G. *The Black Family in Slavery and Freedom, 1750–1925*. New York: Pantheon Books, 1976.

Habermas, J. *The Inclusion of the Other: Studies in Political Theory*. Cambridge, MA: MIT Press, 1998.

-----. "The Public Sphere." Pp. 398–404 in Chandra Mukerji and Michael Schudson, eds., *Rethinking Popular Culture: Contemporary Perspectives in Cultural Studies*. Berkeley: University of California Press, 1991.

Hamburger, Philip. Is Administrative Law Unlawful? Chicago: University of Chicago Press, 2014. Hanson, Victor Davis. "Obama and Revolutionary Romance," National Review Online, April 15, 2015. At: http://www.nationalreview.com/article/416870/obama-and-revolutionary-romance-victor-davis-hanson.

Hartcher, Peter. "Bully-boy Malaysia Immature and Australia's Reaction So Limp." *Sydney Morning Herald,* Feb. 19, 2013, 9.

Harvey, David. *The Condition of Postmodernity*. Cambridge: Blackwell, 1990.

Hayek, Friedrich A. *The Constitution of Liberty*. Chicago: University of Chicago Press, 1960.

-----. *Law, Legislation, and Liberty* (3 vols.). Chicago: University of Chicago Press, 1973–1979.

-----. *The Road to Serfdom*. Chicago: University of Chicago Press, 1944.

Hegel, G. W. F. *The Phenomenology of Mind*. New York: Harper & Row, 1967.

Hetzel, Robert L. *The Great Recession: Market Failure or Policy Failure?* Cambridge: Cambridge University Press, 2012.

Himmelfarb, Gertrude. *One Nation, Two Cultures: A Searching Examination of American Society in the Aftermath of Our Cultural Revolution*. New York: Alfred A. Knopf, 2001.

-----. *One Nation, Two Cultures: A Searching Examination of American Society in the Aftermanth of Our Cultural Revolution*. New York: Alfred A. Knopf, 2001.

-----. "The Panglosses of the Right Are Wrong." *Wall Street Journal*, Feb. 4, 1999, A22.

Hirschman, Albert O. *Exit, Voice, and Loyalty: Responses to Decline in Firms, Organizations, and States*. Cambridge, MA: Harvard University Press, 1970.

Huntington, Samuel P. *The Clash of Civilizations and the Remaking of World Order*. New York: Touchstone, 1997.

-----. *The Third Wave: Democratization in the Late Twentieth Century*. Norman, OK: University of Oklahoma Press, 1991.

-----. *Who Are We?* New York: Simon and Schuster, 2004.

Ibn Khaldun. *The Muqaddimah: An Introduction to History* (3 vols.). New York: Pantheon Books, 1958.

Ignatius, David. "In China, It's All about Prosperity, not Freedom." *Washington Post*, Oct. 21, 2010, A21.

Jacobs, Jane. *The Death and Life of Great American Cities*. New York: Vintage, 1961.

Jones, E.L. *The European Miracle: Environments, Economies and Geopolitics in the History of Europe and Asia*. Cambridge: Cambridge University Press, 1981.

Judt, Tony. *Postwar: A History of Europe since 1945*. New York: Penguin, 2005.

Kagan, Robert. *The World America Made*. New York: Alfred A. Knopf, 2012.

Katz, Michael B. *The Undeserving Poor: From the War on Poverty to the War on Welfare*. New York: Pantheon Books, 1989.

Kimmel, Michael. "A War against Boys?" *Dissent*, Vol. 53, no. 4 (Fall 2006): 65–70.

Klatch, Rebecca E. *A Generation Divided: The New Left, the New Right, and the 1960s*. Berkeley: University of California Press, 1999.

Kotkin, Joel. *The New Class Conflict*. Cantor, NY: Telos Press Publishing, 2014.

Krein, Julius. "The Real Class War." *American Affairs Journal*, Volume III, No. 4 (Winter 2019): 153-72. At https://americanaffairsjournal.org/2019/11/the-real-class-war/

Krinsky, Natalie. *Chloe Does Yale*. New York: Hyperion, 2006.

Kristol, Irving. *Reflections of a Neo-Conservative*. New York: Basic Books, 1983.

Krugman, Paul, Richard N. Cooper, and T. N. Srinivasan. "Growing World Trade: Causes and Consequences." Pp. 327–77 in *Brookings Papers on Economic Activity*, Vol. 1995, no. 1. Washington, DC: Brookings Institution.

Kulke, Hermann, and Dietmar Rothermund. *A History of India*. New York: Dorset, 1986. Kuniholm, Bruce R. *The Origins of the Cold War in the Near East: Great Power Conflict and Diplomacy in Iran, Turkey, and Greece*. Princeton, NJ: Princeton University Press, 1980.

The Last Temptation of Christ. Directed by Martin Scorsese. Universal City, CA: Universal Pictures, 1988.

Leibovich, Mark. *This Town*. New York: Penguin, 2013.

Lemann, Nicholas. *The Promised Land: The Great Black Migration and How It Changed America*. New York: Alfred A. Knopf, 1991.

Lewis, Michael. *Boomerang: Travels in the New Third World*. New York: Norton, 2011.

Lilla, Mark. *The Once and Future Liberal: After Identity Politics*. New York: Harper, 2017.

Lipset, Seymour Martin. *American Exceptionalism: A Double-Edged Sword*. New York: Norton, 1996.

Loewen, James. *The Mississippi Chinese: Between Black and White*. Cambridge, MA: Harvard University Press, 1971.

Long, A.A. and D.N. Sedley, eds., *The Hellenistic Philosophers*, Vol. 1, *Translations of the Principal Sources with Philosophical Commentary*. Cambridge: Cambridge University Press, 1987.

Luce, Edward. *In Spite of the Gods: The Strange Rise of Modern India*. New York: Doubleday, 2007.

Lyotard, Jean-Francois. *The Postmodern Condition*. Minneapolis: University of Minnesota Press, 1984.

Maccoby, Michael. *The Gamesman: The New Corporate Leaders*. New York: Simon and Schuster, 1976.

MacDonald, Heather. "A Window into a Depraved Culture." *City Journal*, January 8, 2017. www.city- journal.org/html/window-depraved-culture-14929.html

MacIntyre, Alasdair. *Whose Justice, Which Rationality?* Notre Dame, IN: University of Notre Dame Press, 1988.

MacKenzie, Donald. *An Engine, Not a Camera: How Financial Models Shape Markets*. Cambridge, MA: MIT Press, 2006.

Maddison, Angus. *Phases of Capitalist Development*. Oxford: Oxford University Press, 1982.

Mannheim, Karl. *Ideology and Utopia*. New York: Harcourt, Brace and World, 1936.

Mallaby, Sebastian. *The Man Who Knew: The Life and Times of Alan Greenspan*. New York: Penguin Press, 2016.

Marini, John. *Unmasking the Administrative State: The Crisis of American Politics in the Twenty- First Century*. Edited by Ken Masugi. New York: Encounter Books, 2019.

Marquardt, Elizabeth, et al. "The President's Marriage Agenda for the Forgotten Sixty Percent." Pp. 1- 46 in *The State of Our Unions*. Charlottesville, VA: National Marriage Project and Institute for American Values, 2012.

Matza, David. *Becoming Deviant*. Englewood Cliffs, NJ: Prentice-Hall, 1969.

McKinley, James C., Jr. "Uganda Leader Stands Tall in New African Order." *New York Times*, June 15, 1997, 3.

McPherson, Miller, Lynn Smith-Lovin, and Matthew E. Brashears. "Social Isolation in America: Changes in Core Discussion Networks over Two Decades." *American Sociological Review*, Vol. 71 (June 2006): 353–75. See also the online supplement to the article at http://www2.asanet.org/journals/asr/2006/smith-lovinerratum.pdf.

Mead, Lawrence M. *Beyond Entitlement: The Social Obligations of Citizenship.* New York: Free Press, 1986.

Mill, John Stuart. *Considerations on Representative Government.* Chicago: Henry Regnery Co., 1962.

Miller, Andrew T. "Social Science, Social Policy, and the Heritage of African American Families." Pp. 254–89 in Michael B. Katz, ed., *The "Underclass" Debate.* Princeton, NJ: Princeton University Press, 1993.

Moore, Barrington, Jr. *The Social Conditions of Dictatorship and Democracy: Lord and Peasant in the Making of the Modern World.* Boston: Beacon Press, 1966.

Morgenson, Gretchen, and Joshua Rosner. *Reckless Endangerment: How Outsized Ambition, Greed, and Corruption Led to Economic Armageddon.* New York: Times Books/Henry Holt and Co., 2011.

Mosca, Gaetano. *The Ruling Class.* New York: McGraw-Hill, 1939.

Moynihan, Daniel Patrick. "Defining Deviancy Down: How We've Become Accustomed to Alarming Levels of Crime and Destructive Behavior." *American Scholar,* Vol. 62 (Winter 1993): 17–30.

-----. *The Negro Family: The Case for National Action.* Washington, DC: Office of Policy Planning and Research, U.S. Department of Labor, 1965.

Murray, Charles A. *Coming Apart: The State of White America, 1960–2010.* New York: Crown Forum, 2012.

-----. "Charles Murray: Hillary Clinton's 'Deplorables' Comment May Have Changed the Course of World History." *RealClearPolitics,* April 25, 2017. At realclearpolitics.com/video/2017/04/25/charles_murray_hillary_clintons_deplorables_commint_ may_have_changed_the_course_of_world_history.html.

-----. "Does Welfare Bring More Babies?" *The Public Interest,* no. 115 (Spring 1994): 17–30.

-----. *The Underclass Revisited.* Washington, DC: AEI Press, 1999.

Mus, Publius Decius [Michael Anton]. "The Flight 93 Election." *American Greatness,* September 5, 2016.

Nielsen Company, The. *Shifts in Viewing: The Cross-Platform Report.* Sept. 2014, 8. At http://www.nielsen.com/content/dam/corporate/us/en/reports-downloads/ 2014%20Reports/q2- 2014-cross-platform-report-shifts-in-viewing.pdf.

Nietzsche, Friedrich. *On the Genealogy of Morals/Ecce Homo.* New York: Vintage, 1969.

-----. *The Will to Power,* ed. Walter Kaufmann. New York: Vintage Books, 1967.

Noonan, Peggy. "The Inconvenient Truth about Benghazi." *Wall Street Journal,* May 10, 2013, A15.

Olson, Mancur. *The Logic of Collective Action: Public Goods and the Theory of Groups.* Cambridge, MA: Harvard University Press, 1965.

Orwell, George. *1984.* New York: New American Library, [1949] 1961.

Packer, George. "The Megacity: Decoding the Chaos of Lagos." *New Yorker*, Nov. 13, 2006, 62–75.

Pareto, Vilfredo. *Sociological Writings*, ed. S. E. Finer. New York: Praeger, 1966.

Parsons, Talcott. *The Evolution of Societies*. Englewood Cliffs, NJ: Prentice-Hall, 1977.

Patterson, James T. *America's Struggle against Poverty in the Twentieth Century*. Cambridge, MA: Harvard University Press, 2000.

Pechatnov, Vladimir O. "The Soviet Union and the World, 1945–1952." Pp. 90–111 in Melvyn P. Leffler and Odd Arne Westad, eds., *Cambridge History of the Cold War*, Vol. 1. Cambridge: Cambridge University Press, 2012.

Piore, Michael J., and Charles F. Sabel. *The Second Industrial Divide*. New York: Basic Books, 1984.

Plato. *Republic*. In *The Collected Works of Plato*. Translated and edited by Edith Hamilton and Hamilton Cairns. Princeton, N.J.: Princeton University Press, [ca. 380 BC] 1961.

Polanyi, Karl. *The Great Transformation: The Political and Economic Origins of Our Time*. Boston: Beacon Press, 1944.

Polybius. *The Histories*, Vol. 3. Cambridge, MA: Harvard University Press, 1923.

Popenoe, David. *Life without Father: Compelling New Evidence that Fatherhood and Marriage are Indispensable for the Good of Children and Society*. New York: Martin Kessler Books, 1996.

Putnam, Robert D. *Bowling Alone: The Collapse and Revival of American Community*. New York: Simon and Schuster, 2000.

Putnam, Robert D., and David E. Campbell. *American Grace: How Religion Divides and Unites Us*. New York: Simon and Schuster, 2010.

Rajak, Svetozar. "The Cold War in the Balkans, 1945–1956." Pp. 198–220 in Melvyn P. Leffler and Odd Arne Westad, eds., *Cambridge History of the Cold War*, Vol. 1. Cambridge: Cambridge University Press, 2012.

Rank, Otto. *Will Therapy*. New York: Alfred A. Knopf, 1936.

Rauschenbush, Walter. *Christianity and the Social Crisis*. New York: Macmillan Co., 1907.

Riesman, David. *The Lonely Crowd: A Study of the Changing American Character*. New Haven, CT: Yale University Press, 1961.

Rosefielde, Steven, and Stefan Hedlund. *Russia since 1980*. Cambridge: Cambridge University Press, 2009.

Sakharov, Andrei. *Progress, Coexistence, and Intellectual Freedom*. New York: Norton, 1968.

Schorske, Carl. *Fin-de-Siecle Vienna: Politics and Culture*. New York: Vintage, 1981.

Schrader, Matt. "In a Fortnight: Xi's Other Amendments." In RealClearDefense, March 13, 2018. At realcleardefense.com/articles/2018/03/13/in_a_fortnight_xix_other_amendments_113180.ht ml

Schumpeter, Joseph A. *The Theory of Economic Development: An Inquiry into Profits, Capital, Credit, Interest, and the Business Cycle*. New Brunswick, NJ: Transaction Publishers, 1983.

Sen, Amartya K. *Development as Freedom*. New York: Knopf, 1999.

Schur, Edwin. *Crimes without Victims; Deviant Behavior and Public Policy: Abortion, Homosexuality, Drug Addiction*. Englewood Cliffs, NJ: Prentice-Hall, 1965.

Sennett, Richard. *The Fall of Public Man*. New York: Vintage, 1978.

Shattuck, Roger. "Morality of the Cool." *The Atlantic*, Vol. 283, no. 1 (Jan. 1999): 73–78.

Shepard, Sam. *The Buried Child*. New York: Dramatists Play Service, 1997.

-----. *The Late Henry Moss; Eyes for Consuela; When the World Was Green: Three Plays*. New York: Vintage Books, 2002.

Siegel, Fred. *The Future Once Happened Here: New York, DC, LA, and the Fate of America*. New York: Free Press, 1997.

Simmel, Georg. "The Metropolis and Mental Life." Pp. 409–24 in Kurt Wolff, ed., *The Sociology of Georg Simmel*. New York: Free Press, 1950.

Social Network, The. Directed by David Fincher. Culver City, CA: Columbia Pictures, 2010.

Der Spiegel Online International. "The Ticking Euro Bomb," no. 39 (Oct. 5–7, 2011).

Stearns, Peter N. *American Cool: Constructing a Twentieth-Century Emotional Style*. New York: New York University Press, 1994.

Steele, Shelby. *White Guilt: How Blacks and Whites Together Destroyed the Promise of the Civil Rights Era*. New York: Harper Perennial, 2006.

Streetwise. Directed by Martin Bell. New York: Angelika Films, 1984.

Stueck, William. *Rethinking the Korean War: A New Diplomatic and Strategic History*. Princeton, NJ: Princeton University Press, 2002.

Suranovic, Steve. *International Trade: Theory and Policy*, Vol. 1.0 (May 2010). Accessed at http//flatworldknowledge.com/catalog/editions/surantrade-international-trade-theory-and-policy-1-0.

Tocqueville, Alexis de. *The Old Regime and the French Revolution*. Garden City, NJ: Anchor Books, 1955.

Vance, J.D. *Hillbilly Elegy: A Memoir of a Family and Culture in Crisis*. New York: Harper Collins, 2016.

Vedantam, Shankar. "Social Isolation Growing in U.S., Study Says." *Washington Post*, June 23, 2006, A3.

Wallerstein, Immanuel. *The Modern World-System: Capitalist Agriculture and the Origins of the European World-Economy in the Sixteenth Century*. New York: Academic Press, 1974.

Wallison, Peter J. "How Regulators Herded Banks into Trouble." *Wall Street Journal*, Dec. 3–4, 2011, A-17.

Walt, Vivienne. "Lagos, Nigeria: Africa's Big Apple." Fortune, issue 8 (June 12, 2014). At http://fortune.com/2014/06/12/lagos-nigeria-big-apple.

Wang, Hui. *China's New Order: Society, Politics, and Economy in Transition*. Cambridge, MA: Harvard University Press, 2003.

Washington Post, "Exit Polls 2012: How the Vote has Shifted." Nov. 6, 2012.

Weber, Max. "Anti-critical Last Word on 'The Spirit of Capitalism.'" *American Journal of Sociology*, Vol. 83, no. 5 (1978): 1105–31.

-----. *Economy and Society: An Outline of Interpretive Sociology* (2 vols.). Berkeley: University of California Press, 1978.

-----. *The Protestant Ethic and the Spirit of Capitalism*. New York: Charles Scribner's Sons, [1905] 1958.

-----. *The Religion of China: Confucianism and Taoism*. Translated and edited by Hans Gerth. New York: Free Press [1922] 1964.

Whyte, William H., Jr. *The Organization Man*. New York: Anchor Books, 1957.

Williams, Rosalind H. *Dream Worlds: Mass Consumption in Late Nineteenth-Century France*. Berkeley: University of California Press, 1982.

Wilson, William J. *The Truly Disadvantaged: The Inner City, the Underclass, and Public Policy*. Chicago: University of Chicago Press, 2012.

Wooldridge, Adrian. "Northern Lights." Special Report on the Nordic Countries in *The Economist*, Vol. 406, no. 8821 (Feb. 2–8, 2013): 3–16.

Wright, Richard. *Black Boy*. New York: Harper and Row, 1966.

Wyatt, Ian D., and Daniel E. Hecker. "Occupational Changes during the Twentieth Century." *Monthly Labor Review*, Vol. 129, issue 3 (Mar. 2006): 48.

X, Malcolm. *The Autobiography of Malcolm X*. New York: Grove Press, 1965.

NOTES

Introduction

1. See Bishop, *The Big Sort*, 87–90, on how pivotal the year 1965 was.

2. Paradigms provide much of the deep structure of eras, societies, and personalities. Since truly fathoming their own complexity and that of circumstances is overwhelming, people finesse the task by assembling and clasping models that guide what they perceive, think, feel, and do. Paradigms stake out positions on the dimensions of the human, pinning down existential abodes for a time. Their basic assumptions are for the most part unconsciously held.

3. This definition utilizes the traditional European sense of the word "liberal" as relatively free and unregulated on all issues. The other major sense of "liberal" is the current American one of being in favor of free markets in social and cultural spheres but being in favor of expanded hierarchy or government activity in the economy. Both senses are used as needed.

4. This work is grounded in notions I have presented in an earlier book, Claassen, *An Inquiry*.

Chapter 1 The Pax Americana

5. Under the Pax Britannica, Britain employed its considerable diplomatic, financial, and military power to discourage aggressive and destabilizing action by countries large and small, upholding a basic peace within which economies and societies could flourish. Not only was military aggression between states largely deterred, but mercantilism was also largely overcome for nearly a century, between 1815 and 1914.

6. The notion of the Pax Americana or "American world order," as Kagan terms it in *The World America Made*, is an extrapolation from Karl Polanyi's notion of the Pax Britannica in his classic work of history and social thought, *The Great Transformation* (chap. 1). One of the strengths of the concept is that it facilitates a distinction between the informal leadership by and of liberal countries from anything that could be fairly described as imperial. The United States has never really had an empire, nor does it today. Its leadership has been achieved by the willing assent and cooperation of its friends and allies.

Those who label U.S. international leadership since 1945 "imperial" (after the British or Roman Empire), such as Niall Ferguson in *Colossus*, fail to distinguish sufficiently between Britain's leadership of developed countries in Europe under the Pax Britannica and its simultaneous colonial domination over India, Rhodesia, and dozens of other less-developed societies under the British Empire. Ferguson's work as a whole is excellent, but on this point he is not helpful. It is as if he were winking at Americans, asking them to acknowledge that they after all have been doing what the British did with their empire. The Pax Britannica was led by a country that possessed a vast colonial empire, but its exercise of leadership in Europe was not an imperial role. Nor is that of the United States vis-à-vis France, Poland, or Indonesia today. The origin and collapse of the Pax Britannica were also quite distinct from those of the British Empire.

Speaking of the Pax Americana is in no way intended to slight the major roles played in the security regime by other important participants, above all the United Kingdom, which has been the United States' co-leader throughout – nor is the term intended to exaggerate the role of the United States. The Pax Americana could not have existed without the core allies. Yet nor could the international security regime have existed without the United States. Even more than in the nineteenth century, one nation has been the security regime's preeminent leader, and without acknowledging and analyzing this fact, one loses touch with reality. Unfortunately, the notion of a Pax Americana also unavoidably evokes the notion of the Pax Romana. That too was a great time of peace under an international security regime, only one of a very different character, which *was* fundamentally imperial.

Polanyi began his book on the international markets with an analysis of the Pax Britannica because he understood the utterly pivotal role international security regimes play in how the markets fare. That is an important additional reason to follow his usage.

7. See Polanyi, *The Great Transformation*, 121. Much of the world languished economically during that decade although the United States did not.

8. Kagan (*The World America Made*, 16) speaks of the unself-consciousness and ambivalence Americans have always felt toward their exercise of power in the world, which paradoxically has made this leadership less threatening to those in other countries. He also refers (61) to Americans' "obvious aversion to ruling others."

9. See Gaddis, *The United States and the Origins of the Cold War*, 336–37. See also Kuniholm, *The Origins of the Cold War in the Near East*.

10. Rajak, "Cold War in the Balkans," 205.

11. Gaddis, *The United States and the Cold War*, 309–12; Pechatnov, "The Soviet Union and the World," 100–101.

12. The Yalta Agreement was the controversial agreement coming out of the summit meeting between Roosevelt, Churchill, and Stalin in February 1945 in the Crimea regarding the shape of postwar Europe.

13. The UN support was made possible solely by the fluke of a Soviet boycott of the Security Council.

14. Stalin also died at this time, removing the man who had been the war's biggest supporter all along (Stueck, *Rethinking the Korean War*, 65).

1.5 Gaddis, *The United States and the Cold War*, 78.

16. Kulke and Rothermund, *A History of India*, 335–36.

17. What proximately nudged the crisis into tectonic motion, however, was the successive hope and then disappointment emanating from Tiananmen Square.

18. *Ibid.*, 221.

19. National-liberal societies were predominantly market based but retained more hierarchy in many respects than did their global-liberal successors. Substantial barriers protected sociocultural conventions from competition, limiting horizons and difference but also conferring familiarity and reassurance.

20. The regime may or may not have known at the outset that proliferation to Iran and other Islamic countries was going to occur, but, if not, they learned this early and continued their course.

21. None of this is to deny that less sinister economic interests involving the supply of various components and technologies, some having peaceful uses, may also have been present.

22. Through the late 1970s and 1980s, it repeatedly sent commandos into the vibrant south to wreak small-scale mayhem. In Yangon in 1983 its agents bombed the podium upon which much of the South Korean cabinet was gathered on a good-will mission,

killing four ministers and badly injuring a fifth. South Korea and the world did essentially nothing in response. Nor did they in 1987 when North Korean agents destroyed a South Korean airliner, killing 115 people. In 2010, a North Korean midget submarine torpedoed and sank a South Korean naval vessel in South Korean waters, killing 46.

23. That does not mean Muslim countries or factions cannot go to war with each other or treat each other terribly – they frequently do. It just means that even while they do, they retain important bonds with each other and, like fighting married couples, easily turn together against outsiders.

24. Islamic nationalism stretches the concept but does not escape it. A "nation" is a self-conscious people possessing a territorial focus and real or longed-for sovereignty whose devotion is nationalist. Islam is a deeply political religion, the most political of all major traditions, and its territory is the Islamic world. Islam's nationalism references not existing states but the *umma*, the socially constructed overarching community that commands so much of its members' ultimate loyalty. The Islamic world's longing for a glorious, unified, sovereign territory is nationalistic though wrapped in religious language. Nationalism in authoritarian societies is inherently dangerous – theirs is not the mild, mostly salutary nationalism of liberal societies. Whether authoritarian nationalism is framed in secular or religious terms, the security concerns remain the same. It is real invasion when disorderly fanatics under religious banners stream or trickle over porous borders into a country with disruption in mind and real warfare when they mount an insurgency and begin taking over.

One should not be misled by and give a free pass to nationalist aggression when couched in religious terms.

25. Even now, his use of balance-of-power language to frame Russian and Chinese aggression subtly erodes the Pax Americana and moves the world toward a security regime of multipolar regional hegemons. See Goldberg, "The Obama Doctrine," 87-88.

26. See Hanson, "Obama and Revolutionary Romance."

27. Gaddis, *Surprise, Security*, 32–33.

28. That this quote is a probable misattribution (see http://en.wikiquote.org/wiki/Leon_Trotsky) takes nothing away from its chilling veracity.

Chapter 2 Global Capitalism

29. See Eichengreen, *Globalizing Capital*, pp. 91ff.

30. Suranovic, *International Trade*, chap. 2.

31. In the primary sense, hierarchy is collectivity within which decisions are made by higher-level command. Markets are collectivity within which decisions are made by the free choice of individuals or lower-level collectivities. Hierarchy is the opposite of markets (see Claassen, *An Inquiry*, 62–68). A hierarchical society or personality is an authoritarian one. In a loose sense, insofar as consensus, agreement, order, or organization exist, hierarchy may be said to exist.

32. As of the third quarter of 2016. See wwwtradingeconomics.com/mexico.gdp-growth-annual.

33. See http://data.worldbank.org/indicator/NY.GDP.MKTP.KD.ZG. See also Goldman Sachs, "2016 Macroeconomic Outlook." www. goldmansachs.com/our-thinking/pages/outlook-2016/index.html. See also https://trading economics.com/brazil/gdp- growth.

34. Luce, *In Spite of the Gods*, 66, 198, and passim.

35. French, *India*, 200–202.

36. Luce, *In Spite of the Gods*, 47–48, 51, 340.

37. Bhagwati and Panagariya, *Why Growth Matters*, 98.

38. See https://data.worldbank.org/indicator/ NY.GDP.MKPT.KD.ZG?locations=IN&view=chart.

39. The first industrial revolution, in spinning, weaving, iron smelting, and steam power began in about 1760 in Britain; the second, in automobiles, steel, the internal combustion engine, and electrification in Germany, the United States, and Britain, began about 1880.

40. Maddison, *Phases of Capitalist Development*, 84.

41. Bureau of Labor Statistics, June 7, 2013. "International Comparisons of Annual Labor Force Statistics, 1970–2012," 1–10. Computed from Table 6. Employment Shares by Sector, p. 7. See http://www.bls/fls/flscomparelf/lfcompendium.pdf. See also World Bank, "Industry Value Added (percent of GDP)." www.data.worldbank.org/indicator/NV.IND.TOTL.ZS.

42. See data.worldbank.org.

43. Between 1970 and 2000, the occupational category of stenographers, typists, and secretaries declined from approximately 5 percent of the U.S. labor force to about 3 percent (Wyatt and Hecker, "Occupational Changes," 48).

44. See Hirschman, *Exit, Voice, and Loyalty*.

45. For example, one might find a unitary organizational pyramid having a functional division of labor together with a couple of semi-autonomous, product-oriented divisions geared to innovation and flexibility. Or there might be a matrix form in which dual authority structures are superimposed upon each other, as when two different equally critical problems like the need for specialized technological expertise and for rapid change within product lines both simultaneously require emphasis. The result in this case might be interpenetrating functional and semi-autonomous divisional forms. See Daft, *Organization Theory and Design*, 129–31, 229.

46. Kotkin, *The New Class Conflict*, 145.

47. See Whyte, *Organization Man*, chap. 1, 130, 155–60, and passim.

48. See http://stats.oecd.org/Index.aspx?DataSetCode=ANHRS#.

49. See Riesman, *The Lonely Crowd*.

50. Bureau of Labor Statistics, "Union Members – 2016," January 26, 2017. http:// bls.gov/news.release/union2.nr0.htm.

51. Mead, *Beyond Entitlement*, 28–29. This is a comprehensive measure of welfare, including "spending by all governments on social insurance, public assistance, health, veterans, education, housing, vocational rehabilitation, and community action programs" (p. 29fn). With a less comprehensive definition, the OECD reports total U.S. welfare expenditures at 7 percent in 1960 and 14 percent in 1982 (and 20 percent in 2012) (OECD, "Social Spending during the Crisis," 5, accessed at http://www.oecd.org/els/soc/ OECD-2012SocialSpendingDuringTheCrisis8pages.pdf).

52. Patterson, *America's Struggle against Poverty in the Twentieth Century*, 166.

53. Mead, *Beyond Entitlement*, 132–33.

54. Gilbert, *Capitalism and the Welfare State*, 34.

55. Kristol, *Reflections*, 121.

56. The underclass is made up of those without either self-control or a stable, traditional setting to keep them in line. It comprises those who are present-oriented and radically improvident. Approximately the bottom 10 percent in the United States today, the underclass is analyzed in chap. 7.

57 See data.worldbank.org.

58. Bureau of Labor Statistics, "Databases, Taxes, and Calculators by Subject." See data. bls.gov/timeseries/LNS11300000.

59. See Rea S. Hederman, Jr. and Robert Rector, "Two Americas: One Rich, One Poor? Understanding Income Inequality in the United States," 2004. www.heritage.org/research/reports/2004/08/two-americas-one-rich-one-poor-understanding- income-inequality-in-the-united-states. See also Center on Budget and Policy Priorities, "A Guide to Statistics on Historical Trends in Income Inequality," 2015. At www.cbpp.org/poverty-and-inequality/a-guide-to-statistics-on-historical-trends-in-income- inequality.

60. Of the advanced European economies, Switzerland's alone stayed out of the war and continued strong throughout.

61. See Judt, *Postwar*, pp. 453–64.

62. Spiegel, "The Ticking Euro Bomb."

63. *Ibid.*

64. See http://data.worldbank.org/indicator/NY.GDP.KD.ZG.

65. Piore and Sabel, *The Second Industrial Divide*, 36.

66. See http://data.worldbank.org/indicator/NY.GDP.KD.ZG.

67. Wooldridge, "Northern Lights," p. 3.

68. *Ibid.*

69. *CIA, The World Factbook: Japan.* See http://www.cia.gov/library/publications/ the-world-factbook/geos/ja.html.

70. Computed from http://data.worldbank.org/indicator/NY.GDP.KD.ZG.

71. See www.tradingeconomics.com/japan/government/debt-to-gdp. See also Zawatsky, "Tokyo Time Bomb." See http://nationalinterest.org/.commentary.tokyo-time-bomb-japans-looming-debt-disaster-8885.

72. See Packer, "The Megacity"; see also Walt, "Lagos, Nigeria."

73. I owe this insight to the late David M. Rubinstein, Professor Emeritus of Sociology, University of Illinois, Chicago Circle.

74. De Soto, *Mystery of Capital*, 209.

75. Krugman, Cooper, and Srinivasan, "Growing World Trade," 331.

76. The presence of a liberal security regime protecting international markets from the reach of state authority is the ultimate source of capitalism that Marx never understood.

77. These have included Modigliani and Miller's discovery that a firm's capital structure is irrelevant to its stock price, the Capital Asset Pricing Model's recognition of the effects of randomness in the price movements of financial instruments (see MacKenzie, *An Engine, Not a Camera*, e.g., 40–45), and the elegant Black-Scholes-Merton equations for options pricing.

78. See MacKenzie, *An Engine, Not a Camera*, 132, 249–50.

79. Bell, *The Cultural Contradictions of Capitalism*, 82–84.

80. Baudrillard, *Consumer Society*, 77. Consider also his statement that "the alienation peculiar to the last half century" is one in which our "'deep tendencies are mobilized and alienated in the process of consumption, in exactly the same way as labor power is alienated in the process of production" (Baudrillard, System of Objects, 192).

81. Olson, 141-48 and passim; Buchanan and Tullock, chap. 19.

82. See Kotkin, *The New Class Conflict*, 53.

83. Cf. Lemann, *The Promised Land*, e.g., 148–49, 155–57, 179.

84. Hayek, *Road to Serfdom*, 119.

85. Hayek, *The Constitution of Liberty*; cf. Mead, Beyond Entitlement, 207.

86. See Friedman and Schwartz, *Monetary History,* in particular, where they examine (a) the monetary cliff that the economy fell over during late 1930 and early 1931 and why it did so, and (b) the extraordinary role of Benjamin Strong at the Fed (respectively chap. 7, and pp. 225–28, 231–35, 254–56, and 411–16).

87. See Hetzel's authoritative *The Great Recession*, especially pp. 204-223.

88. Congdon and Hanke, "More Bank Capital Could Kill the Economy."

89. I.e., the ruinous hyperinflation of that year in Germany.

90. Morgenson and Rosner, *Reckless Endangerment*, 42–45.

91. See Mallaby, *The Man Who Knew.*

92. See *Ibid.*, 31–40.

93. Wallison, "How Regulators Herded Banks into Trouble."

94. Morgenson and Rosner, *Reckless Endangerment*, 232–36.

95. See, e.g., Friedman, *Free to Choose*, 81.

96. Namely, the Netherlands, Belgium, Switzerland, Great Britain, Sweden, Norway, Denmark, and France, together with the United States, Canada, Australia, and New Zealand.

97. De Soto, *Mystery of Capital.*

98. *Ibid.*, 6.

99. *Ibid.*, 32.

100. *Ibid.*, 157.

101. *Ibid.*, 86, 93–94.

102. See *Ibid.*, chap. 3.

103. Fallows, *Postcards from Tomorrow Square*, 202.

104. Wallerstein could not have been more wrong in *The Modern World-System.*

105. Economic Research Service, USDA. International Macroeconomic Data Set, "Real GDP (2010 Dollars) Historical," Dec. 18, 2014.

106. "Creation and destruction" is a more accurate and salubrious way of expressing Schumpeter's great insight into the functioning of the markets than "creative destruction" (see Schumpeter, *The Theory of Economic Development*).

107. Tocqueville, *The Old Regime and the French Revolution,* 118.

Chapter 3 The Advent of Multiculturalism

108. Lemann, *Ibid.*, 7.

109. See Abrams, *America Transformed*, chap. 10.

110. See Robert Caro, *The Passage of Power,* chap. 23. After passage of the Civil Rights Act, President Johnson astutely observed, "I think we just gave the South to the Republicans" (quoted in Lemann, *The Promised Land*, 183).

111. Lemann, *The Promised Land*, 172.

112. See Lilla, *The Once and Future Liberal*, 66-67.

113. By the social ethic I mean the secular, post-Christian version of the Catholic- Socialist opposite to Max Weber's Protestant ethic and spirit of capitalism, which Weber only mentions in passing in *The Protestant Ethic*. See Rauschenbush, *Christianity and Social Crisis* on the origins and flavor of the national era's classical social ethic.

114. Durkheim, *The Division of Labor*, pp. 127–28, 136, 234. As a modernist, he was too sanguine about the ease and automaticity with which such splintering is overcome in development.

115. Claassen, *An Inquiry*, 158.

116. Lyotard, *The Postmodern Condition*, 10, 16, 17.

117. Habermas, *Inclusion*, 117–18.

118. Ali, *Infidel*, 109.

119. *Ibid.* (passim.).

120. Luce, *In Spite of the Gods*; French, *India*, 21.

121. French, *India*, 51.

122. See Anand and Sharma, "For India's Lowest Castes."

123. Huntington, *The Clash of Civilizations*.

124. See Dunlop, *The Moscow Bombings of September 1999*.

125. In this work, the Jews are treated as a variably distinct ethnic group, much as Italians and Armenians are. One does not have to practice Judaism religiously to be Jewish, although being such may intensify the ethnicity.

126. Abrams, *America Transformed*, 125-26.

127. Quoted in Shelpy Steele, 53.

128. *Ibid.*, 53-60; quote from 55-56.

129. *Ibid.*, 45.

130. *Ibid.*, 68, 62.

Chapter 4 The Rise of the Gamers

131. Weber's work presented exemplary analysis of the paradigmatic roles of the middle class of early capitalism, the Mandarins of ancient China, the Brahmins of ancient India, and the warrior chieftains of early Islam. See, for example, his *The Protestant Ethic* and *The Religion of China*.

132. The original inspiration and notion of the gamers come from psychiatrist Michael Maccoby's excellent book, *The Gamesman*, of 1976, but I have long worked with the concept and further developed it. See Claassen, *An Inquiry*, 32–34. Many others have used the term as well but mostly in passing.

The most powerful way to define the social classes is on the basis of their members' character or personality. It is more common to define them in terms of income, wealth, occupation, education, power, and prestige, but those are relatively superficial features and tend to follow the attributes of character up or down.

133. Heraclitus, *Fragment 119*, in Freeman, ed., Ancilla, 32.

134. Claassen, *An Inquiry*, 32.

135. Weber, *The Protestant Ethic*.

136. *The Social Network*, directed by David Fincher (2010).

137. Dalton Conley sees the gamers as having "multiple selves competing for attention within his/her own mind, just as, externally, she or he is bombarded by multiple stimuli simultaneously.... as we navigate multiple worlds." Today we "function with split-screen attentions" (*Elsewhere, USA*, 7, 18).

138. Brooks, *Bobos in Paradise*, 209, 212.

139. This way of looking at the new American upper and upper-middle classes owes certain general features to Murray's *Coming Apart*.

140. Michael Lewis has also noticed this. See *Boomerang*, 20.

141. See, for example, Baltzell, *The Protestant Establishment*.

142. George Friedman, "Crisis of Interdependence."

143. Murray, "Hillary Clinton's 'Deplorables' Comment May Have Changed the Course of World History."

144. Regarding leadership and the incapacity of the gamers to lead, see William Deresiewicz's outstanding lecture to the West Point plebes in October 2009, "Solitude and Leadership."

145. Congressman X, *The Confessions of Congressman X*, 42.

146. Liebovich, *This Town*, 237.

147. Julius Krein, *American Affairs*. Volume III, Number 4 (Winter 2019): 153-72. https://americanaffairsjournal.org/2019/11/the-real-class-war/#notes

148. Claassen, *An Inquiry*, 32–33.

149. Murray, *Coming Apart*, 55.

150. *Ibid.*, 118.

151. Hegel, G.W.F., *Phenomenology of Mind*, 246ff.

152. I mean by "overcoming" oppositions (such as that between the gamers and the middle class) rising above and reconciling them, Hegel's aufheben. See Claassen, *An Inquiry*, chap. 9.

Chapter 5 Democracy Embraced, Contested, and Exploited

153. Democracy is the making of collective decisions by means of relatively open markets in political influence. Democratic regimes include, listen, and respect rights.

Citizens may speak their minds in them, expose themselves to any views, advocate any cause, participate in any political organization, and vote for any candidate and/or party they wish. Democracy entails the vibrant, tumultuous, political airing of differences, vetting of political interpretations, thoughts, and proposals, and contesting of individual and organizational actors. Insofar as it is full and unrestricted, democracy extends adult citizens the right to participate in politics. Democracy requires elections, the civil liberties that enable these to be meaningful, and the rule of law, which protects the rights of citizens and enforces their decisions upon officials.

Democracy is the political analog to capitalism. In it various public officials, coalitions, and parties – the individual and collective analogs to business firms in the economy – compete with each other, both directly and indirectly through interest groups and parties, for the support of citizens who are the consumers of policies. However, where it is normally private goods that are exchanged in the economic markets, it is public goods that are in the political ones, policies under which we must all live. The word "democracy" is misleading, for it is not essentially rule by the people, but a political system within which the people or a major subset of them are allowed to participate, much as in the economic markets the people are free to participate. Like economic markets, political ones do not guarantee participants any particular outcome, except insofar as they are restricted by law.

154. Diamond, *The Spirit of Democracy*, 42, 52.

155. See Kagan, *The World*, 3; and Freedom House, *Freedom in the World 2015 – Electoral Democracies*. The latter accessed at www.freedomhouse.org/sites/default/files/Electoral%20Democracy%20Numbers%2C%20FIW%201989-2014.pdf.

156. Diamond, *The Spirit of Democracy*, 54. The italics are my emphasis.

157. *Ibid.*, 47.

158. That is, when Freedom House's misattribution of democracy to Russia is reversed, as it should be. Calculated by utilizing the population figures for 1973 by country (from

http://www.geoba.se), with regime types (as determined by taking the freedom scores assigned for each country by Freedom House for the year 1973 ["Freedom in the World Country Ratings 1972-2014," https://freedomhouse.org] and counting as a democracy any country with a combined score of 7 or better on political rights and civil liberties while receiving no worse than 4 on civil liberties [a score of 1 being the most democratic and 7 the least democratic on each scale]).

159. Calculated from Freedom House, List of Electoral Democracies, FIW 1989-2015.xls (www.freedomhouse.org), but reversing their misattribution of democracy to Russia for that year. Population figures from UNFPA, as presented by photius.com, Total Population by Country. Accessed at www.photius.com/rankings/world2050_rank.html. If Russia were scored as a democracy in 2000, as Freedom House would have it, the balance for that year would become 60-40 between populations under democratic and authoritarian regimes respectively.

160. An authoritarian regime or political hierarchy is a relatively closed market in political influence, one that excludes, dictates, and coerces. Democracy and authoritarianism lie on a continuum of political openness versus closedness, at the democratic end of which are found developed democracies and at the authoritarian end, totalitarian regimes.

161. Putnam, *Bowling Alone*, 37.

162. Peggy Noonan, "The Inconvenient Truth about Benghazi," A15.

163. Bellah et al., *Habits of the Heart*, 173–74.

164. See Baltzell, *The Protestant Establishment*.

165. Bishop, *The Big Sort*, 62.

166. See Klatch, *A Generation Divided*.

167. Didion, *Political Fictions*, 9.

168. Leibovich, *This Town*, 143.

169. See Duverger, *Political Parties*.

170. Lipset, *American Exceptionalism*, 212.

171. "Electoral Democracies: Freedom in the World 1989–90 to 2015." At https://freedomhouse.org.

172. Dobson, *The Dictator's Learning Curve,* chaps. 1, 2, and passim.

173. *Ibid.,* 22–24.

174. Diamond, *Spirit of Democracy*, 82.

175. Barbieri, "Lesson in Crony Capitalism," A11.

176 I.e., the free-floating intellectuals of Mannheim's *Ideology and Utopia*.

177. Compare *Ibid.,* 99.

178. Mill, *Considerations on Representative Government*, 7.

179. See Moore, *The Social Conditions*, 458–59.

180. See Sen, *Development as Freedom,*16, 51–53, 156–57.

181. Kagan, *The World*, 29.

182. Cf. *Ibid.,* 33.

183. Diamond, *Spirit of Democracy*, 103–104, 160.

184. *Ibid.,* 158.

185. *Ibid.,* 130.

186. Sakharov, *Progress, Coexistence, and Intellectual Freedom*.

187. Fukuyama, *The End of History*, 41.

188. Rosefielde and Hedlund, *Russia since 1980*, chap. 10.

189. See Wang, *China's New Order*, 54–61.

190. Ignatius, "In China, It's All About Prosperity."

191. Ibn Khaldun, *The Muqaddimah*.

192. Considerably more so than it was in socially democratizing, late-nineteenth- century Austria. See Schorske, *Fin-de-Siecle Vienna*.

193. McKinley, "Uganda Leader Stands Tall."

194. Diamond, *Spirit of Democracy*, 75.

195. Huntington, *The Third Wave*, 65.

196. *Ibid.*, 74–75.

197. See, for example, Peter Hartcher, "Bully-boy Malaysia Immature and Australia's Reaction So Limp."

198. Marini, *Unmasking the Administrative State*, 150-51, 234.

199. *Ibid.*, 294.

200. See Kotkin, *The New Class Conflict*, 129.

201. "The fact that congressional candidates are largely on their own, that their parties have little to do with nominating or electing them, and that they must raise campaign resources personally, leaves them dependent on and vulnerable to influence from those who can produce money and campaigners for them" (Lipset, *American Exceptionalism*, 44).

202. For class characters are ideal types, and many fall in between them.

203. Aristotle, *Politics*, 160.

204. Dobson, *The Dictator's Learning Curve*. See Introduction and passim.

205. *Ibid.*

206. See Adrian Chen, "The Agency."

207. I owe this observation to the late David M. Rubinstein.

208. Bartlett and Fischer, "The China Conundrum," 1–10.

209. Huntington, *Who Are We?* 324-35.

210. Hayek, *Law, Legislation, and Liberty*, Vol. 2, 138.

211. If the Senate majority is obdurate and cannot be persuaded to end the filibuster, either the President or any Senator should have standing and a strong case with which to sue in the Supreme Court to rule the filibuster in violation of the constitution, for it contradicts both the letter and the spirit of that document. The Senate has a constitutional right to make its own procedural rules but only insofar as those rules do not contravene basic provisions of the Constitution, including the right of a simple majority to enact legislation in either house. Nor may any procedural rule bind it in perpetuity but only for a single Congressional term (see Fisk and Chemerinsky, "The Filibuster," 181-254).

Chapter 6 Devastated Community

212. The wonderfully apt term "chaotic-exotic" is from Williams, *Dream Worlds*, 69 and passim.

213. Putnam, *Bowling Alone*, 86.

214. *Ibid.*, 63.

215. *Ibid.*, 61, 112, and passim.

216. Baumeister, *Identity*, 70–72. See also Sennett, *Fall of Public Man*.

217. McPherson, Smith-Lovin, and Brashears, "Social Isolation in America," 358. See also the online supplement to the article.

218. Vedantam, "Social Isolation Growing in U.S."

219. *Ibid*.

220. *Ibid*., 100.

221. Putnam, *Bowling Alone*, 101–102.

222. McPherson, Smith-Lovin, and Brashears, "Social Isolation in America," 362. The difference is substantial, but precisely how much less socially isolated the better educated have been than the less educated is uncertain. See also the online supplement to the article.

223. Putnam and Campbell, *American Grace*, 454.

224. Putnam, *Bowling Alone*, 66.

225. *Ibid*., 67.

226. Putnam and Campbell, *American Grace*, 472.

227. Putnam, *Bowling Alone*, 71–72.

228. *Ibid*., 72.

229. I would like to thank Conrad Claassen and Jennifer French for suggesting this to me regarding the respective venues.

230. Nielsen *Company, Shifts in Viewing*.

231. Popenoe, *Life without Father*, 6–7.

232. Putnam, *Bowling Alone*, 100–102.

233. Ibid., 2–3; Current Population Survey 2013.

234. Katz, *The Undeserving Poor*, 132.

235. Calculated from U.S. Census Bureau, "Households and Families: 2010," 8. Accessed at www.census.gov/prod/cen2010/briefs/c2010br-14/pdf.

236. Popenoe, *Life without Father*, 6; DeParle and Tavernise, "The New Normal," A1 (L).

237. *Ibid*.

238. Gutman, *The Black Family*, 519.

239. Murray, *The Underclass Revisited*, 2.

240. DeParle and Tavernise, "The New Normal," A1 (L).

241. Murray, *Coming Apart*, 154–56.

242. *Ibid*., 161–62.

243. *Ibid*., 4–5.

244. *Ibid*., 15.

245. Popenoe, *Life without Father*, 43; 2012 Statistical Abstract of the United States, Table 597.

246. See Moynihan, *The Negro Family*; Murray, "Does Welfare?"

247. See Bogle, *Hooking Up*.

248 Krinsky, *Chloe Does Yale*,

249 Ibid., passim.

250. *Ibid*., chap. 7.

251. Murray, *Coming Apart*, 69.

252. Quoted in *Ibid*., 70.

253. Bishop, *The Big Sort*, 5, 15, 44–45.

254. *Ibid.*, 100–101.

255. *Ibid.*, 43.

256. Banfield, *The Unheavenly City Revisited*.

257. See *Ibid.*

258. Dalrymple, *Life at the Bottom*, 25.

259. Murray, *The Underclass Revisited*, 2.

260. These are the familiar Freudian terms but with somewhat distinct usages. See Claassen, *An Inquiry*, chap. 3 for more detail. Here I am ignoring the superid dominant (about whom see Ibid., pp. 27-33)

261. Scholars vary widely in their definitions of the underclass and therefore in their sense of its scale. My high estimate of how many are so afflicted flows primarily from my character-based rather than income-based definition of the underclass. Like Murray's, it also draws loose corroboration from many indicators: percentage illiterate, dropping out of high school, able-bodied but out of the labor force, raised in single-parent families, in the criminal justice system, and behaviorally disqualified from the military (see Murray, *The Underclass Revisited*, 2).

262. Wilson, *Truly Disadvantaged*, 43.

263. Mead, *Beyond Entitlement*, 22.

264. See e.g. Shepard, *The Buried Child* and *The Late Henry Moss*, and Dalrymple, *Life at the Bottom*.

265. *Streetwise*, directed by Martin Bell; *Bombay Beach*, directed by Alma Har'el; and

266. See Brown, *Manchild in the Promised Land* and X, *The Autobiography of Malcolm X*.

267. Eurostat, "Marriage and Divorce Statistics," n.d. Accessed at http://epp.eurostat.ec.europa.eu/statistics_explained/index.php/Marriage_and_divorce_statist ics. National Vital Statistics Report, Vol. 58, no. 25 (Aug. 27, 2010). Accessed at http://www.CDC.gov/nchs/products/nvsr/monthly_provisional_notice.htm.

268. Bishop, *The Big Sort*, 100.

269. Luce, *In Spite of the Gods*, 14.

270. *Ibid.*, 142.

271. See Simmel, "Metropolis and Mental Life."

272. Durkheim, *Suicide*, 208–16.

273. See Putnam, *Bowling Alone*, e.g., 62.

274. Weber, *Protestant Ethic*, 182; Adorno, *Minima Moralia*, 230.

275. See, e.g., Becker, *A Treatise on the Family*.

276. See Putnam, *Bowling Alone*, 161ff.

277. See Popenoe, *Life without Father*, 132–33.

278. *Ibid.*, 4

279. See Ehrenreich, *Hearts of Men*.

280. Cherlin, *Marriage-Go-Round*, 181–83.

281. Riesman, *Lonely Crowd*, chap. 6.

282. See Bogle, *Hooking Up*, 54, 101–102, 175.

283. Ibid., 97–98, 100.

284. It has also seemed natural to many female teachers to overemphasize fiction, underemphasize nonfiction, and nearly eliminate science from elementary school curric-

ula.

285. I owe these insights mostly to conversations over the years with my wife, Ruth Weick, an astute and outstanding elementary school teacher.

286. Kimmel, "A War against Boys?"

287. Murray, *Coming Apart*, 25.

288. See *Ibid.*, 28.

289. See Murray, *The Underclass Revisited*, p. 34.

290. Wright, *Black Boy*, 43. See also Glazer and Moynihan, lxiv.

291. See Marquardt et al., "The President's Marriage Agenda," xii.

292. *Ibid.*, p. 2.

293. See Murray, "Does Welfare?" In some respects, blacks have been canaries in the mine, manifesting common American problems earlier and at a more advanced state than other groups. By approximately 2010 the white rate of nonmarital births passed what that of blacks had been in 1965 (Marquardt et al., "The President's Marriage Agenda," 4).

294. See Moynihan, *The Negro Family*, chap. 3. It is also true that had the burden of southern discrimination been less onerous, blacks would have moved out of the South in fewer numbers and less rapidly, thereby undergoing somewhat less family disruption (see Lemann, The Promised Land, on the circumstances of the migration).

295. Wilson, *The Truly Disadvantaged*, chap. 3.

296. The data were available only for 1992 through 2011. The numbers for the year 2011 were $34,355 for married white individuals, $31,236 for black ones (Calculated from census data presented in "Historical United States Income Data by Marital Status, Race, and Sex." <web.grinnell.edu/dasil/resourceprograms/dasilsoft/Income%20Stratification%20by%20Ma rital%20Status.html> Accessed 1-7-16.)

297. See, e.g., Popenoe, *Life without Father*, 9.

298. See, e.g., Loewen, *The Mississippi Chinese*.

299. The aggregate median household incomes in 2014 dollars for other groups are 40,337 for Hispanics of any race and 35,398 ("Income and Poverty in the United States: 2014," Carmen DeNavas-Walt and Bernadette D. Proctor. Current Population Reports, US Census Bureau, September, 2015, 7).

300. See *Ibid*, passim.

301. Dalrymple, *Life at the Bottom*, 143.

302. Wilson, *Truly Disadvantaged*, 7–8, 55–56, 143, 198, 253, 281, and passim.

303. In Hirschman's words, if sufficient voice is not possible, exit may be necessary (see Hirschman, *Exit, Voice, and Loyalty*).

304. See Goody, *The Logic of Writing*, 86.

Chapter 7 Embattled Morality

305. For further detail and justification see Claassen, *An Inquiry*, chap. 7.

306. Siegel, *The Future Once Happened Here*, chap. 14 and passim.

307. Moynihan, "Defining Deviancy Down."

308. See Bourdieu, *Distinction*, 47.

309. Himmelfarb, *One Nation, Two Cultures*, 118.

310. Himmelfarb, "The Panglosses of the Right Are Wrong."

311. Burnham, *Bad Habits*, 166–68.

312 See Ibid., 120–21, 142.

313. Burke, *Reflections on the Revolution*, e.g., 108–109.

314. The shift from consensus toward politics parallels that from community toward economy.

315. Habermas, "The Public Sphere," 403–404.

316. Putnam and Campbell, *American Grace*, 37, 50.

317. Berlin, "Two Concepts of Liberty."

318. See Burnham, *Bad Habits*,138 and passim.

319. The phrase is Raban's (quoted in Harvey, *The Condition of Postmodernity*, 299).

320. Stearns, *American Cool*. See also Roger Shattuck, "Morality of the Cool."

321. MacIntyre, *Whose Justice?* 397.

322. See Parsons, *The Evolution of Societies*, 184.

323. See my earlier book's philosophical argument grounding and justifying an ethics whose criterion of absolute morality is that which optimally contributes to the long-term well-being of the whole (Claassen, *An Inquiry*, chap. 11; see also chaps. 9 and 18). I distinguish there between absolute morality so understood and the particular moral norms, virtues, and ways that societies proffer which to varying degrees and in varying ways approach or depart from that criterion. Just as a company or family's sociocultural forms patently affect its performance advantageously or adversely, so do a society's. Radical relativism is in gratuitous denial of this empirical reality and its consequences.

324. Popenoe, *Life without Father,* 13.

325. See Claassen, 66-67, 144-45. I used the terms expansionary and contractionary in that book but prefer now to speak of expansive and repressive with the same intended meaning. The distinction is rooted in Otto Rank's fear of death versus fear of life, his fear of going backward versus fear of going forward (Rank, *Will Therapy*, chap. 10).

326. Fallows, *Postcards from Tomorrow Square*, 21.

327. See Fan, "Chinese Slough Off."

328. I would like to thank Chien Lin for these observations.

329. Fallows, *Postcards from Tomorrow Square*, 21.

330. I would like to thank James Shinn for this.

331. See Brooks, "Teen-Age Infidels."

332. Although high in income and remarkably entrepreneurial, a large part of why two-thirds or more of American Jews have been supporting the Democrats is because social issues are of overriding importance to them (see, for example, *Washington Post*, "Exit Polls 2012." Nov. 6, 2012; Emily Chow et al., "Exit Polls." *Washington Post*, Nov. 5, 2014).

333. Hayek, *Law, Legislation, and Liberty*, vol. 2, 12.

334. Although it also covers the economic gamers, Kotkin's notion of the "Clerisy" emphasizes the cultural gamers and nicely captures many of the problems they pose (Kotkin, *The New Class Conflict*, chap. 3.

335. See Gurevitch, "Globalization of Electronic" 192.

336. Schur, *Crimes without Victims*.

337. See Bell, *Cultural Contradictions*, 16.

338. *A Clockwork Orange*, directed by Stanley Kubrick.

339. *Easy Rider*, directed by Dennis Hopper.

340. In 1940, only 4.6 percent of 25-year-olds were college graduates, but by 2009, 31

percent of people between the ages of 25 and 64 were (National Center for Education Statistics, Digest of Education Statistics, table 422. Accessed at http://www.nces.ed.gov/programs/digest/d11/tables/dt11_422.asp). By 2010, just over half of 18- to 21-year-olds were attending college (U.S. Census, 2010. Current Population Survey. Accessed at http://www.census.gov/hhes/school/data/cps/2010/tables.html). As a consequence, the numbers of university faculty have also gone from truly minuscule in 1940 to more than 1.4 million distributed across thousands of institutions of higher learning today (U.S. Census, 2012, table 296. Accessed at http://www.census/gov/compendia/statab/2012/tables/12s0297.pdf).

341. *The Last Temptation of Christ*, directed by Martin Scorsese.

342. *Barton Fink*, directed by Joel Coen.

343. See Burnham, *Bad Habits*, 129.

344. See, for example, Carroll, *The Basketball Diaries*.

345. That is to say, they often become superid dominant (see Claassen, *An Inquiry*, 27-32).

346. See Burnham, *Bad Habits*, 138.

347. See Wilson, *Truly Disadvantaged*, 74–75.

348. Durkheim, *The Division of Labor in Society*, 235.

349. Berger, *The Sacred Canopy*, 127.

350. Ibid., 125. I use the word perturbing not only because it is apt but because the seeking of imperturbability carried poignantly through so many Hellenistic philosophies, none more so than Epicureanism, that arose during the chaotic conditions of that earlier Western period of extraordinary sociocultural mixing, to provide good people reassurance and direction during the centuries immediately before Christianity (see Long and Sedley, *The Hellenistic Philosophers*, e.g. 58-59, 128-29, and passim.).

351. See Claassen, *An Inquiry*, 66–67, 144–45.

352. This is to consider the third Great Awakening beginning in the 1850s as part of a larger movement that began several decades earlier in the United States and in 1793 in Europe.

353. Mosca, *The Ruling Class*; Pareto, *Sociological Writings*; Ibn Khaldun, *The Muqaddimah*; Augustine, *City of God*; and Polybius, *The Histories*.

354. See Mosca, *The Ruling Class*, 416.

355. Fallaci, "An Interview."

356. Mill, *Considerations*, 82.

357. Nietzsche, *On the Geneology of Morals*, 113, 328; *Will to Power*, 252.

Chapter 8: Trump's American Restoration Meets Asymmetric Top-Gamer Resistance

358. That is to say, it is an empirical historical law that if an upper class does not provide leadership, terrible things will happen to it and to the society. It is a moral law because the very meaning of morality is that which contributes to the long-term wellbeing of the whole (see Claassen, *An Inquiry into the Human Sciences*, chap. 11). New York: Peter Lang, 2007.

359. Golding, *Lord of the Flies*.

360. See Publius Decius Mus [Michael Anton], "The Flight 93 Election." See also Anton, "The Empire Strikes Back."

361. I take my sense of the *Megaphone* from Publius Decius Mus's powerful essays of 2016 and especially "The Flight 93 Election."

362. Quoted in Cleveland, "Schumer: Intelligence Agencies."

363. George Orwell, *1984*, 69.

364. *Ibid.*, 231.

365. Plato, *Republic*, 336b-354b.

366. For the key sources of Steele's bad fiction were FRS assets. See the dogged, outstanding reporting of John Solomon and Andrew McCarthy on this.

367. Hayek, *The Road to Serfdom,* 72, 83, 84. See also *Constitution of Liberty*, 214-15, 222, 257.

368. Marini, *Unmasking the Administrative State*, 324-25.

369. There were two exceptions: Seeking "to restore representative government," Nixon was determined to contest the administrative state head on in his second administration, and the Watergate "scandal" was socially constructed with which to oust him (See Marini, *The Administrative State Unmasked*, 150 and Anton, "The Empire Strikes Back"). Reagan also sufficiently threatened the administrative state and its allies that his elite opponents socially constructed another scandal in Iran-Contra with which to at least trim his sails. The top gamers and DPASM have been running and rerunning the same fraudulent gambit on Trump, with the full support of the *Megaphone* (ibid.).

370. Cf. Claassen, *An Inquiry,* 158.

371. Schrader, "In a Fortnight: Xi's Other Amendments."

Epilogue: The Historical Context That Is Never Provided

372. This reading of the circumstances of early-liberal America is heavily influenced by the story of the slow emergence of early-liberal Europe, especially as recounted by North and Thomas, *The Rise of the Western World*; Pirenne, *Democracy in Belgium*; and Thrupp, "The Gilds."

373. Caldwell, *Age of Enlightenment.*

374. MacDonald, "A Window."

375. Shepard, *The Late Henry Moss.*

376. Koestler, *Darkness at Noon*

377. Hamilton, *The Roman Way*, 203.

Index

R

ACKNOWLEDGEMENTS

I would like to thank Frank Bergon, Thomas Hiller, Patrick Finley, Joel G. Best, James W. Shinn, my wife Ruth Weick, the late David M. Rubinstein, and several anonymous readers for having read and offered invaluable critique of some or all of the manuscript in earlier draft form, some of them through multiple drafts. I would also like to thank Jennifer French and an anonymous reader for their helpful copyediting, as well as Trine Day publisher Kris Millegan for his work on many fronts in bringing this book to press. Among the above, I dedicate this book to Frank Bergon, Thomas Hiller, and the late David Rubinstein, men with whom I have had the good fortune of meaningful, formative intellectual friendships spanning respectively more than sixty, more than fifty, and almost fifty years. None of this is to say that any of those mentioned necessarily agree with interpretations, explanations, or judgments expressed in this book.